Performing HISTORY

STUDIES IN

THEATRE HISTORY

& CULTURE

Edited by Thomas Postlewait

Performing HISTORY

THEATRICAL
REPRESENTATIONS
OF THE PAST IN
CONTEMPORARY
THEATRE

Freddie Rokem

University of Iowa Press
Iowa City

University of Iowa Press,
Iowa City 52242
Copyright © 2000 by the
University of Iowa Press
All rights reserved
Printed in the
United States of America
Design by Richard Hendel
http://www.uiowa.edu/~uipress

The publication of this book
was generously supported by the
University of Iowa Foundation.

Printed on acid-free paper

Library of Congress
Cataloging-in-Publication Data

Rokem, Freddie, 1945–
    Performing history: theatrical
representations of the past in
contemporary theatre / by Freddie
Rokem.
        p.   cm.—(Studies in theatre
    history and culture)
    Includes bibliographical references
and index.
    ISBN 0-87745-737-5 (cloth)
    1. Historical drama—20th
century—History and criticism.
2. Holocaust, Jewish (1939–1945),
in literature.   3. France—History—Revolution, 1789–1799—
Literature and the revolution.
I. Title.   II. Series.

PN1879.H65R65   2000
809.2'9358—dc21

                        00-039248

00 01 02 03 04 C 5 4 3 2 1

FOR NAAMA & ARIEL,

AND IN MEMORY OF AMITAI

CONTENTS

Preface
Quoting Histories . . .

Revolution is the mask of death.
— *Heiner Müller*

Engel und Puppe dann ist endlich Schauspiel.
— *R. M. Rilke*

During the first years of my university studies I had a fantasy that the ultimate goal of academic scholarship was to compose a study consisting of quotes so perfectly put together that no one would notice that this was an act of plagiarism. Only afterward did I read Jorge Luis Borges and study Walter Benjamin and recognize that even this fantasy was basically intertextual, a quotation. My "project" was interrupted by more menial tasks, and also by some much more important ones. Now, when trying to understand what I have done in this book, it seems that this fantasy still has a grip on me. That is why I start with a series of quotations which I have brought with me as fragments "rescued" from different textual pasts, pasts with which the theatre, in its attempts to "perform history," also has to come to terms. This is a more speculative way to approach my subject, not yet the introduction to the book itself.

History is an organization of time: "An insight: in one hour's time, sixty minutes will have passed," says Danton in Georg Büchner's *Danton's Death*. The question is: How will this "insight" be understood after this hour has passed? And will it still be an insight then? Or just a painful recognition of a routine which must be repeated over and over again every sixty minutes?

In Shakespeare's *As You Like It* (II, 7, 20–28) Jaques reinforces the sense that quotations carry a unique force, referring to the wisdom about the passage of time he once heard from a "motley fool":

. . . he drew a dial from his poke,
and looking on it with lack-lustre eye
Says very wisely "It is ten o'clock."
"Thus we may see," quoth he, "how the world wags.
'Tis but an hour ago since it was nine,
And after one hour more 'twill be eleven.
And so from hour to hour we rot and rot;
And thereby hangs a tale."

Besides the sexual expenditure which serves as the subtext for the sense that time organizes not only our lives but the tales about it, here the hours are consecutively numbered, while Danton, measuring time on the basis of his own subjective position, will always, at every moment, place himself in an anguished, unidentified present.

The vision of the Israeli playwright Hanoch Levin is informed by an anguish about history to which he gives a cynical expression. The mother, Tsescha, says:

If I did not know that we are living [in] history
I wouldn't be able to stand it [manage/stay alive].

These are the very last lines of Levin's grotesque play *Shitz* from the mid-1970s. The question they raise is: When is the life of an individual transcended in order to become included in that form of continuous linear "eternity" we call history? And under what circumstances does the individual within this flow become aware (à la Hegel) that this is the case? And not least, does such an awareness bring consolation? Tsescha's proud pronouncement, after her daughter has lost her husband in one of the wars, is a kind of reversed (or even ironic?) "threat," based on a conditional structure (If . . . then): since Tsescha knows that she is living "[in] history," life is worth living, which means that without this "absurd" certainty, life would become totally meaningless. To live is to live in history. And history as we know it consists of a series of threats.

The anonymous (last) hours of Danton's life, as they have been captured by Büchner in his play, were always at the point of a new start for the next hour, and for Danton they probably did not even enter the more organized spheres of history. Paradoxically, he was unable to perceive the kind of causal chain of events and consequences that we generally call history. That was his tragedy. But at the same time Danton's own death, through Büchner's play, created the rhythm and the movement we consider necessary for such an awareness of history. Otherwise, repeating Tsescha's triumphal conclusion as a question, how could we be able to stand it all?

"I'm not a historian," says Gogo in Samuel Beckett's *Waiting for Godot*. In a world where Godot does not appear (again tonight) and where there is no continuity and causality, it is indeed impossible to be a historian. There is room for historians only in a world where it is possible to establish relations between the past and the present. And history can be performed, in the world and on the theatrical stage too, when different structures of time (besides the daily reappearance of the sun), can be distinguished, making it possible to ask not only if the things that appear again are natural phenomena but if they are triggered by some kind of agency, creating a pattern, not just a mechanical repetition.

That is no doubt why Marcellus (in the Folio and First Quarto of *Hamlet*) or Horatio (in the Second Quarto) asks: "What, has this thing appeared again tonight?" This, I believe, "is *the* question" when beginning to explore different plays and performances about specific historical events. What does it mean to present these events *again* on the stage? What can be seen in *Hamlet* is how a burden (some kind of unfinished business from the past) becomes transformed into an actor's being and doing "this *thing*" on the stage, appearing again in tonight's performance, continuously performing a return of the repressed on the theatrical stage. History can only be perceived as such when it becomes recapitulated, when we create some form of discourse, like the theatre, on the basis of which an organized repetition of the past is constructed, situating the chaotic torrents of the past within an aesthetic frame. This is probably true of the more conventional forms of historiography too, as practiced in history books.

The ghost in *Hamlet* appears on the stage as a disturbance of the efforts to create meaning and order after the death of the old king, breaking the patterns that have, perhaps too soon, already been established. The other world imposes itself, and this invasion of a new occurrence immediately has to be explained. It is Horatio, who has witnessed the arrival of the ghost (and reports it to Hamlet) and is asked to watch the king during the performance of *The Mousetrap*, who becomes the historian in Shakespeare's *Hamlet*.

Beginning from a totally different point of departure, Roland Barthes wrote in his *Camera Lucida* that the life of someone whose existence has somewhat preceded our own encloses in its particularity the very tension of History, its division. History is hysterical: it is constituted only if we consider it, only if we look at it — and in order to look at it, we must be excluded from it. As a living soul, I am the very contrary of History, I am what belies it, destroys it for the sake of my own history (impossible for me to believe in "witnesses"; impossible, at least to be one . . .).[1]

By "performing history" it is possible to confront this sense of separation and exclusion, enabling us to believe in the witnesses who have seen what in some way has to be told again. What other possibility remains unless we are willing to submit ourselves to a discourse or a theatre totally devoid of references? The theatre "performing history" seeks to overcome both the separation and the exclusion from the past, striving to create a community where the events from this past will matter again.

What this book shows by looking at theatre performances presenting events from the French Revolution and the Second World War is that the theatre can seduce us to believe that it is possible for the actor to become a witness for the now dead witnesses. This contests Paul Celan's historigraphically untenable "position" (but emotionally probably the only one possible), expressed in his poem "Aschenglorie." In this poem he reflected on the possibility of bearing witness about the Shoah after the "natural" death of the survivors:

> Niemand
> zeugt für den
> Zeugen

Nobody can bear witness for the witnesses, Celan says. No one but the survivors themselves can become a witness about what happened in the Shoah. The attempt to represent Auschwitz by aesthetic means is, as Theodor Adorno claimed, one of the most difficult moral and aesthetic issues of our time.

Primo Levi, in *The Drowned and the Saved*, takes an additional step with regard to who can bear witness about that past. He claims that even

> we the survivors, are not the true witnesses . . . We survivors
> are not only an exiguous but also an anomalous minority: we are

those who by their prevarications or good luck did not touch bottom. Those who did so, those who saw the Gorgon, have not returned to tell about it or have returned mute, but they are the "Muselmans," the submerged, the complete witnesses, the ones whose depositions would have a general significance.[2]

It is this muteness of the "complete witnesses" that the theatre, when it is performing history, constantly tries to rescue. The complex paradoxes and tensions created by the efforts to bring the historical past and the theatrical present together through different forms of witnessing is, when everything else has been said, the main subject of this book.

Walter Benjamin, in his most impressive collection of quotations or "found" statements, the *Passagen-Werk* (*The Arcades Project*), reflected on what still makes the past legible for us:

> It's not that what is past casts its light on what is present, or what is present its light on what is past; rather, image is that wherein what has been comes together in a flash with the now to form a constellation.[3]

The theatre performing history, as this book shows, can become such an image, connecting the past with the present through the creativity of the theatre, constantly "quoting" from the past, but erasing the exact traces in order to gain full meaning in the present.

When looking back at the writing of this book, my thanks go first of all to my students at the Universities of Tel Aviv and Helsinki for the inspiration they have given me to pursue this subject; to Pirkko Koski and my collegues at the International Centre for Advanced Theatre Studies at the University of Helsinki (ICATS) for sharing their ideas on the topics it deals with; and to Erika Fischer-Lichte for organizing the symposium which led to the volume *Theater seit den 60er Jahren*, where the European chapter in this book was published in an earlier version.[4] There are also many other friends and colleagues I would like to thank: Linda Ben-Zvi, Daniel Boyarin, Gabrielle Brandstetter, Marvin Carlson, Sofia Gluchowitz, Stephen Greenblatt, Bruce McConachie, Jeanette Malkin, Janelle Reinelt, Eli Rozik, Stuart Schoffman, Claude Schumacher, Yehoshua Sobol, Dan Urian, Christel Weiler, and Bill Worthen. To Tom Postlewait I offer not only thanks for his editorial care and confidence, but my great appreciation; to Herbert Blau, as will become clear in the following pages, my admiration; to Yvonne Rock, my gratitude for her deep and lasting friendship; and to Galit Hasan-Rokem, as much as I can give. This book is dedicated to our three children.

Introduction

The Notions of "Performing History"

This book examines the ways in which the theatre after the Second World War has presented different aspects of the French Revolution and the Shoah on its stages.[1] The reason for choosing these specific events, as they have been represented through performances, is that they have formed our modern consciousness, in particular our sense of the historical past as a series of tragic failures of basic human values. Even if the French Revolution initially fostered such universal ideals as freedom, equality, and brotherhood, it also in many ways directly betrayed these values; and the Shoah has cast its awesome shadow on almost every possible form of human agency since the Second World War. Although the French Revolution and the Shoah took place on European soil, both of them have no doubt profoundly influenced the whole world. This study thus not only confronts the ways in which such historical pasts have been represented on the stage but also examines the significance of such representations in different national contexts: in the United States and in Europe in performances about the French Revolution and in Israel in performances about the Shoah.

The specific overview of theatre performing history presented here in a way reflects my own personal "history." I was born in Europe after the end of the Second World War, more specifically in Stockholm, Sweden, a country which (after having made some serious moral compromises) was actually spared from Hitler's atrocities during the war itself. But many of the positive ideals of the French Revolution have after all become quite deeply rooted in that northern European outpost. The issue I want to examine in this book is how the heritage of the French Revolution has been perceived in the (Western) European theatre after the Second World War.

Most of my life, however, I have lived in Israel. I came to Jerusalem in the mid-sixties, driven by a curiosity to explore my Jewish background and culture. That was before the country had to face the moral dilemmas of its own existence which became so painfully apparent in the wake of the Six-Day War in 1967, with the gradually growing oppression of the Palestinian people. I point this out because much of the thinking underlying this book is an attempt to confront the question why, after Auschwitz, it has still not been possible to solve the moral issues resulting from the foundation of a homeland for the Jews. In what follows I show how the theatre has confronted these issues.

Today, at the turn of the millennium, United States hegemony in the world has become a fact. This creates both curiosity and suspicion for a relatively informed outsider like myself, after having spent several years in the United States both as a student and on sabbaticals. The aspect of American culture and theatre which has drawn my attention here — reconsidering the heritage of the French Revolution as it has been presented on the stage — is perhaps different from those that my American colleagues in the field have generally considered in their work. But by looking at phenomena which previous academic research has left unexplored I hope to be able to point out something which perhaps has not been seen "over there." Finally, this book also brings me back to Europe, more specifically to the city of Berlin, which at least for me represents both the burden of the past and the possibility of a new beginning.

On the basis of approximately a dozen specific performances, which occurred on three different continents, in Israel, in Europe, and in the United States, this book analyzes a number of strategies employed by the theatre, through which events and figures from these particular pasts (which in different ways are situated in the heart of the national consciousness of these places) have been "resurrected" in the *here* and the *now* of theatrical performances. Although I focus on plays that feature the French Revolution when considering European and U.S. productions, I do not mean to suggest that the Second World War has not deeply affected these continents. Aspects of this specific past have of course also been widely represented on their stages.[2] My aim here, however, is not to cover all possible forms of performing history, but rather to examine performances from different contexts, pointing out the great diversity of this form of theatre but also its common features. In analyzing such performances I draw attention to the complex collective efforts of playwrights, directors, designers, and actors in creating what I refer to as theatrical energies connecting them to a specific historical past. I also try to say something about the ways in which these performances have been received by their respective audiences and how they have been affected by and have even influenced the ideological debates in these different national contexts.

Collective identities, whether they are cultural/ethnic, national, or even transnational, grow from a sense of the past; the theatre very forcefully participates in the ongoing representations and debates about these pasts, sometimes contesting the hegemonic understanding of the historical heritage on the basis of which these identities have been constructed, sometimes reinforcing them. By performing history the theatre, at times even more forcefully than other discourses about the past like historiographic writing or novels about historical events, engages in such ideological debates, frequently intervening in them directly. What may be seen as specific to the theatre in dealing directly with the historical past is its ability to create an awareness of the complex interaction between the destructiveness and the failures of history, on the one hand, and the efforts to create a viable and meaningful work of art, trying to confront these painful failures, on the other. This awareness is enhanced by the live presence of the actors on the stage. They perform the historical figures from the past on the stage, relying on different kinds of theatrical energies, a notion that is central for this study. It refers to the restorative potentials of the theatre in trying to counteract the destructive forces of history. The creative energies of the theatre not only are central for the impact of a performance on its spectators, but are crucial for the ways in which such a performance confronts the issues of collective identity and transgression.

In order to examine the complex notion of performing history this study does not attempt to present a comprehensive survey of the post–World War II historical drama. Instead I consider a limited number of performances about the French Revolution and the Shoah which have been produced in different contexts and for very diverse aims. What they all have in common, though, is that in each of them historical figures and events from the past have been given a new "life" through theatrical performances. I recognize, of course, that the productions I have chosen, as well as the texts they were based on, provide a seemingly arbitrary selection of this subgenre loosely called the "history play" or "history performance." My aim here, however, is not to cover this genre completely, but rather to examine several typological characteristics of this specific form of theatrical performance, pointing out its ideological and aesthetic potentials as well as its limitations. When the themes and issues are examined more in detail, I hope to be able to demonstrate that my own idiosyncratic understanding of this form of contemporary theatre also reflects some of the more general concerns, not only of this specific genre, but in some respects even of the post–World War II theatre in general.

Chapter 1 carefully examines Israeli productions about the Shoah and also presents the general issues that recur throughout this book. Chapter 2 turns to three European productions of plays about the French Revolution which were written after the Second World War. Chapter 3 focuses on three American productions of *Danton's Death*, the first major (and now classic) drama written about the French Revolution. Georg Büchner completed this play in 1835, less than fifty years after the events themselves — basically the same time-span that separates us today from the end of the Second World War. This chapter ends with a "performative reading" of Büchner's play, leading directly into chapter 4, which elaborates on the notions of theatrical energies and witnessing and the ways in which they contribute to our understanding of the notion of performing history. This in turn leads to a theoretically oriented discussion of the manner in which such performances about history can affect the spectators, creating what has traditionally been termed *catharsis*. The epilogue brings me to Germany and to the city of Berlin.

Except for the first U.S. Danton production, directed by Orson Welles in 1938, all the productions examined here were produced after the Second World War; except for *Danton's Death*, all the dramatic texts were written after 1945. But Welles' production of *Danton's Death*, like his production of *Julius Caesar* in 1937 (which in his own adaptation was simply called *Caesar*), was influenced by the growing horrors of fascism under Hitler. The two additional U.S. productions of *Danton's Death* which are examined here were directed by Herbert Blau in 1965 and by Robert Wilson in 1992. Wilson also directed *Danton's Death* in 1998, at the Berliner Ensemble (in cooperation with the Salzburg Festival). None of these Danton productions has previously received any scholarly attention. Of the three European productions about the French Revolution, two have already been more or less canonized by previous theatre research: the 1964 production of Peter Weiss' *Marat/Sade* directed by Peter Brook and Ariane Mnouchkine's performance *1789* in 1970. The third European example dealing with the French Revolution, Ingmar Bergman's Swedish production of Yukio Mishima's play *Madame de Sade* in 1989, the year of the revolutionary bicentennial, has not yet been extensively analyzed in an academic context, even though it has toured to a large number of major cities and theatre venues throughout the world.

Of the three Israeli plays and performances about the Shoah analyzed here, Yehoshua Sobol's *Ghetto*, which premiered in 1984, is probably the most widely known. It has been produced at more than fifty theatres all over the world, mainly in the German-speaking countries. Dudu Ma'ayan's production of *Arbeit macht frei vom Toitland Europa*, which was performed between 1991 and 1996 at the Akko Theatre Centre in Israel, has also received some international attention, being performed both in Germany and in Switzerland. It has also been analyzed in some scholarly reviews and articles. The other Israeli performance examined here, Hanoch Levin's *The Boy Dreams*, published in 1991 and first performed in 1993, is still more or less unknown outside of Israel. Levin died of cancer in 1999 at the age of fifty-six. He was Israel's most prolific writer for the stage and one of the country's most original and inventive directors. The Levin production not only deserves attention in itself, but also adds a very significant contribution to the complex theatrical responses to the Shoah on Israeli stages.

This study attempts not only to examine how these two seminal historical events, the French Revolution and the Shoah, have been represented on the stage in theatrical performances, but also to say something about the ways in which these performances have communicated in different national and ideological contexts. Since the spectrum of issues is very broad, and since the ways in which the different historical materials have been transformed into theatrical performances are quite diverse, it is first necessary to clarify what I believe to be at stake when the theatre takes on the difficult and complex task of performing history.

Poetry and History

The notion of performing history, chosen for the title of this study, is intentionally ambiguous because the terms "performance" and "history" can align in a number of different ways. On the most basic level the notion refers not to the representations of the past staged in the theatre but to the historical events and actions themselves as they have been performed in the past (in the "past perfect" tense). A historical event, moreover, is a form of "doing" or performing just like a "drama," and drama of course means "the thing done" in the original Greek. The aim of the historians, on the basis of the available documentation of these past events, is to present their authorized version of that past, usually in different forms of narrative writing. Theatrical performances about historical events are aesthetic adaptations or revisions of events that we more or less intuitively (or on the basis of some form of general knowledge or accepted consensus) know have actually occurred. The theatre, by performing history, is thus redoing something which has already been done in the past, creating a secondary elaboration of this historical event.

It is obviously never the event itself we see on the stage. When the historical figures reappear on the stage through the work of the actors on the basis of a dramatic text, the historical events are, rather, performed again. This understanding of the notion of performing history even contains a "ghostly" dimension — enabling the dead heroes from the past to reappear — just as when Marcellus or Horatio (depending on which edition of Shakespeare's text is consulted) asks: "What, has this thing appeared again tonight?" in the opening scene of *Hamlet*.[3] This portentous question primarily refers to the appearance of the ghost of Hamlet's father on the "platform" where the sentinels watch and wait for this thing which appears every night. On the metatheatrical level, however, this question also implies that the repressed ghostly figures and events from that ("real") historical past can (re)appear on the stage in theatrical performances. The actors performing such historical figures are in fact the "things" who are appearing again tonight in the performance. And when these ghosts are historical figures they are in a sense performing history, just as the dead king Hamlet does when he tells his son, prince Hamlet, how he was murdered. Even more directly, this is what prince Hamlet asks the troupe of actors to do when he produces *The Mousetrap*, an allegorical rendering of the murder of the old king as it has been told to Hamlet by the ghost.

One of the main features that characterizes the notion of performing history is the time lag between the *now* of the performance and the *then* of the historical events themselves. Seen from this perspective, the notion of performing history can clearly be distinguished from documents exhibited in a museum, where something from the past, instead of being reenacted on the stage, is preserved, displayed, and perhaps even reconstructed like an archaeological site. It can also be distinguished from different forms of documentary theatre which have developed from the traditions of theatrical realism, presenting a "slice" of almost contemporary life or reality on the stage. Attilio Favorini, for example, stresses that the performance materials for documentary drama have, as he terms it, actually been "'found' in the historical record."[4] "Docu-drama" and its closely related forms of stage realism, however, are not primarily interested in drawing attention to the time-lag between the "real" events and their theatrical re-enactment. They are more like newspapers, which report events as closely as possible in time to their occurrence. Today on television they are preferably presented "live." Sometimes they become so-called media-events, where the event itself is defined by the fact that it has been reported. For the notion of performing history which I develop here, however, the gradually growing time-lag between the historical event and the performance is of central importance.

Since performing history is obviously a hybrid notion — creating a bridge between performance and history — at times it moves closer to the fictional and even allegorical pole (like *The Mousetrap* and Levin's *The Boy Dreams*) and at others closer to the pole of historical accuracy and documentation (like Sobol's *Ghetto*). In order to cope with this kind of hybridity, performances about history frequently also draw attention to different metatheatrical dimensions of the performance, frequently showing directly on the stage how performances about history are constructed. The making of a performance about history and the making of history as a "theatrical" event are themes frequently dealt with in the performances I examine here. This metatheatrical awareness with regard to the theatre as well as history enables them to communicate directly to the audience that, even if what is presented on the stage is a theatrical performance, it actually presents or refers to events that have really taken place. This is also one of the reasons why the notion of performing history can, I believe, illuminate certain more general aspects of the theatre after the Second World War. In struggling to overcome the realistic heritage while at the same time trying to say something relevant about the world we live in, it has developed aesthetic discourses whereby the performances become transformed into a critical and frequently even theoretical examination of the theatrical medium itself. In this sense the notion of performing history perhaps is paradigmatic of much that has happened in the post–World War II theatre.

Furthermore, we must also accept that the historical past can be told in a number of different ways; that the narrative presented by a historian may be based on a specific point of view and on different vested interests; that it is this historian's individual version of what actually happened, whatever the notion "wie es eigentlich gewesen war"—the motto coined by the German historian Ranke—really means. Only when such forms of subjectivity are clarified is it possible to understand that a playwright and, on the basis of his or her script, the directors, scenographers, and actors are also presenting their specific version of what actually happened or what is significant. In some cases, they present an intentional revision or even an allegorization of that past. As I intend to show, theatrical performances of and about history reflect complex ideological issues concerning deeply rooted national identities and subjectivities and power structures and can in some cases be seen as a willful resistance to and critique of the established or hegemonic, sometimes even stereotypical, perceptions of the past. They can also provide a direct critique of certain historical figures and their actions. When we move from these forms of ideological critique to blunt revisionism, the moral issues concerning the performances of history become a burning issue. As we know, it is usually the victors, not the victims, who write history. The question is to what extent this is true of those who "perform" it on the stage as well.

In dealing with these issues it is possible to argue that the notion of performing history is closely related to the basic model for an epic theatre developed by Bertolt Brecht in his theoretical writings, most poignantly perhaps in his 1938 essay called "The Street Scene." The important point in this context is not the ways in which the actor creates a sense of detachment or alienation (the famous V-Effekt)— how the actor's involvement in the theatrical action affects the spectator (an issue I take up from a somewhat different perspective later) —but rather how the theatrical event itself is constituted. What Brecht terms a "'natural' epic theatre" consists of "an incident such as can be seen at any street corner: an eyewitness demonstrating to a collection of people how a traffic accident took place. The bystanders may not have observed what happened, or they may simply not agree with him, may 'see things a different way'; the point is that the demonstrator acts the behaviour of driver or victim or both in such a way that the bystanders are able to form an opinion about the accident."[5]

Without violating Brecht's intentions in this text too much it is

possible to insert "historical event" instead of "traffic accident," because — and this is not an irony — they have many characteristics in
common. The only proviso that has to be made for this exchange to
work is that the actor-demonstrator performing history need not
necessarily have witnessed the events directly, but may have learned
about them in other ways, as a historian or a student of history.
Brecht's formulations serve my purposes very well for several reasons. The notion of performing history emphasizes the fact that the
actor performing a historical figure on the stage in a sense also becomes a witness of the historical event. As a witness the actor does
not necessarily have to strive toward complete neutrality or objectiv-
ity in order to make it possible for the spectators, the "bystanders" in
the theatre, to become secondary witnesses, to understand and, in particular, "to form an opinion" about the forces which have shaped the
accidents of history. Not even the facts about the past are completely
"pure" or unambiguous; they can be contested on different levels, in
particular when seen from the gradually growing time-perspective
from which the notion of performing history operates. But it is the
actor's role as a witness which determines the kind of relationship a
certain production develops with the historical past. One of the aims
of performances about history is to make it possible for the spectators to see the past in a new or different way, as Brecht formulates the
general aims of the theatre, just as his Galileo — the scientist/witness
— makes us see the movements of the heavenly bodies in a new way.
The manner in which the witness functions on the stage is examined
throughout this study.

Besides presenting various authentic documents or objects most
historians today also consider themselves in one way or another to be
"storytellers" involved in piecing the past together through narrative
in a manner which is closely related to the notion of performing history. Aristotle's distinction in *The Poetics* between the historian and the
poet relates directly to this issue: "one tells of what has happened, the
other of things that might happen."[6] But Aristotle's conclusion that
"poetry is something more philosophical and more worthy of serious
attention than history," since it deals with universal truths rather than
particular facts, is something which the notion of performing history
seriously questions.

Aristotle, who was born in 384 B.C., based his distinctions on a theatre which had almost exclusively relied on mythical narratives and

thus no doubt saw the significance and relevance of historical events in a very different light. For Aristotle, history "is not the exposition of a single action that is required [in epics], but of a single period, and of everything that happened to one or more persons during this period, however unrelated the various events may have been."[7] Aristotle adds, however (and in this has been echoed in our own time by "meta-historians" like Hayden White), that in spite of this seeming diffuseness of history "most of our poets use the methods of the historian,"[8] making selections from the seemingly unrelated events and emphasizing their significance in relation to each other. Thus, any process of telling or writing a version of what has happened is a form of performing history and of resurrecting that past.

Aristotle repeatedly returns to the principles of narrative selection and goes on to argue that, "although the Trojan War had a beginning and an end, he [Homer] did not attempt to put the whole of it into his poem; it would have been too large a subject to be taken in all at once . . . [A]s it is, he has selected one part of the story, and has introduced many incidents from other parts as episodes."[9] In themselves, the events in history, as they "really" took place in the past, lack a coherent narrative structure, according to Aristotle. Any narrative version of these events is based on some form of selection. The historical realities do not have a beginning, a middle, and an end; therefore, the notion of performing history inevitably confronts the tensions between such narrative principles of selection, on the one hand, and the seemingly chaotic and sometimes unimaginable dimensions of these historical events and their catastrophic characteristics, on the other. This tension between the principles of selection and the chaotic nature of what happened has no doubt been reinforced by our understanding of the past after the Second World War. Spectators of theatre performances based on historical events, however, are always aware that beyond the aesthetic principles on the basis of which this historical past is selected and performed there was once a historical reality which was totally unrelated to the concepts of beauty, art, and any kind of aesthetic form. These tensions between the historical past as a chaotic and frequently unmediated reality and the performance have to be confronted on the stage when performing history.

Among the classical Greek dramas which have been preserved there exists only one text with a recent historical subject, *The Persians* by Aeschylus, which was written in 472 B.C., less than twenty years after the war began. It is true, of course, that the Trojan War was a historical event for the Athenians; but by the fifth century it had been transformed into epic and myth by the Homeric poets and rhapsodists. On the basis of Aristotle's insistence on drawing distinctions between poetry and history, Jean-Pierre Vernant has argued that the characters of Greek tragedy usually belong "to a sphere of existence quite different from that of the audience. By being set on stage, they are made to seem present, characters truly there, although at the same time they are portrayed as figures who cannot possibly be there since they belong to somewhere else, to an invisible beyond."[10] This is not the case in dramas based on historical events, however. Such plays present characters who, even if they belong to the past, possess a reality or a veracity which does not exclusively confine them to the fictionality of the stage. Vernant's distinctions are thus also based on the ways in which an actor-character is perceived to be present on the stage during the performance. For us today (as I show more in detail in the chapter on Israeli Shoah performances), certain events in the past like Auschwitz or the ghettos and what happened to people there are perceived as such an "invisible beyond"— as something almost unimaginable or fantastic, which even as a recent historical fact has incorporated something of the mythological and otherworldly. It may perhaps seem paradoxical that the theatre, giving form to historical events on the stage, resorts to this kind of strategy. But that is exactly one of the reasons why the notion of performing history is so interesting.

It is, admittedly, very difficult to draw a sharp line between the veracity of a historical reality and the sense that the characters belong to this kind of "invisible beyond" of fiction and myth. The genre of historical drama — as it has developed from Shakespeare, French Neo-Classical drama, and the Romantics (in particular the German ones) through Büchner, Strindberg, and Brecht (to sketch just one of the possible lines of development) to the theatre after the Second World War — is extremely varied and multifaceted.[11] This complexity is one of the reasons why I have chosen to examine the ways in which two specific historical events, the French Revolution and the Shoah, have been represented on post–World War II stages, as performances, rather than trying to characterize the developments of historical drama and theatre on the basis of genres or authors in a systematic way.

It is also important to stress in this context that contemporary academic authorities like Hayden White have argued eloquently that historiography is always subjected not only to scientific methodologies and theories, but also to distinct narrative structures which in turn rely on complex rhetorical and aesthetic conventions. Michel de Certeau, who basically holds the same position, has suggested that fiction and historiography are closely related and even in some respects identical. De Certeau's point of departure, which is also very suggestive when examining performances about historical events, is that historians and creative writers not only rely on similar rhetorical strategies, but also hold the same basic assumption concerning the status of their discourses in relation to the "real" events in the past which they depict. This assumption is made quite clear through de Certeau's claim that "[h]istoriography (that is 'history' and 'writing') bears within its own name the paradox — almost an oxymoron — of a relation established between two antinomic terms, between the real and discourse. Its task is one of connecting them and, at the point where this link cannot be imagined, of working *as if* the two were being joined."[12] There are no doubt many easily identified differences between scientific historiographic representations of the past, on the one hand, and the "fictional" and "theatrical" modes of such representations, although these two narrative modes are perhaps not always positioned as a clear-cut dichotomy. What they have in common is that theatre and performance are also constituted by creating an "as if" situation, similar to that articulated by de Certeau. This aspect of the theatrical performance has been developed in particular by Konstantin Stanislavsky, who in his work with the actor on the stage also sought to link something that was "real" — the emotional memories of the individual actors — to different forms of aesthetic discourse (or semiotic systems).

We must wonder, though, if the borders between what de Certeau terms the "real" and the "discourse" become blurred or obliterated in such "as if" situations. The theatre, as well as film and television, is no doubt able to create modes of representation where this blurring happens. The main reason for this does not seem to be thematic, but rather semiotic, relating to the fact that the basic material from which theatrical performances are created is the human body of the actors, as they appear and move in an architectural-theatrical space, constituting what is termed the *mise-en-scène*. Of course, this does not imply that the actors performing history are transformed into historical figures or believe that they are such figures, because that would make it necessary to transfer them to the mental ward where the "Napoleons" are supposedly kept. Rather, the actors serve as a connecting link between the historical past and the "fictional" performed

here and *now* of the theatrical event; they become a kind of historian, what I call a "hyper-historian," who makes it possible for us — even in cases where the reenacted events are not fully acceptable for the academic historian as a "scientific" representation of that past — to recognize that the actor is "redoing" or "reappearing" as something/ somebody that has actually existed in the past. Performing history means to reenact certain conditions or characteristic traits inherent in such historical events, presenting them to the spectators through the performance, but it can never become these events or the historical figures themselves. In order to understand the notion of the actor as a hyper-historian when performing history, we have to examine how the aesthetic potentials of the actor's body as well as emotions and ideological commitments are utilized as aesthetic materials through different kinds of embodiment and inscription.

The postwar theatre, and in particular the theatre performing history, can no doubt be seen as an attempt to create restorative energies, in the sense of recreating something which has been irretrievably lost and attempting, at least on the imaginative level and in many cases also on the intellectual and emotional levels, to restore that loss. These creative attempts aim at overcoming the destructive energies without necessarily becoming (at least in performances about the French Revolution) a direct process of mourning for that loss. It is not always possible to distinguish clearly between a more uninterested, informative representation of the past and one which is restorative or based on processes of mourning. It is even possible to argue that the theatre as a medium, in a Hamletian mode, always contains different processes of mourning for a loss. In a way, as a ritual experience, this is also what the theatre implicitly demands of all of us when the fictional world disappears at the end of the performance, at the final curtain or blackout. When examining performances about the Shoah, however, it seems that the creative energies are to a large extent determined by the still ongoing processes of mourning in the social extra-theatrical spheres. This is perhaps also dependent on our perception of the Shoah and the atom bomb as the ultimate forms of destruction. But this possibility of integrating the theatre performances about historical events in the ongoing social processes of interpreting and reinterpreting these events on the stage can perhaps give us an additional opportunity to try to balance the almost unimaginable destructive deficits from our more immediate past.

Temporal Perspectives

The ideas engendered by the French Revolution contain some form of universal truth or value even today, more than two centuries later. The complex conceptual and ideological construct of a utopian civil society based on liberty, freedom, and brotherhood as well as the destructiveness and violence to which the implementation of these ideas eventually led are no doubt still relevant for us. In the performances examined here the theatrical stage is the locus, the site where the dialectical tensions between the revolutionary utopia and the terror can be demonstrated by theatrical means. We can see this, for example, in the long ideological discussions between Sade and Marat in Weiss' play or in the tensions between the new rulers and the common people in Mnouchkine's *1789*.

Even the horrors of the Second World War and the Shoah are actually the results of a revolutionary movement. Mainly because these horrors are so much more openly destructive, but also because they are much closer to us in time than the French Revolution and are still real experiences and memories to a gradually diminishing community of survivors, they have been continuously reexamined by all possible scholarly, pedagogical, and creative means. We are still at the stage where we learn and try to "understand" what happened and in particular how it could happen. With regard to the Shoah the rational means of inquiry fostered by research and education still seem not fully able to grasp the dimensions or the "significance" of this event, as if it has a significance of some kind. It is no exaggeration to claim that the Shoah has challenged and even radically changed some of our notions of history and historiography. The forms of documentation from the Shoah and the Second World War, the immense number of people killed or executed during this period, the decisions made about how and who to kill, the helplessness of the victims facing their death, and many other factors create an almost unsurmountable challenge not only for professional historians, but for every human being. Yet even when the complexity of these events is understood, it does not mean that they will become meaningful in any way, as we assume that works of art, including the theatre, are.

This book examines the force through which the tragic events of the Shoah became organized within the more comprehensive narrative of the establishment of the state of Israel (just three years after the end of the Second World War, in 1948). The murder of six million Jews was very soon counteracted by the building of the new country, through which an ideological narrative integrating this past was created. In this hegemonic national Israeli narrative, the degradation of the Shoah was constructed in opposition to the "resistance" and "heroism" in the ghettos and camps, as instances of Jewish bravery and self-determination in the face of the systematic murders, as well as to the "resurrection" or the "redemption" that was realized through the subsequent establishment of the state of Israel. These hegemonic narrative structures are constantly reworked and even contested on the stage in view of the gradually developing events in the country, in particular in relation to the Israeli-Palestinian conflict, showing how the former Jewish / Israeli victims for different reasons are perceived as perpetrators in the present (see chapter 1). The Israeli theatre has no doubt become one of the important institutions to confront these complex issues within the even more complex ideological and national cultural discourses.

Our relationship to the French Revolution is as a rule more open to different points of view. Here we are even willing to admit that the historical events from this period are like the theatre. The theatricality of revolutions and the ways in which revolutionary situations lead to different kinds of "spectacles" and theatrical performances have been extensively dealt with.[13] The forms of violence which erupted during the time of the French Revolution and their aestheticization in the practices surrounding the guillotine, for example, have been analyzed in detail by Daniel Arasse, who (in a chapter suitably entitled "The Theatre of the Guillotine") points out that

[t]he fall of the blade was the last episode of the second phase of a ritual spectacle comprising three phases. The first was the procession from place of detention to place of execution; the sudden change of rhythm at the end of this slow, preliminary procession added to the production-line effect. The third phase testified to the moral and political efficiency of the spectacle. The people shouted, whereupon the executioner picked up the detached head and held it up to the crowd. The gesture consecrated the sacrifice and marked the end of the ritual. The rite

could be allegorized by being given a setting that functioned like a theatrical backdrop.[14]

The historical event is thus being "performed" within the legal and ritual frameworks, in the form of a three-act play, established by the revolutionary practices themselves.

While the events of the French Revolution often seem to have been staged in a theatrical mode as public spectacles, the Shoah, as several critics and historians have already observed, defies representation.[15] The Nazi atrocities, as well as those committed in Stalin's gulags, during more or less the same time and even later, were significantly removed from the public gaze; even though the practices in some of the Nazi extermination camps were meticulously documented, they were not spectacles in the public sense which characterized the official cruelties of the French Revolution. This is no doubt one more important reason, in addition to the dimensions of the atrocities themselves, why the more recent events of the Shoah have so radically problematized the notion of representation and even of narrativity itself. For Adorno, this was a moral issue. In addition, the dimensions of the human suffering inflicted defy most forms of narration. These issues are no doubt also relevant in the context of the Brechtian epic narrative. For Brecht, the fact that the "accident" was a public event, witnessed by passersby in the street, seems to be an implied precondition for its being theatrically representable as a basis for this notion of epic theatre. Whether historical events are public or private is a difficult issue. Even the private diary of Anne Frank contains a public dimension — the familiar qualities of family life and community values — which made it very effective when it was dramatized and presented on the stage, not only because of what it tells us about the larger context of the period. In order to create some form of narrative order in the chaotic universe of the Shoah, we have to rely on the subjective experiences which in different ways contextualize the private suffering within the public sphere in the form of some kind of testimony. This places the private suffering in a larger context. That is also the process through which the victim becomes a witness in the Brechtian sense.

It is thus possible to see the Israeli productions about the Shoah as an expression of the processes through which the private pains and memories from the past are brought to the attention of the public sphere in different ways. I am of course aware of the fact that this is the point of view of the victims, where the hoped-for healing of the scars and traumas from the suffering of these events is frequently even formulated as a kind of utopian situation. This utopian wish ideally not only affects the private individuals involved, but can even have a redemptive effect for the Jewish people, and in particular for Israeli society, symbolically at least bringing some kind of apocalyptic closure to history. In view of this, the ironic dystopian dimensions expressed by some of the Israeli Shoah productions, as a critique of such a Messianic (and even fascist) yearning, are even more striking. It is thus no exaggeration to claim that the Israeli Shoah performances "read" or interpret this specific past on the basis of the most fundamental ideological issues faced by Israeli society from its establishment until today.

In addition, and this is another important aspect of performing history, when examining theatrical representations of the French Revolution after the Second World War, it is also necessary to confront various aspects of politically organized violence in different post-1789 contexts as well, in particular the Shoah. The theatrical *here* and *now*, showing an aspect of the French Revolution on the stage, inevitably seems to link such a performance to more recent political and ideological issues by its capacity to "step out" of the theatrical representation in order to participate in the discursive activities and debates within the specific context of this performance. The performances about the French Revolution examined here thus also attempt in different ways not only to confront the much bigger bloodsheds which followed (for which the French Revolution, at least in retrospect, was no more than an "innocent" preview), but also to engage the ongoing ideological debates when and where they were performed. History never repeats itself, of course, but at the same time it seems inevitable that different historical events will be compared and measured against each other, for pedagogical, rhetorical, or ideological reasons. Though the French Revolution was certainly not the first event in history to demonstrate that the intentions of radical reform eventually became tranformed into fanaticism and organized official cruelty, it is probably the historical event which has most significantly shaped the modern European imagination in this respect. And at the same time it is no doubt also still remembered because of the civic reforms it led to.

There is, it seems, also a deeper connection between the French Revolution and the Shoah, which has influenced not only performances about the French Revolution but also certain aspects of more academic historiographies and philosophical reflections. The budding forms of "industrialization of death," through the use of the guillotine for executions during the French Revolution, were brought to almost unimaginable dimensions by the establishment of the "factories of death" in the concentration camps established by the Nazis and by the invention and use of the atom bomb. The guillotine and the twentieth-century modes of destruction are not causally related, of course; but they often become superimposed in the post–World War II imagination as different stages or degrees of destruction. The Marquis de Sade, who appears as a dramatic character in two of the performances examined here (*Marat/Sade* and *Madame de Sade*), is one such link, and his ideas have frequently been analyzed in the post-Auschwitz context, where both similarities and differences between these two events have been examined. The interesting point, however, is the way in which they are frequently brought together in the same discursive context.

In his introduction to Pierre Klossowski's *Sade My Neighbour* Alphonso Lingis claims that

> [t]he libertine, in his sodomite perversion, is the materialization of the theological sign of sodomy, a sign within rational discourse of the destruction of the generic substrate for all generality . . . Klossowski shows that rational discourse contains the intrinsic possibility of such a sign, such a black hole in the medium of discourse. Rationalism itself, then, contains the possibility of such a rationalist project of the destruction of rational man.[16]

And he goes on to ask: "Could it be that such a rationalism is in effect not only in the banned writings of Sade but in the history writ large of our time of holocaust and thermonuclear extinction?"[17] Timo Airaksinen, who claims that de Sade "is divine" because of the suffering to which he submits himself in order to entertain his readers,[18] argues that Sade wanted to

> sabotage any idea of what Hannah Arendt was to call "the banality of evil." The ultimate recourse of countless helpless victims, including those who were persecuted by the Nazis, has been the idea that cruelty is a small, gray, boring, and undistinguished thing. As such, it not only lacks value in itself but value for any others; it is unrewarding to the agents of evil themselves. From this standpoint, even the most powerful cruelty would be a matter of the agent's error and psychological weakness. Sade's project is to combat any such notion. He paints wicked-

ness as a strong and grand phenomenon which provides glory and spectacle.[19]

Perpetrators have probably never considered their actions to be banal; nor is the suffering or the pain, as Elaine Scarry has convincingly argued,[20] at all banal for the victims. Protesting against banality, de Sade in this sense has become an allegorical "model" figure who is no longer directly bound to any specific historical period.

But different periods, seen from an ideological or even pedagogical perspective, not only merge or overlap in historical drama. By performing history a double or even triple time register is frequently created: the time of the events and the time the play was written and in some cases also (if this does not coincide with the time of writing of the play) the later time when it was performed. As mentioned before, most forms of documentary drama and theatre tend to bring all of these as close together as possible, while the notion of performing history is based on strengthening or reinforcing the dialectics between them. In all the performances dealt with in this book, except those of *Danton's Death*, there is not a significant distance between the time of writing and the time of the performance. Peter Weiss' *Marat/Sade*, however, very clearly problematizes the significance of such time-lags by showing a semifictional situation in the past where another performance is presented, the play written by the Marquis de Sade about the murder of Marat, which took place in 1793. According to the fiction set up by Weiss, this theatrical performance was presented by the inmates at the Charenton hospital for the director of the hospital, his wife, and his daughter in 1808. The spectators of *Marat/Sade* are thus, on one level, asked to take the position of the 1808 audience; yet, on another level, they are invited to see the events from — and within the context of — a modern perspective, shaped in part by the events of the Second World War.

The assassination of Marat while he was sitting in his bathtub had already been made famous by the painter David, who "documented" this event the same year it took place. Weiss specifically indicates in his stage directions for *Marat/Sade* that after his death "Marat hangs as in David's classical picture, with his right hand over the edge of the bath. In his right hand he still holds his pen, in his left his papers."[21] The imaginary performance of this event, the performance-within-the-performance, written and directed by the Marquis de Sade, was performed fifteen years after the event took place, just as Weiss wrote his own play in 1964, less than twenty years after the end of the Second World War, just before the revolutionary spirit of the New Left started to become apparent. This is also reflected in the play by its early productions. But *Marat/Sade* also bridges the much longer time-gap between the French Revolution and the period we are now living in; subsequently, every performance or reading of the play will have to confront these cyclical repetitions of history as they have been constructed by Weiss.

For example, the Marquis de Sade's words in Peter Weiss' play (in his conversation with Marat concerning life and death in scene 12) very clearly exemplify how these discrete events are accumulated to assume common or more inclusive significances. These lines show that we are in fact dealing with some form of complex superimposition of several apparently discrete historical events. What Sade says in Weiss' play about the executions during the terror following the French Revolution also refers more or less directly to the mass-killings during the Shoah, creating an implicit analogy between these two distinct historical events:

Every death even the cruellest death
drowns in the total indifference of Nature
Nature herself would watch unmoved
if we destroyed the entire human race
I hate Nature
this passionless spectator this unbreakable ice-berg-face
that can bear everything
this goads us to greater and greater acts
Haven't we always beaten down those weaker than ourselves
Haven't we torn at their throats
with continuous villainy and lust
Haven't we experimented in our laboratories
before applying *the final solution*.[22]

Here the Marquis de Sade, as a refraction of Peter Weiss, directly refers to the historical developments which took place 150 years after the French Revolution, but are, no doubt, relevant to both the playwright and his audiences after the Second World War.

In this context it is also important to note, however, that the expression translated as the "final solution" in the last line of the English translation of Sade's speech in *Marat/Sade* is "letzten Behandlung" in the German original. This rather means "last treatment," which perhaps in the German context can be seen more as an understatement or even as a euphemism. In Geoffrey Skelton's translation, which was used by Peter Brook in his production of this play, this expression was thus given a much more pointed formulation than in the original, thus creating a much stronger analogy than Weiss himself probably intended. The "final solution" as a rule is the expression used for the German term "Endlösung," the planned killing of all Jews as it was conceived and carried out by the Nazis.

In 1964, when Peter Brook staged *Marat/Sade* with the Royal Shakespeare Company at the Aldwych Theatre, Susan Sontag noted that the play evoked, even required, a modern understanding: "The heart of the play is a running debate between Sade, in his chair, and Marat, in his bath, on the meaning of the French Revolution, that is, on the psychological and political premises of modern history, but seen through a very modern sensibility, one equipped with the hindsight afforded by the Nazi concentration camps."[23] Opening up such possibilities by creating analogies is an important discursive strategy for performing history in the theatre.

Such analogies can no doubt also be seen in the setting for Brook's production created by Sally Jacobs. The performance put on by de Sade takes place in the the mental hospital of Charenton. In the prologue of Weiss' play, Coulmier, the director of the hospital, extends his thanks to the inmates and in particular to Sade and adds:

I agree with our author Monsieur de Sade
that his play set in our modern bath house won't be marred
by all these instruments for mental and physical hygiene
Quite on the contrary they set the scene
For in Monsieur de Sade's play he has tried
to show how Jean-Paul Marat died
and how he waited in his bath before
Charlotte Corday came knocking at his door.[24]

Marat, of course, is killed in his home, while sitting in his bathtub. But de Sade's performance takes place in the bathhouse of the hospital, where all the "instruments for mental and physical hygiene" can supposedly be seen. Thus the setting is based on a double image of the "bath," superimposing two periods: the historical event, where Marat is sitting in the bathtub (as "documented," e.g., by David in his painting) and de Sade's fictional performance in the mental hospital, where there are also baths for the treatment of the patients.

Sally Jacobs's model for the production of Peter Weiss's Marat/Sade *at the Aldwych Theatre, London, 1964. The showers are clearly visible on both sides of the stage. Photo by and courtesy of Sally Jacobs.*

In the stage performance as well as in the model of the set preserved at the Theatre Museum in London (but not in the much more widely distributed film version of the Brook production) two quite large showers frame the stage on both sides of the proscenium arch. Sally Jacobs, who designed the sets for this production, has stated that this primarily placed the director of the hospital in a vulnerable position under one of them,[25] also indicating that the bathhouse somehow "came out of the proscenium." The explicit aim of this could have been to create a "smooth" transition between stage and auditorium. According to Jacobs, however, this was not specifically intended as a conscious reference to the Shoah. But she added that since Peter Brook was interested in "opening up" the interpretative possibilities, not directly conceptualizing any one of them, such an interpretation could no doubt have been subliminally possible, depending on who the specific spectators were. In the film version of this production the proscenium showers were removed, being replaced by the "curtain" of bars which can clearly be seen. There are showers inside the stage, but these, I think, are less immediately associated with the gas-chambers than the showers situated close to the proscenium arch. Inside the fictional space they are more functional than symbolic. When they are part of the proscenium arch, as in the stage version, they become a symbol for the ways in which the production communicates with the spectators. Such historical analogies, based on the real or sometimes even imagined similarities between discrete events in history, seem to be rhetorically much stronger than the forms of analogy created by purely fictional genres of theatre. For a liberal French audience, the analogies between the different "industrializations of death" developed in Weiss' play, and reinforced by Sontag's critical observations, may perhaps even seem offensive. But such discursive strategies for performing history are quite frequently practiced on the stage, raising contested ideological issues.

Historical analogies also have been frequently activated in many Israeli theatre performances. Pointing out similarities between the behavior of the Nazis toward the Jews during the Second World War and the behavior of the Israelis toward the Palestinians less than fifty years after the end of that war, which several theatre productions about the Shoah implicitly or even explicitly do, may seem offensive to many Israelis. Such analogical strategies frequently contest discursive practices used in political and more official ideological contexts, where it is usually the Palestinians who have been compared to the Nazis. Regardless of which form such analogies have been given, this is a

Production photo from Peter Weiss's Marat/Sade *at the Aldwych Theatre, London, 1964. Directed by Peter Brook, designed by Sally Jacobs, costumes by Gunilla Palmstierna-Weiss. Photo by and courtesy of Sally Jacobs.*

rhetorical strategy which has to be very carefully examined and analyzed. Analogies, no matter how effective they can be in polemic contexts, can be both misleading and facile in key ways. But this is a risk which theatre performing history in some way will always have to take.

The pedagogics of teaching history in schools and universities is no doubt also based on such analogical-narrative strategies between different periods, set up in order to make it possible for students to "learn" from history. Furthermore, such analogies also serve as the conceptual basis for the commemoration of certain aspects of history through museums or exhibits. In the Beit Hashoah Museum of Tolerance in Los Angeles, for example, it is quite openly employed. This is a museum telling about the Shoah which begins by asking its visitors to look at pictures from the Los Angeles riots. No effort is made to hide the analogies made between different forms of racial discrimination and intolerance. I want to emphasize that there is nothing inherently "wrong" in using such analogies. When visiting this museum, I was very impressed by the seriousness with which young Afro-American schoolchildren reacted, no doubt because of the issues this museum raised for *them*. However, it is necessary to examine carefully how they are employed and what they mean in this specific context.[26]

While examining the Israeli performances about the Shoah and the planned total extermination of the Jews as understood in the Israeli context and considering the performances about the French Revolution in Europe and in the United States, we have to make room for the expressions of optimism which the foundation of Israel and the storming of the Bastille evoked at their respective times. In turn, we also have to question the significance of this initial revolutionary optimism within the specific contexts in which the different productions took place. Performances about historical events very directly reveal their ideological preferences and position within the specific social and the cultural context in which they have been created and performed.

Theatre performing history partially takes over the role of the professional historian. But the means used by the theatre are indeed very different from those used by academic historiographers. Instead of relying on the documents used by the historian, the theatre relies primarily on the ability of the actors, during the performance itself, to convince the spectators that something from the "real" historical past has been presented on the stage. And the actors in turn have to rely on the creativity of the playwrights, directors, designers, etc., to create an aesthetic experience for the spectators which at the same time says something about that past. What distinguishes the theatre

performing history from other forms of performance is the way in which it enables the actor to be transformed into what I have called a hyper-historian, functioning as a witness of the events *vis-à-vis* the spectators. This transformation both relies on and creates different kinds of theatrical energies which are central to the notion of performing history. Finally, though, the analysis of the specific productions performing history reveals that they have a great deal in common with other modes and genres of theatre. But it is primarily the differences between them that I am interested in here.

Refractions of the Shoah on Israeli Stages
Theatre and Survival

It was very theatrical: in go people at one end and out comes smoke at the other.
—*Danny Horowitz*

Niemand
zeugt für den
Zeugen
—*Paul Celan*

Israeli culture and its public discourses resonate powerfully with stories and memories from the Shoah. They have been central for the creation of a collective Israeli identity. The awesome dialectics between Destruction and Revival—*Shoah ve'T'kuma* in Hebrew—has been inscribed in the consciousness of every Israeli. As might be expected, the Israeli theatre is one of the many seismographs measuring and confronting the extreme complexities of these stories from and about the Shoah as they are constantly retold from our own gradually growing time-perspective in relation to that past. Israeli society is obsessed by the efforts to understand the Shoah and what significance it holds for the survivors. The Israeli theatre performances dealing directly or indirectly with the Shoah must therefore be seen as an integral aspect of the more comprehensive "work of mourning" and "working-through" which is an important element in the Israeli ideological texture, occupying Israeli society and culture in innumerable ways.[1]

The representations of the Shoah presented on Israeli stages are quite different from the ones which have been created in other places, including the United States and Germany. When making such a claim it is necessary to keep in mind that the Jewish majority of the Israeli society perceives itself as a direct continuation of the survivors of the Nazi genocide; the Shoah has been constructed as a collective experience, even for those who did not experience it directly. These "secondary" survivors, the Israeli Jews who were not directly or biographically affected by the Shoah itself, have integrated that trauma as a basis of identification with the state founded only three years after the end of the Second World War. Even the Palestinians who are Israeli citizens, as well as those living in the occupied areas or under the rule of what is now called the Palestinian Authority (the future Palestinian state) or in exile, have also been affected in different ways by the trauma experienced by the Jewish people. One of the questions raised by some of the performances about the Shoah, like *Ghetto* and *Arbeit macht frei vom Toitland Europa*, is how the sufferings of the Palestinians as a result of the foundation of the state of Israel are related to the extermination of six million Jews during the Second World War. Can all the actions carried out by the Israelis be justified on the basis of that threat; or should Israelis, on the basis of the "Holocaust-experience," be more sensitive to the sufferings of others?

There are, of course, survivors of the Shoah and relatives of victims living in countries other than Israel, but the Israeli society has fostered a self-perception through which its very existence provides the "proof" that in spite of its horrendous toll of human suffering and degradation, the "Final Solution" did not triumph. The history and the experience of the Shoah in Israel must necessarily be written from the perspective of the victims. Schematically, it is possible to claim that the American understanding of the Shoah will primarily be dominated by the role of the United States, together with the other Allied countries, as liberators. The first image which meets a vistor in the Holocaust museum in Washington, D.C., is of American soldiers arriving in one of the death camps. The German perspective, in trying to cope with the murder of six million Jews during the Second World War, has inevitably been influenced by the fact that these actions were initiated by people who spoke German. These clearly different national perspectives on the past have no doubt also deeply influenced the strategies in these respective cultures for creating aesthetic representations of this particular past.

In the Israeli context, which this chapter examines, the Shoah serves as a very charged focal point, a kind of filter for the collective Israeli consciousness through which most of the major events of present-day Israeli life are experienced and interpreted, thus superimposing these events on the already existing collective framework of what a "threat" is and what its results can be. During times of crisis the notion of the Shoah as the ultimate form of threat is automatically activated by Israelis as an almost "genetically" coded reaction or defense mechanism. The mention of a name, a place, or a person connected to the Shoah in a contemporary context activates a whole set of intellectual and emotional responses, which, like a chain reaction, trigger and even manipulate not only the discourse about the past but the understanding of the present-day situation as well. Thus Saddam Hussein's threat during the Gulf War in 1991 to bomb Israel with SCUD missiles equipped with poisonous gas was both cognitively and emotionally interpreted by many Israelis in the context of the Shoah experience, repeating that threat. Moshe Zuckerman has shown how the Israeli press, partly on the basis of the fact that certain components for the manufacture of the Iraqi gas had been supplied by German companies, developed the equation "Saddam = Hitler."[2] And as the discussion of *The Boy Dreams* shows, for Hanoch Levin the notion of *threat* became a central feature of his theatrical world.

If the equation between "Hitler" and different Arab leaders has mainly been nourished by right-wing politicians, a complementary discourse concerning the relationship between the present and that specific past has also developed among the Israeli left. The Israeli occupation of East Jerusalem, the West Bank, and the Gaza strip (inhabited by more than two million Palestinians) in 1967, the Israeli occupation of Lebanon in the early 1980s directed mainly against the Palestine Liberation Organization (PLO), when the right-wing Israeli prime minister Menahem Begin called Yasir Arafat the "Hitler of Beirut"; and the Intifada, the Palestinian revolt against the continuing Israeli occupation, have led to significant changes in the Israeli self-perception as victims. These events have, at least among the left, led to the painful understanding that Israelis are not necessarily the victims, but in these situations are actually the perpetrators, while it is the Palestininans who have become the victims. From having been two more or less separate issues, the Shoah and the Palestinian "problem" have become, since the beginning of the 1980s, closely connected and even significantly and painfully dependent on each other in many of the Israeli public discourses.

No matter which of the two basic ideological commitments or modes of action has been chosen in relation to the Palestinian issue, denying the national rights of the Palestinian people and their aspirations for self-determination or affirming them, these attitudes have more and more frequently become an extension of the confrontation with the experience of the evil, pain, and suffering experienced during the Shoah and a test-case for how the "lessons" of history ought be learned. On the other hand, the Shoah has become the scale by which the intentions of Israel's enemies are measured, as a direct continuation of the Nazi "Final Solution"; on the other, a dangerous warning that the state of Israel is committing atrocities which, if they are not stopped in time, may gradually develop into actions which will in some way resemble those previously committed against the Jews. The late Israeli philosopher and scholar Yeshaiahu Leibovitz has probably been most extreme in this respect, classifying the actions of the Israeli soldiers toward the Palestinians as "Judeo-Nazi." The fact that he was an orthodox Jew and a Zionist drew a lot of attention to this claim.

The Israeli theatre has almost exclusively expressed the left-wing position. It is no exaggeration to claim that these gradual changes of sensitivity — perceiving the Palestinians as the victims of the former (Jewish) victims, looking at history as a constant recurrence of the repressed and at aggression toward others as something the Israelis have tragically inherited from their own experiences during the Shoah — have become an important subtext of the Israeli theatre during the 1980s, and not only in performances about the Shoah. This complex subtext even became visible on the stage before it was so clearly formulated in most other cultural discourses, except in journalistic writing. It is, however, difficult to say at this point what the ideological and political impact of these perceptions has been. It seems to me that since the early 1990s, when two of the performances examined here premiered, the more established Israeli theatres have undergone some significant structural and economic changes which have made it much more difficult for them to intervene in or even change the cultural discourse to the same extent as some of the earlier performances did in the mid-1980s. The Israeli theatre has in many ways become more "careful" and less provocative or "subversive."

Regardless of how the ideological and political reverberations of the issues themselves are resolved (and they usually remain inconclusive on the stage), the overwhelming presence of the Shoah in the Israeli consciousness is at the same time both a challenge and a burden for the Israeli theatre. It is no doubt a truism to say that the French

Revolution has become a general concept of noble ideals and lost opportunities, of dreams destroyed by fanaticism. When representing different aspects of the Shoah and its results, however, the theatre has a much more difficult task. The concreteness of the theatrical medium itself and primarily the terrible realities of the Nazi era — still real as private memories to many Israelis and passed on to the second and third generations as an unsurmountable trauma — make this an almost impossible mission. This chapter examines how the Israeli theatre has confronted a subject ominously charged with destructive energies, which at the same time forces us to confront the most important and most painful ideological and political issues the country is struggling to solve.

The Theatrical Modes of Israeli Shoah Performances

Beginning in the theatre of the early 1980s, it is possible to distinguish a simultaneous mixture of at least three different genres or modes of representation in Israeli plays and performances about the Shoah — the testimonial, the documentary, and the fantastic. Previously these modes of representation had been much more separated, each appearing more or less by itself. It is very difficult to understand exactly how and for what aesthetic and ideological reasons such hybrid generic forms of theatre evolve. In this particular case it seems clear, though, that as the trauma of the Shoah gradually became more distant in time the incomprehensibility of the events themselves was growing. The inherent difficulties in communicating what had happened on "the planet Auschwitz," as Ka-Tsetnik (Yechiel De-Nur), one of the central witnesses at the Adolf Eichmann trial in the early 1960s, termed it, became an even more urgent problem, which works of art, like performances, had to cope with. Paradoxically, in a move which in a way even contradicted its ominous concreteness, this transformed the Shoah into a kind of "extraterrestrial" event, which underwent a strong mythologization in the more official Israeli discourses. It was surrounded by the aura of "never again," a slogan which separated the event from the present reality, as if it belonged to a different kind of temporal existence.

One possible reason for casting performances from the early 1980s as first-person testimony of a survivor was to give them a subjectively based specificity. Michael Bernstein has rightly argued that one of the most pervasive myths of our era, a myth perhaps even partially arising out of our collective response to the horrors of the concentration camps, is the absolute authority given to the first-person testimony. Such narratives, whether by camp survivors or by those who have endured rape, child abuse, or any devastating trauma, are habitually regarded as though they were completely unmediated, as though language, gesture, and imagery could become transparent if the experience being expressed is sufficiently horrific. Testimony wrung out of a person under extreme duress is thus seen as the most true, the most unmediated, the most trustworthy. In contemporary aesthetics, for example, the force of much "performance art" relies precisely — and I think precariously — on just such a faith in the authenticity of first-person testimony.[3]

To this day any attempt to question the events in the concentration camps can be dismissed by a witness-victim, whose words and experiences still carry much more weight than any other form of documentation. But at the same time, Bernstein argues, there is something precarious about such testimonies; they are one of "the most pervasive myths of our era." What I argue here is that the theatre about the Shoah can probably not do without some form of testimony and witnessing and that they are even central to the very notion of performing history. The theatrical-aesthetic aspects of this argument are developed in the last chapter of this book; here I focus primarily on their thematic and generic dimensions.

Shoshana Felman, writing about Claude Lanzman's film *Shoah*, has taken a similar position, arguing from what I understand to be an essentialist position that

> the *necessity* of *testimony* it [this film] affirms in reality stems, paradoxically enough, from the *impossibility of testimony* that the film at the same time dramatizes. I would suggest that this impossibility of testimony by which the film is traversed, with which it struggles and against which it precisely builds itself is, in effect, the most profound and most crucial subject of the film. In its enactment of the Holocaust as the *event-without-a-witness*, as the traumatic impact of a historically ungraspable *primal scene* which erases both its witness and its witnessing *Shoah* explores the very boundaries of testimony by exploring, at the same time, the historical impossibility of witnessing and the historical impossibility

of *escaping* the predicament of being — and having to become a witness.[4]

Felman's position is not primarily determined by Lanzman's manipulation of his witnesses, an aspect of his film which has been severely criticized by Dominick LaCapra,[5] but rather by the impossibility of grasping what she terms this "primal scene" of history. If this is a primal scene in the Freudian sense, it suffers from the same kind of uncertainty which Freud argued that this scene has. Even if it did not actually occur, Freud claimed, every individual will construct such an "experience," while the Shoah is history. The problem, however, with the first-person witnesses, in the case of *Shoah* and in theatre performances, is not the "impossibility of witnessing" because the Shoah was too horrendous (what Felman terms a "primal scene which erases" the witness), but the ways in which the testimony itself, the words of the witness, can become embedded within a theatrical discourse or a performance.

In many Israeli performances about the Shoah one of the characters is a witness drawing his or her authority from some kind of direct experience of the Shoah, in spite of the problematic status of such first-person narratives. In analyzing the specific examples below I draw attention to the manner in which such a fictional character is presented on the stage, in order to function as a witness. But the witness is not the only element of a theatre performance, no matter how central he or she is in creating a basic authenticity. Therefore the more comprehensive discursive contexts within which a first-person testimony is presented on the stage and what actually happens to the witness as a dramatic character also have to be examined. In the early 1980s a form of theatre developed in Israel in which the testimony gradually became embedded within two additional modes or genres of theatrical representation. One of these modes featured a documentary drama, which focused either on a situation from the Second World War, presented "in medias res," or on the subsequent fate of the survivors in the present. In both cases, the events were presented in the "objective," realistic style. In contrast to these documentary possibilities, a self-reflexive dramatic mode was introduced, creating various forms of metatheatre. This mode also created the basis for the fantastic in performances about the Shoah. In the performances examined here the relations between these three modes of representation (testimony, documentation, and metatheatre/the fantastic) vary from case to case, placing a different emphasis on each.

A brief discussion of two 1981 performances may clarify these distinctions: *Uncle Artur*, a monodrama by Danny Horowitz, directed by the author and performed by Yossi Yadin at the Bet Lessing Theatre, and *Adam's Purim Party*, a group-work, based on a novel by Yoram Kaniuk, directed by Nola Chilton at the Neve Zedek–Theatre Centre (both in Tel Aviv). This Kaniuk novel also served as the basis for the 1993 performance *Adam ben Kelev* (Adam Son of a Bitch/Dog) by the Gesher Theatre. The Gesher performance takes place in the circus tent of Adam, a Shoah survivor who once owned a circus and who tells his personal narrative of survival and degradation, having been forced to "play" the dog of the concentration-camp commander.

Both of the 1981 performances were based on testimonies presented from the point of view of the survivor. They also contained some form of direct address by a survivor-witness, who in a sense has "too much" knowledge or experience. He or she usually speaks to a "naive" listener inside the fictional world or on its borders who has not experienced the Shoah directly. This strategy of transmitting the painful knowledge and experience of the past to a listener, which actively includes the real spectators in the communication through various rhetorical means, is examined more closely below. The main aim of this device, however, is basically to make it possible for "naive" listeners to understand, and at the same time also to show implicitly that they probably never *really* will. The realities of the Shoah are too ominous to be rationally understood.

In the Horowitz performance of *Uncle Artur* Peter Stone, who is a survivor, not only wants to explain, but also wants to show his uncle, who fled from Prague on the last train before the borders were closed for Jews, how it was possible for the Jews to react like "cattle brought to slaughter," the expression frequently used to describe the passivity of the Jews facing the Nazi atrocities. And in the Neve Zedek production of *Adam's Purim Party* the inmates of a mental hospital in contemporary Israel, who are all Shoah survivors, have invited their "relatives" (the spectators) to a Purim party, where they perform the traditional story from the book of Esther in the Bible — a story of almost miraculous survival in ancient Persia — while at the same time telling about their own survival from the concentration camps. Adam himself, who had been a circus clown before the war, survived because he was willing to serve as the dog of the commandant. But, like all the other inmates in the present-day mental hospital, he has paid a heavy price for this survival.

According to Mendel Kohansky, the critic of the English daily newspaper *Jerusalem Post* who reviewed this performance, its message was "that the Holocaust, which ostensibly came to an end in 1945, still lives with us, not only as a nightmarish memory, but as a horrifying presence in those who had the misfortune to survive."[6] Ironically, Purim, as it is told in the book of Esther, is the holiday celebrating the survival of the Jews in ancient Persia who faced extinction. The Purim party in the mental hospital poses an awesome balance between physical survival and spiritual disintegration. While the world goes on living normally, at least on the surface — and the establishment of the state of Israel in 1948 is supposedly the proof of this normality — it is in fact still a madhouse. In this madhouse the mental patients, who have enabled their souls to integrate the pain, are perhaps reacting to the Shoah in the only "normal" way possible. In addition to establishing a direct communication inside the fictional frame between a survivor and a naive listener, both of these productions also presented documentary material dramatized in a more or less realistic-objective mode, either by presenting experiences from the Shoah itself or by situating the testimony in the present-day situation in which this testimony was presented.

In *Uncle Artur* the playwright-hero Peter Stone, with the help of four dolls, presents a scene from a play he has written about the first Nazi selections of the Jews in Prague. This little play (within the play), a documentary bringing us back to the event itself, is performed for the uncle, who, many years after the Shoah, is still unwilling or unable to understand how the threats and the sudden violence forced the Jews to comply with the cruel orders given by the Nazis. This reenactment, through which Uncle Artur is in a sense forced to cope with and understand how such things really were possible, is at the same time both a "rehearsal" of a play and a "return" to the actual events themselves. This double meaning is implied by the Hebrew title of a play by Gabriel Dagan, *Hazara*,[7] which had been rejected by several Israeli theatres and served as the source of inspiration for the Horowitz version. The documentary aspect of *Adam's Purim Party* was expressed through the realistic presentation of the inmates' stories in the present-day mental hospital. Through these Purim performances the characters were reenacting and reliving their traumas. Some of the critics even felt that this was uncannily realistic.

In both of these performances the humiliating and painful stories
m the past are retold as a kind of documentary realism. But at
same time they also discuss events that are in a way "unimagin-
e," as if they had actually taken place on another planet. Therefore
:y contain elements that could even be termed fantastic in Tzvetan
Todorov's sense of the word. According to Todorov, "the very heart
of the fantastic" appears when "in a world which is indeed our world,
the one we know, a world without devils, sylphides, or vampires, there
occurs an event which cannot be explained by the laws of this same
familiar world."[8] Since the early 1980s Shoah performances have in
different ways integrated this notion of the fantastic in an everyday
world. The fantastic elements are probed as a means to address and
confront the issue of the incomprehensibility and the incommunica-
bility of the Shoah. One of the aims of these performances is no doubt
also to show that what may seem too fantastic to be true has in fact
taken place. This aspect indirectly and paradoxically implies that some
kind of aestheticization of the narrative is necessary in order to tell
what really happened. The Shoah can never be brought onto the theatrical stage in a direct and unmediated form. Only through a combination of first-person narrative and a strong emphasis on the performative, the metatheatrical aspects of the historical narrative, can
the story of that past be told on the stage. The forms given to this kind
of performance of history in the Israeli theatre, on both thematic and
structural levels, have paradoxically also integrated elements which
Todorov termed "fantastic."

How can the most inclusive and tragic Jewish experience of the
twentieth century be termed fantastic? Todorov argues that the person who experiences an event which cannot be explained by the laws
of our familiar world "must opt for one of two possible solutions: either he is the victim of an illusion of the senses, of a product of the
imagination — and the laws of the world then remain what they are;
or else the event has indeed taken place, it is an integral part of reality
—but then this reality is controlled by laws unknown to us."[9] The
testimonies of survival from the Shoah, as they have been represented
on the stage (as well as in film), very clearly communicate a strong
sense that the victims in the ghettos and camps were living in a world
controlled by laws which were unknown or incomprehensible to
them. This in turn implies that their testimonies must in a way also
be viewed as expressions of the fantastic, a position which these per-

formances also attempt to reproduce in their relationship *vis-à-vis* the spectator-participants. The performances about the Shoah have developed various rhetorical and aesthetic strategies through which a victimized witness, a survivor of the Shoah, communicates directly to a present-day audience about the almost inconceivable events he or she has experienced. This audience has also become integrated into the performance itself in different ways, as characters and as on-stage spectators who in turn become witnesses of the testimony of the survivor. The performance sets up a chain of witnesses, beginning with the survivor-witness who passes on a painful experience.

The performances about the Shoah insist on creating a very direct and intimate relationship with the spectators. This insistence on intimacy, which to a lesser extent is present in performances about the French Revolution like *Marat/Sade* and *1789*, can also be considered in relation to the notion of the fantastic. In the performances about the Shoah this intimacy is much more obvious, however. Todorov argues that the fantastic "implies an integration of the reader into the world of the characters; [and] that world is defined by the reader's own ambiguous perception of the events narrated."[10] The Shoah performances create an ambiguous condition for the spectators because they situate the spectators both inside and outside the fictional frame. The spectator is in various ways urged to become an active participant in the performance. When the stories from the past are presented, the reader, Todorov argues (or the spectator in our case), experiences a hesitation, which is based on the incomprehensibility of these events. Todorov adds the important remark that "the reader's role is so to speak entrusted to a character, and at the same time the hesitation is represented, it becomes one of the themes of the work."[11]

According to Todorov's structuralist-functional formula, which I have basically adopted here, the key to the fantastic (and I repeat Todorov's own words) lies in the representation of hesitation as one of the themes in the work itself. The articulations of such hesitations in Shoah performances are manifold. One such recurrent articulation is the device of a performance within the performance. As the examination of the performances about the French Revolution shows and a quick glance at contemporary world drama probably also confirms, this metatheatrical device is of course not restricted to performances about the Shoah. But in Shoah performances, more clearly than in other performances, this device serves as the basis for an epistemological critique of the events and a measure for the dialectics between the real and the fantastic.

In the Horowitz production Peter Stone presents what in Hebrew is called a *hazara*, a simultaneous "rehearsal of" and "return to" the past, a repetition, in order to change the preconceived ideas of the old uncle. Such an inherently ambiguous performance-return, which is at the same time also an obsession, is also the basic concept on which the Purim party is based. There Adam plays the impresario presenting the actors in his Shoah show. The whole performance raises the question whether the characters we are seeing on the stage — the mental patients in the hospital — really have survived or if their degraded and deranged state actually shows that what they experience is not a form of survival at all. And in both of these performances the present moment of helplessness and pain is powerfully penetrated by the seemingly fantastic elements of the past and the incomprehensibility of this past, which become embodied by the theatrical representation itself. That past haunts the survivors and, as a result, the spectators as well.[12]

Yehoshua Sobol, Ghetto

Yehoshua Sobol's *Ghetto* tells the story of the establishment of the theatre in the Vilna ghetto during the Second World War and in particular the role played by the female singer Chaya in order to make this possible. According to the narrative presented in Sobol's play, it was her voice which seduced the Nazi officer Kittel to agree to establish this theatre; but after she flees to join the partisans hiding in the forests, all the members of the theatre are killed except Srulik, who becomes the witness in Sobol's play. The play was first performed in 1984 at the Haifa Municipal Theatre in Israel, where it was directed by Gedalia Besser, and since then has been produced all over the world. It is by far the most often produced Israeli play ever, with more than sixty productions in major theatres including the Volkstheater in Berlin in 1984 (directed by Peter Zadek) and the National Theatre in London in 1989 (directed by Nicholas Heitner). It has also had more than forty university and school productions. The play has been published in two Hebrew editions, in 1984 and 1992. The second edition contains several significant changes, adding passages as well as discarding several passages from the first edition. In his introduction to the second edition Sobol notes that these changes are based primarily on the productions in London and at the Municipal Theatre in Essen, Germany, in 1992, the latter of which was directed by the playwright himself. Sobol has so far directed the play four times, most recently in 1998, also at the Haifa Municipal Theatre. The more recent production was based on a shortened version of the second edition. The play has been published in several languages; each such publication contains small variations, which are generally based on a specific local production.

Sobol's *Ghetto* is a work which has been in constant progress since it first appeared more than fifteen years ago; each production can in some way be considered a new version of the play. Sobol has always been very flexible with regard to his dramatic texts. Since he has often been directly involved in the production process, he is interested in making such changes so that the specific performance reacts to the time and place in which it is produced. In a 1986 interview Sobol emphasized the immediate contact between himself as a writer and his audience, which later no doubt also led him to direct his own plays. For Sobol, "[t]heatre is a social medium and you create for a live audience experiencing the same kind of things which led to the writing of the play. Plays lacking this kind of immediate implication or relevance . . . are worthless. A theatre cannot present plays without reference to a contemporary social reality. What happens to the play after that is another matter."[13] Not only the performance, but the dramatic text itself is in constant flux, depending on and reacting to the specific conditions and contexts of its presentation.

It is not possible to examine the changes in all the versions of the play here. For many of the performances Sobol himself has rewritten sections of his play. Here I focus on some of the passages from the first Hebrew edition of the play which have *never* been performed on the stage and have not been included in the second Hebrew edition. The reason for paying attention to these discarded (or seemingly unplayable?) passages is that they give us an interesting indication of what Sobol initially imagined and what his "first" intuitions were as he was writing the earliest version of the play, before it had been tested on the stage. In some respects his writing is more "fantastic," in Todorov's sense, than the performances of these texts have been. This is a dramaturgical discussion which shows how sensitive the performance medium is to variations. But before examining these more specific issues I want to take a more general look at Sobol's *Ghetto* and to consider some of his other historical plays in order to clarify the historiographic position he expresses in his drama.

Ghetto is the first part of a trilogy about the Vilna ghetto, called "The Ghetto Triptych 1983–1988" (the years when it was written). The other plays are *Adam* and *In the Underground*.[14] Between 1941 and 1943 the Vilna ghetto where the Jews were forced to live had been decimated to seven small streets in less than one square mile in the center of the city. In December 1942 the ghetto had a population of 17,000 Jews, less than a quarter of its original population. The three plays are an attempt to document minutely the life in the ghetto in the shadow of the Nazi threat. All three plays are based on several first-hand testimonies and accounts from its inhabitants, those who survived as well as those who did not. The dramatic framework created by Sobol for his trilogy is fictional, however, and the three plays are not directly related to each other chronologically. They are different selections based on the well-documented historical realities of the ghetto, and they take place more or less simultaneously, with some of the characters appearing in all three parts.

The central dramatic conflict in all three plays focuses on the struggle between Gens, the head of the Judenrat (the Jewish council of the ghetto), and Kittel, the Nazi officer in charge. The three plays are all deeply informed by a sense that the Jewish community as a collective, the Jewish culture and its traditions, was stronger and more viable than the attempts of the Nazis to bring about the "Final Solution." The common theme in all of the plays is the struggle to survive. In each play Sobol explores in detail the moral dilemmas of the Jewish leaders who face the cruel certainty that it is not possible to save all the inhabitants in the ghetto. Because of the inhuman demands of the Nazis it is necessary to sacrifice some people in order to save others. Sobol's plays about the ghetto focus on the fact that the Jewish leaders became partly responsible for this selection. The theatre depicted in *Ghetto*, the underground movement depicted in *Adam*, and the ghetto hospital, which is the focus of the third part of the trilogy, are all perceived as different strategies for survival inside the ghetto walls. *Adam* and *In the Underground* have not, however, reached the same degree of popularity as *Ghetto*. One possible reason for this could be that theatre about theatre is somehow more effective than other themes in performances dealing with the Shoah. There are indeed a large number of Shoah plays with this kind of metatheatrical framework.

The understanding of the Shoah that Sobol brought to the foreground — which had not been so explicitly formulated in the Israeli public discourse before *Ghetto* appeared in 1984 — was that the Jewish leaders in the ghetto, who had been appointed by the Nazis, to some extent became integrated into the Nazi system and even cooperated with it, or rather pretended that they were cooperating with it, in order to survive. According to Sobol's plays about the Vilna ghetto, to achieve their aim of saving a viable part of their community and culture, the Jewish leaders in different ways tried to resist the Nazi system by a kind of "cooperation" which was in essence a form of both deception and resistance. Sobol presents their partly successful efforts to subvert the intentions of the Nazis by a delicate balancing act between cooperation and deception. The ghetto theatre functions in Sobol's play as such a form of deception — and theatre is in itself a form of deception — which at the same time is based on a form of creativity. Even though all of its members except one are finally executed, the theatre in the ghetto is presented as a successful revolt against oppression and thus a form of survival. From our own present-day perspective, Israeli actors performing *Ghetto* are perceived as a kind of victory against the Nazis and serve to construct the ideological statement about the state of Israel as the direct heir to the destroyed Jewish people of Europe.

But while the cooperation with the Nazis during the war itself is portrayed as a heroic revolt based on deception, Sobol's project must also be seen as an attempt to analyze and integrate the experience of the Shoah within the complex Israeli experience of the 1980s and to criticize the Israeli government from such a perspective. When *Ghetto* was performed in 1984, the Israeli army was still occupying large parts of Lebanon. This occupation led to tragic events, including the Sabra and Shatila massacres, which, although not directly carried out by the Israelis, at least received some kind of approval or even encouragement from the Israeli occupation authorities. The painful issue Sobol raised is to what extent the Israeli society had unconsciously absorbed the values of its previous persecutors, the Nazis, and whether the previous victims were now creating new victims, the Palestinians.

The former "cooperation" with the Nazis, notwithstanding that it had been carried out for the sake of survival through sophisticated strategies of cooperation and deception, was now interpreted by the predominantly left-wing-oriented dramatists and theatre institutions as a form of "infection," an unconscious integration of values which during the war had been directed toward the annihilation of the Jews. The first production of *Ghetto* at the Haifa Municipal Theatre in 1984 clearly pointed to these issues by casting an Israeli Palestinian actor, Yusuf Abu Varda, as Gens, the Jewish leader of the ghetto, while the Nazi officer Kittel was played by an Israeli Jewish actor, Doron Tavori. Tabori even said in an interview at the time, for which he was severely criticized in most media, that there is a little Nazi hiding inside every Israeli. The production itself, because of the freshness with which it presented the familiar materials about the Jewish resistance but mainly because of its very high production values, was highly appreciated by the audiences and received a lot of media attention. The main stage image was a heap of clothes, an image of loss and absence, which the theatre tried to give new life, making the memories of Srulik come alive again. The final scene of this production was extremely strong. Since Chaya the singer has joined the partisans in the forests, Kittel has threatened to kill all the other actors. They try to cover up this fact by performing a play with only clothes; when Kittel brings in a big jar of food for them to eat, they think he has not dis-

First Haifa production of Yehoshua Sobol's Ghetto, *1984. The Nazi officer Kittel (Doron Tavori) and the singer Chaya (Riki Gal). Photo by Morel Drefler. Courtesy of Haifa Municipal Theatre.*

First Haifa production of Ghetto, *1984. The librarian Kruk (Ilan Toren, left) and the Nazi officer Kittel (Doron Tavori, right). Photo by Morel Dreßer. Courtesy of Haifa Municipal Theatre.*

covered their trick. When the actors have overcome their uncertainty and hesitation, however, eating fervidly from the jar, Kittel kills them all except Srulik, who has survived to tell the story. The surprise of the sudden ending, alleviating the threat for a few moments and suddenly changing the whole situation again, was quite impressive in this production.

The second Israeli production, also at the Haifa theatre, was directed by Sobol himself fourteen years later, in 1998. On the whole it presented a much more sentimental understanding of the past, implying that in the ghetto — as opposed to the present-day situation of the Israelis — the moral conflicts were much more clearly defined. There was one remarkable moment in this production which went by almost unnnoticed. When the Jewish policemen are ordered by the Nazis to participate in a massacre of other Jews, one of them shouts "Acharai!"—"Follow me!"— as he leaves the stage. This is the command Israeli officers supposedly give their soldiers in battle, lending this situation an uneasy touch. But this short moment of protest, implying that Israelis are ultimately committing atrocities against themselves, was not contextualized in any other way in the production.

Second Haifa production of Ghetto, *directed by Sobol himself, 1998. In the photo Gens (Asher Zarfati) is facing the inhabitants of the ghetto. Photo by Eyal Landsman. Courtesy of Haifa Municipal Theatre.*

Many of the plays about the Shoah written during the 1980s — including an earlier Sobol play about Otto Weininger, *The Soul of a Jew*, which premiered in October 1982 at the Haifa Municipal Theatre (less than six months after the beginning of the Israeli occuption of Lebanon) — attempted more or less directly to cope with the moral dilemmas of the war in Lebanon. *The Soul of a Jew* also reflected a sense that the former victim had now become a persecutor of another people. The significant differences in degree between the two historical situations, the Second World War and the war in Lebanon, were no doubt clearly perceived, but at the same time they were linked by the perception expressed by the character Selma in another Shoah performance, *Arbeit macht frei vom Toitland Europa* (examined in detail below). Selma says: "It begins with a yellow star."

In his earlier play Sobol had shown how the Jewish soul of the *fin-de-siècle* philosopher Otto Weininger, who was posthumously highly admired by Adolf Hitler (for which Weininger himself can of course not be held responsible), was tragically torn between its Jewish/female and Aryan/male halves. Weiniger as well as the Israelis at the time favored masculine force — i.e., fascism. The present-day solution of the moral and ideological dilemmas suggested by all of

Sobol's plays dealing with the painful memories of the past was not to deny or condemn what Gens had done, "collaborating" with the Nazis in order to save the Jewish community and culture, but rather to undo or change the political situation. This was a protest against Israelis oppressing and degrading another people, calling for an end to the occupation of the homeland of another people in order to prevent the Israelis from becoming like the Nazis in any way.

Another important issue connected with these moral sensibilities and deliberations raised, at least indirectly, by many of the Israeli Shoah performances is the problematic implication that on some level every survivor of the Shoah actually cooperated with the forces of evil in order to survive. On an existential-psychological level the very "act" of survival has brought with it some form of vague guilt, mixed with pride and self-assertion, for having deceived the most effective death-machinery ever invented. This is also what makes the idea of witnessing so ambiguous, but also so interesting. What Sobol often implies in his plays is that the Israelis, as survivors, have internalized something of the ideology of oppression and are now exercising this horrible lesson on another people or that evil in itself somehow contaminates anyone who is in contact with it—albeit as a victim. This complex set of contradictory emotions can at the same time develop into different forms of vengeance and anger as well as a fervent denial or repression and even a refusal, particularly in moments of crisis, to look honestly into the mirror, to confront the fact that Israeli military power, supposedly created for self-defense, is also an instrument for the continuing repression of the Palestinians.

All the plays in Sobol's trilogy about the Vilna ghetto contain a mixture of the three genres or modes of representation distinguished above. Here too, the testimony of a witness is very prominent; they all begin with a survivor who is speaking directly to the spectators in a vaguely defined contemporary Israeli context. In all three plays, moreover, this initial testimony very quickly becomes transformed through flashbacks into a historical documentary drama. The central dramatic actions in the plays are based on minute research involving many different documentary sources. According to the stage directions of the first edition of *Ghetto*, which was published after the premiere at the Haifa Municipal Theatre in 1984, the action starts in "[t]he living room of a middle class apartment in Tel Aviv. 1983."[15] In the second edition this has been changed to a more abstract scene in a city in a fog, which is perhaps more suggestive as a locus for remembering, but less concrete with regard to where the person who is remembering is located.

In both editions, however, Sobol indicates that the "real time and place of the action is the Vilna ghetto, 1941–1943," while the "place of the events," as he terms it, is "[t]he memory of the narrator, who has situated the stage of the theatre and scenes from plays written in the ghetto, which never were performed, and manuscripts that have been lost."[16] This narrator, who is called Srulik, is the sole survivor among the members of the theatre company, and the dialogue in both of the Hebrew editions begins with Srulik's answer to a question from an unidentified interviewer about the activities of the theatre: "The last performance? No, I don't remember anymore . . . the last performance, you asked? It was on the evening before . . ."[17] This is the brief moment of hesitation, after which Srulik briefly describes this last performance, on "the evening before Kittel killed Gens,"[18] and some of the other activities of the theatre in the ghetto. This introductory section ends with Srulik saying that he will look in his library for one of the texts which was performed at the theatre during the war. At this point the ghetto itself appears on the stage; the act of trying to remember has created the place of memory, or what Pierre Nora has termed the "Les lieux de mémoire."[19] It is only through such a flashback technique that the place of memory itself is brought back, the place where it happened.

This rhetorical device, which includes a moment of hesitation before the act of remembering itself and which involves the spectators directly, represents that moment during which, according to Todorov's scheme, the spectators pass the threshold between the "normal" and the "fantastic." The "fiction" created by Sobol is that the spectators are carrying out an interview with a survivor, just as Sobol himself actually did while conducting his own research for the play. We are all trying to understand how it was possible to create a theatre in the ghetto, which still seems almost unbelievable in light of the systematic efforts of the Nazis to exterminate the Jews. The performance of Sobol's play on the stage can thus be seen as an answer to the question not only about the last performance of the ghetto theatre, but also about how it was possible to establish a theatre under these circumstances at all. At the end of Sobol's performance the question about the tragic end, literally the *last* performance, echoing the Nazi efforts in reverse to bring about the "Final Solution," has been at least partially answered. While there was a last performance in the ghetto, by performing Sobol's play *Ghetto* every night, again and again, this last performance at least has been symbolically postponed as it is being repeated in today's theatre. When we look at the impressive list of productions of this play, it is perhaps not an exaggeration to claim that since the play opened in 1984 it has been performed every night somewhere in the world. This "thing," the performance, indeed appears again and again.

The rhetorical structure of Sobol's *Ghetto* thus brings out the idea that we are witnessing a testimony which ends at the same point where it began. The bracketing sentence with which the play opens and closes shows that Srulik has given testimony, while his memory, which has been dramatized on the stage, constitutes the report of the activities of the ghetto theatre, a documentary reconstruction. The more or less realistically presented document has been triggered by the memory of the individual; and the work of art, the art of today's theatre, is an attempt at the same time both to liberate and to communicate this memory.

While Srulik, the only survivor from the theatre, is addressing his first-person testimony to today's audiences, he gradually begins to remember. Through the act of memory he is brought back to the ghetto itself, which now appears on the stage and is dominated by big heaps of clothes, constantly reminding us of the victims who used to wear them. This is an obvious change of genre from the first-person narrative to the multivocal realistic dramatic situation. This realistic documentary presentation also includes the first-person testimony of the librarian Herman Kruk, a central figure in the ghetto who did not survive the Shoah. But his remarkable diary describing the events in the ghetto has been salvaged. In this diary, sections of which are included in Sobol's play, he expresses his objections to giving "performances in a graveyard," as he puts it; thus Kruk's testimony is also contained within Srulik's memories of the past, presenting another point of view. This means that Srulik's testimony is multivocal, as he "remembers" other memories and testimonies. This device clearly shows that testimonies are ideologically conditioned, since the play revives the debates in the ghetto about the most suitable strategy for survival — open revolt or the tactic of cooperation that Gens favored.

When the walls of the Tel Aviv apartment crumble, noises of locks and chains can be heard. According to the stage directions in the first edition there is also a piece of gray cloth hiding a shrine for the Tora-scrolls at the back of the stage. The stage directions indicate that this shrine, which can hold all the members of the theatre group, is situated at a height of three meters and has to be entered with a ladder. The first scene in the memory/ghetto begins by opening a large gate (another obvious symbol for the act of remembering), through which the shadow of a man who wears nothing but torn underwear appears. He approaches the heap of clothes and, according to the stage-directions, "picks up the uniform of a German officer . . . gets dressed, and is transformed, in front of the eyes of the audience, into the German officer Kittel."[20] After getting a machine gun and a suitcase from the heap of clothes, the now clearly distinguishable Nazi officer takes a flashlight from his pocket and shouts "Tohu va-vohu," the Hebrew words for the primordial chaos in the biblical creation story. The scene implies that God also acts in the world through agents like Kittel, who create nothing but chaos and destruction instead of introducing order into chaos as God supposedly did through his creation. When another character enters, Kittel immediately commands: "Or," which means light in Hebrew, just as God did in the biblical creation story. But this light is at the same time also the light of the theatre, and the opening sequence shows how Kittel has "created" the space in the ghetto which will eventually become the theatre, which he will also eventually destroy.

Before examining in detail how this initial sequence has actually been performed on the stage, and in particular which features have never been staged, I want to stress that the third modal aspect of theatre performances about the Shoah, their metatheatricality (the obvious self-referentiality through which the fantastic develops, according to Todorov), is also very clearly present in *Ghetto*. Sections from actual and planned performances are shown on the stage, as they were supposedly presented for their original audiences in the ghetto. This aspect of Sobol's play also emphasizes that this remarkable episode in the history of the Vilna ghetto — the creation of a full-fledged theatre with regular performances during a time when the Jews were subject to Nazi oppression — is almost too fantastic to be true. Or as Sobol himself wrote in his program note to the production of the play at the Haifa Municipal Theatre in 1998 (which he also directed):

Anyone who reads the documents about the ghetto, the diaries of the victims, and immerses himself in the details of the daily life in the Vilna ghetto is immediately struck by the vitality which emerges from them, a kind of vitality without which it is impossible to imagine the victory of survival of these defenseless people, who succeeded in sticking to their desire for life and their humanity while facing their tormentors who, fully armed, humiliated them. To the mystery of that vitality I owe my play.[21]

There is obviously something almost irrationally fantastic, Sobol argues, in the fact that it was possible to establish a theatre in the Vilna ghetto which actually functioned under these extreme circumstances.

These fantastic elements are also implicitly related to this metatheatrical dimension of Sobol's play. A person running through the wall and a figure in underwear dressing up in a Nazi uniform who uses language from the biblical creation story, as if he were a divine figure, and who begins to give orders to the others, would no doubt make the spectators uncertain as to what kind of reality they are watching. The Tora shrine in the synagogue where the scroll of the five books of Moses is kept (appearing in the background already in the first scene), which according to the stage-instructions serves as the refuge of the actors in the last scene of the play, when they are actually presenting their last performance just before their execution by Kittel, is also somewhat fantastic in the context of the ghetto. In his first conception of the play, Sobol wanted the Tora shrine to remain on the stage throughout the performance. This could be seen as a constant reminder of the kind of ambiguity from which the fantastic, as an otherworldly or even supernatural presence, stems. The Tora shrine, representing the presence of a "supernatural" alternative to Kittel, whereby the Jews in the ghetto can be saved, is a potential *deus ex machina* which is supposed to be present throughout the whole performance of Sobol's play. But rather than being a source of redemption as the divine "witness" of the events in the ghetto, it is actually an ironical reminder of the absence of God in this world. According to the written version, when the actors try to find a refuge in the Tora shrine, all but one are killed. Since the theatrical device of the *deus ex machina* is usually employed for the purpose of saving the dramatic characters, here it actually emphasizes the absence of such a possibility. It is important to note that the *deus ex machina* frequently has been used in ironical ways in the modern theatre, as in Brecht's *Threepenny Opera*, for example.[22]

"The last performance" in *Ghetto* is a ghost-play performed only by clothes, which are the recurring symbol in the play of what remains of the victims after their extermination. This is a darkly satirical presentation of how these clothes have miraculously "survived" the poisonous gas of the washing machines where they have been "cleansed." This performance takes place just after the singer Chaya has escaped from the ghetto to join the partisans in the forests. Kittel has threatened to kill the actors if anyone is missing. This (last) performance, presenting nothing but the clothes, is a deceptive (i.e., theatrical) way to hide the fact that Chaya has run away. According to Sobol's stage-directions in the first edition, after the last performance has been completed Kittel wants to determine if any of the actors are missing. At this point the clothes approach the ladder leading to the Tora shrine, open its doors, and throw the holy scrolls on the heap of clothes which has been lying on the stage throughout, finally hiding themselves inside the shrine. Kittel, who has also been watching this part of the performance, where the actors are trying to escape, understands that something is wrong and asks the actors to return and to take off the clothes behind which they have been hiding.

When Kittel realizes that one of the costumes is empty because Chaya (for whom he has developed a strong liking because of her beautiful voice) is missing, he makes all the preparations for the execution of the actors. Instead of carrying out his threat he surprises them by his own sardonic deception, bringing a pot of jam with bread for the frightened actors. When the actors feel secure again, however, it becomes clear that Kittel has merely postponed his threat: he begins to shoot. Only one of the actors, Srulik, survives the massacre, because Kittel has aimed his machine gun at the human-sized doll constantly accompanying Srulik. Srulik is a ventriloquist who has been speaking through this doll, his other half or "persona." All of these elements, except for the Tora shrine, have appeared in one way or another in all the productions of *Ghetto*. One of the interesting changes, though, is that in the first edition the doll does not have a defined gender identity, while in the second edition it has been given the name "Lina" and is supposed to be played by an actress. What survives of Srulik's ventriloquism after the "death" of his doll-companion is his more daring and outspoken half, because it is Srulik who becomes the witness telling the audience in today's theatres about the last performance in the ghetto.

The issue I want to examine in summing up my discussion of Sobol's *Ghetto* is the fact that the dressing of Kittel in the first scene of the play and the constant presence of the Tora shrine as part of the set (from the first edition of the play) have not been realized on the stage in any of its numerous productions. Such an analysis raises some very interesting methodological issues concerning the relations between a newly written and innovative play about the Shoah and its "performability." On the one hand, this methodological approach — examining the significance of those passages in the text which have not been performed — sharpens the issue of how the impossible, the unnamable, can be represented on the stage. On the other hand, I do not believe that the fact that certain passages or aspects of the first edition of this play in 1984 have not been performed necessarily signals a failure. Indeed, *Ghetto* is the most-performed Israeli play ever written. The fact that the Nazi uniform and the Tora shrine — the horror of the uniform and the sacredness of the holy books — have been so problematic as theatrical signs points at some very basic issues of representation in plays of this kind, and perhaps in the theatre in general. These two objects apparently contain forbidden messages which the form of theatre that Sobol writes for is not able to contain.

As a playwright Sobol clearly had some initial intuitions which for several reasons were not "applicable" on the stage. By trying to understand what the aesthetic and ideological implications of these initial intuitions were and by examining the second edition of the play (which was published after the play had been performed for almost a decade, in more than forty productions), we can draw some tentative conclusions about some of the limits in what a performance of this specific play about the Shoah could apparently show at a given time. It seems that the dressing of Kittel and the presence of the Tora shrine, precisely because they make some very clear statements about the significance of the Shoah for us today, are somehow (at least from the point of view of the theatres where they have been produced and the directors of these productions) beyond that limit.

Making an actor enter the stage dressed in underwear, pick up a Nazi uniform from the heap of clothes on the stage, and get dressed in front of the audience, thus being transformed into the Nazi officer Kittel, shows how somebody lacking power and authority appropriates these by his clothing. It is a device that Brecht used very effectively in the pope-dressing scene of *The Life of Galileo*. When Kittel appears he could even be one of the actors who is getting dressed for a performance of the theatre in the ghetto, maybe even "the last performance" itself, where all the actors except Srulik are massacred. The act even implies that when somebody dresses up in a military uniform he becomes a cruel persecutor. This is a very strong and provocative statement in the Israeli context, considering the political background against which the play was written and performed for the first time. That was also apparently an aspect of Sobol's dramaturgical statement which Gedalia Besser, the director of the first production of the play at the Haifa Municipal Theatre in 1984, was not willing to present on the stage. And since then nobody has tried to realize this idea on the stage in any of the many productions. The question is what such an initial statement in the performance — that a Jew is putting on a Nazi uniform — communicates to the spectators, and in particular to a German audience. It would no doubt cancel most forms of identification between the present-day German audiences and their relationship to their own problematic past if the Nazi was a dressed-up Jewish actor in the ghetto. But at the same time, the fact that anybody can become a victimizer by putting on a certain uniform is no doubt relevant as a warning to audiences all over the world, including the Germans.

The dressing of Kittel on the stage is no doubt an interesting case in many respects. It would introduce a theatrical dimension from the very beginning of the performance, creating a strong sense of doubt about the "reality" or "historicity" of the events which the performance wishes to document as historical facts. But it is exactly this vaguely defined borderline which Shoah performances always in one way or another have to confront, because what actually happened was in some sense too "fantastic" for anyone to believe it actually occurred. While Shoah performances seem to stress the fantastic dimension, they also have to present some form of historical "reality" as objectively as possible. For Besser, who directed the first production of the play in Haifa, the need for a clear documentary statement was so strong that he even canceled the frame-story of Srulik remembering. As far as I know, all the other productions have begun with the interview with Srulik about "the last performance." It is interesting to note, though, that in Sobol's own 1998 production in Haifa Srulik was already positioned in the set of the ghetto during his initial interview as he tried to remember this last performance. This is a compromise between the present and the past, combining the historical figure with the witness/survivor looking back at his experiences in the past. Here the first-person narrative, the documentary, and the fantastic modes are actually contained within one image on the stage.

An examination of several productions of Sobol's *Ghetto* as well as the second edition of the play shows that the dressing of Kittel —

symbolizing the fact that even a Jew can "become a Nazi"— has been moved to "the last performance" of the clothes at the end of the play. In the second edition the use of the Nazi uniform has in fact undergone an interesting metamorphosis. In the first edition Sobol states in his stage-directions and in the dialogue itself that all the costumes in this last performance except one, a German uniform, are the clothes of the gas-chamber victims. In the second edition, however, all the actors in "the last performance" are dressed up in Nazi uniforms with the easily identifiable hairstyle and mustache of Hitler. In the 1998 Haifa production it was clear that this was a parody, rather than the much more threatening version of the uniform in the first edition. During this parodistic performance, only Lina the doll, who is already a total theatrical sign by herself, is dressed in the clothes she has been wearing throughout the performance.

To a certain extent, dressing all of the actors except Lina in Nazi uniforms and making them look like Hitler carries a much stronger message than having only one actor appear in the beginning getting dressed in a uniform. The appearance of an anonymous figure in the very first scene of the play is much more ambiguous and open to different and even contradictory interpretations than the clearly marked Jewish actors in the ghetto who become multiplied caricatures of Hitler in the last scene. The Hitler figures and the emphasized framing of the Nazi costume in the performance within the performance in the second edition of the play create a parodistic dimension of the same message, while the initial version of the play seriously implied that every person can become not only a Nazi in a performance, but a Nazi who persecutes victims until they are killed. However, there were already enough hints in the play about the possibility that Germans and Jews will continue their "fruitful" cooperation after the war to provoke the Israeli audiences at the time, when the conflicts surrounding the Israeli occupation of Lebanon in 1982 were at a peak.

The Tora shrine also has not been realized on the stage in any of the productions of *Ghetto*, and this image is also absent from the second edition of the play. This well-known visual image, representing a metaphysical dimension within the Jewish tradition, raises some fundamental questions about the use of traditional ritual objects on the theatrical stage in general and the use of Jewish symbols on the Israeli stage in a performance about the Shoah in particular. The use of the Tora shrine in the first edition of *Ghetto* is no doubt a clear intertextual reference to the first act of the famous Evgeny Vakhtangov production of *The Dybbuk* at the Habima Theatre which premiered in Moscow in 1922. This specific production moved with the theatre from Moscow to Tel Aviv, where the Habima Theatre settled in 1931 and later became the Israeli National Theatre. It was performed for more than forty (!) years on the stage, with some of the same actors in the major roles throughout. This production clearly belongs to the collective associations of an Israeli audience. In the first act of this performance, which takes place in the synagogue, the two lovers Leah and Hanan meet for a short moment in front of the Tora shrine, just before Hanan dies. The reason given for his death is Leah's planned marriage to another man in spite of the fact that their respective fathers had actually sworn an oath before the children were born that they were to be married. But at Leah's wedding to the other man Hanan returns as a Dybbuk — the soul of a dead person who has not come to complete rest — possessing her body with his voice (with obvious erotic implications), speaking through her mouth under the wedding canopy and thus violently interrupting the ceremony.

This is also a metaphysical form of ventriloquism, whereby the spirit of the dead lover speaks through the mouth of his beloved. It is not a theatrical form of ventriloquism, which is so central in *Ghetto*, when Srulik speaks through Lina. There is, however, an important similarity between *The Dybbuk* and *Ghetto*, because both plays are about a "voice" or a witness from the "country" of the dead who returns and is still able to communicate in the "country" of the living. The voice of the dead, just like a theatrical ghost (e.g., Hamlet's father) keeps reappearing. From a psychological perspective this is what Srulik is doing by remembering the ghetto theatre. Lina, the rebellious and "chutzpe-like" doll, who is "killed" by Kittel in the last scene, throughout the play also speaks with Srulik's voice, just as the dead Hanan speaks through the body of Leah in *The Dybbuk*. In both of these plays it is the voice of the man who speaks through the body of a female figure. This empowers the female figures, since they are enabled to give "voice" to the fate of the man, but at the same time it is a weakening of the female figures, because the voices of the men occupy or penetrate the female bodies, turning them into victims. It is also the beautiful voice of the singer Chaya which led to the establishment of the theatre in the ghetto.

There is also an aspect of *The Dybbuk* which can be related to the Shoah. In this performance the true lovers, Hanan and Leah, are brought together in voice and spirit in a mystical union with strong

Kabbalistic and erotic subtexts, but they have no offspring in this world. The renowned Habimah production, which was also performed during and after the Second World War, actually tells the story of the gradual waning of the Galut, the Jewish Diaspora. When the play premiered in Moscow, seventeen years before the outbreak of the war, it was impossible to foresee which meanings would eventually become integrated in this performance. When the Habimah Theatre settled permanently in Tel Aviv, it continued to perform *The Dybbuk* for another thirty years. After the war, however, with six million Jewish souls who had not been properly buried, and who had thus not reached complete rest, the Israeli cultural discourses gradually developed an unconscious obsession with becoming possessed by these Dybbuks. I do not think it is an exaggeration to argue that this is one of the reasons why this particular play, first in Vakhtangov's production and later in several other productions, has continued to have such a strong hold on Israeli audiences.[23]

The issue implicitly raised by this intertextual interpretation is whether works of art which do not directly deal with the Shoah can be read as allegories about it (see the discussion of Levin's play *The Boy Dreams* below). Thus, it is possible to argue that the presence of the Tora shrine in the first version of *Ghetto* is perhaps too ambiguous or allegorical for the theatre, just like the dressing of Kittel in the first scene. The ritual space of the synagogue, where the Tora shrine originally belongs, is very different in all respects from the mental space of the ghetto recalled by Srulik. And I do not think that Sobol wished to transform the space of the ghetto — with everything that this space implies in terms of degradation and suffering — into a sacred or a ritual space that goes beyond the theatre. Whereas the Tora shrine on the stage in *The Dybbuk* signifies a divine presence which is actively influencing the lives of the humans, this divine "place" in the first edition of *Ghetto* (the version where it appears) has become totally vacuous and powerless. It has been emptied of its holy books, giving room and power instead to the satanic figure of Kittel. According to Sobol's original script, the actors try to find refuge in the remains of this holy place, but to no avail. Instead all except Srulik are massacred.

The dialectical tensions between the traditional Jewish sacred space and the ghetto during the Second World War contain modalities which can no doubt also become effective on the theatrical stage. I will not attempt here to speculate about what forms they could have taken had the original script of *Ghetto* with the Tora shrine been used as the basis for a production. However, the discourses about the Shoah in Israel as well as in many other countries are constantly occupied with creating spaces of remembrance and commemoration. Shoah memorials and museums, not to mention the sites of extermination themselves, are no doubt the kinds of spaces which in various ways contain the dialectical tensions between "sacredness" and "theatricality," while the sites of extermination in a way are also cursed. These sites, especially the objects and images from that particular past, have frequently been assigned ritual functions which are much more inclusive than the graveyards that were never erected for the victims. It is the very absence of traditional forms of commemoration which assigns such an important function to theatre performances about the Shoah, creating their own sense of ritual and commemoration. The first half of the performance examined in the next section of this chapter, *Arbeit macht frei vom Toitland Europa*, takes place in a Shoah museum and confronts the issue raised by the presence of the Tora shrine in the never-performed version of Sobol's *Ghetto* from a different perspective: how is it possible for a Shoah play to represent and state the impossible?

While the Nazi uniform and the Tora shrine are objects beyond the limits of representation in the theatre for which Sobol writes (repertory theatres with large audiences, usually with a subscription audience), *Arbeit macht frei vom Toitland Europa* is in many ways able to transgress these theatrical borders. Sobol as a writer is clearly more radical in *Ghetto* than the theatres he has been writing for. In *Arbeit macht frei vom Toitland Europa*, however, it seems nothing has been suppressed on the stage.

Dudu Ma'ayan, Arbeit macht frei vom Toitland Europa

The almost five-hour-long performance work *Arbeit macht frei vom Toitland Europa* (Work Liberates from Deathland Europe) was produced by the Akko Theatre Centre,[24] a free theatre group located in Akko, a small town 15 miles north of Haifa on the Mediterranean coast. It is one of the few cities in Israel with a mixed Jewish and Arab population. The production was directed by Dudu Ma'ayan, the director of this theatre, but it was created as a collective work by the whole group and won first prize at the Akko fringe theatre festival in 1991. It was performed there until 1996 and has also been shown in European cities, including Berlin and Hamburg. The title of the production refers directly to the inscription over the gate of Auschwitz, but also to the "work" which liberates *from* Europe, the land of death and the ultimate Galut or Diaspora of the Shoah, implying that this production itself could perhaps be seen as a kind of redemptive activity — a creative and theatrical "working through" of the Shoah trauma in order to become free of it.

This attempt at liberation from the country of death no doubt also implicitly refers to the famous Habimah production of *The Dybbuk*, which ends with the unification of Leah and Hanan in the "Igra Rama," designating the high mystical abode (i.e., in the realm of the dead). When *The Dybbuk* premiered in 1922, eleven years before Hitler came to power, the country of death pointed toward a utopian sphere in terms of the Zionist ideology at that time, implicitly referring to a Jewish national state, the high abode where the young couple could become unified. Hanan, who dies in his efforts to regain his lost beloved Leah after she has been betrothed to another man, returns under the wedding canopy in the form of a Dybbuk, speaking through her mouth. When Leah is brought to the rabbi to free her from the spirit, she refuses, and in her death she becomes unified with her true lover in the country of death. After the Shoah, however, in a performance like *Arbeit mach frei vom Toitland Europa* as well as in Hanoch Levin's *The Boy Dreams*, Toitland, the country of death, is obviously dystopian. Selma, the main character of *Arbeit macht frei vom Toitland Europa*, is no doubt a contemporary transformation of Leah, possessed by the dead, unburied spirits.

The ominous title of *Arbeit macht frei vom Toitland Europa*, which joins German, the language of the persecutors, with Yiddish, the almost dead language of the Jews (in particular of Eastern Europe), could thus even be read as an allegory of the Zionist utopian dream, where work will liberate the Jews from bondage. When it was realized in 1948, less than three years after the end of the Second World War, this dream no doubt held a promise both of liberation and of redemption. In 1991, however, it had been seriously compromised by new expressions of the Diasporic nightmare which the production in various ways tries to confront.

Moving from the relatively organized Israeli everyday realities to the surrealistic regions of a collective subconscious where chaos and madness reign, this production was exceptional because of its directness and immediacy in dealing both with the memories of the Shoah and with the Israeli-Palestinian conflict. But instead of reconfirming the generally accepted notions of Israel as the realization of the utopian longings of the Jewish people, the Akko performance subverts them, just as it subverts the inscription from the gates of the extermination camps and creates a theatrical discourse showing how intimately connected the two issues are in the minds and memories of its two main characters — Selma and Haled.

Two documentary films have also been made about the production, *Balagan*,[25] directed by Andres Viel for German television, and *Don't Touch My Holocaust*,[26] independently produced by the Israeli director Asher T'lalim. In both of these films Dudu Ma'ayan and the actors are interviewed and different sections from the production itself are shown. Since these documentaries only present small fragments from one performance, interspersed with the interviews and other background materials, they do not enable us to understand the complexities and sophistication of this production as a whole. They must rather be seen as personal "viewings" or even interpretations of a performance, which in turn reflect the interests of a German and an Israeli director, respectively. But even if they fragment the production, they still give us some very vivid glimpses of it.

As a generalization one could say that T'lalim's film focuses on the processes the actors went through to prepare for their roles, while Viel stresses the political implications of the work, in particular its relation to the Israeli-Palestinian conflict. In this context it is also necessary to mention that the genesis of both these films was a proposal by Asher T'lalim, who had been following the rehearsals of the production, to a German TV channel to make a documentary about the performance. When the project was accepted, however, the assignment was given to the German director Andres Viel, while T'lalim went on to make his own independent film, indirectly referring to his struggle in the title of his own documentary, *Don't Touch My Holocaust*. The two films no doubt present Ma'ayan's production as well as the actors from two very different perspectives. In the film by T'lalim it is possible, however, to see some glimpses of how the work was created collectively; even if some of these sections are not documentary in the strict sense of the word, they give an indication of such a collective creative process.

My critical reading of *Arbeit macht frei vom Toitland Europa* here is based on the two performances of this work that I myself have seen in Akko, in 1992 and in 1996. Even if there were several significant differences between these two occasions, the main "performance script" and its structure were basically the same. The performance begins in the parking lot outside the Hall of Knights built by the Crusaders in the Old City of Akko, where the theatre center itself is situated. The Crusaders who conquered Palestine almost a millennium ago are also intimately connected to that dark European past, culminating in the Shoah, which today's Israeli society in different ways is trying to liberate itself from. The Crusades, as a historical parallel that casts its shadow on the present, also figure frequently in the political-ideological discourses of the Middle East conflicts, most prominently in anti-Israeli propaganda, comparing the temporality of the Jewish state to that of the Crusader invasions of Palestine, which will end in the same fashion, by expulsion.

The performance of *Arbeit macht frei vom Toitland Europa* begins when the approximately twenty spectator-participants have gathered outside the medieval stone fortress in Akko; with a "guide" they board a bus headed for the Holocaust museum at the Kibbutz Lochamei Hagettaot (the Kibbutz of the Ghetto Fighters). The first time I saw the production this "guide" was a young female soldier and, as it turned out later, one of the actresses, while the second time it was one of the actors, giving the ride a more neutral nature. The soldier's uniform made the ride much more official and "educational." It is less than half an hour's ride to the Shoah museum at the kibbutz. The implicit oppositions between the Crusader fortress (signifying the efforts of the Europeans to liberate the Holy Land from the heathens) and the Shoah museum (outside of which an aqueduct built by the Romans serves as a very prominent landmark) and between these and the gates of Auschwitz in "Deathland Europe" serve as the constantly recurring geo-conceptual subtext of the performance, creating both its real and conceptual scenographic space. The kibbutz and the museum were established by survivors of the Shoah, two of whom were very prominent among the resistance fighters in the Warsaw ghetto during the war itself. James E. Young, writing about this kibbutz, notes that "[n]ot only do the fighters who live here embody the link between the memorial sites and an actual past, but their experiences have left an unmistakable imprint on the very forms remembrance takes here."[27] It is this unmistakable, almost mythical, imprint which the Akko production wishes to examine critically.

When *Arbeit macht frei vom Toitland Europa* was performed in Hamburg the museum tour was conducted in KZ Neuengamme, a concentration camp near the city; and in Berlin the Wannsee villa,

where the "Final Solution" was engineered, was the site for this conducted tour! These places are indeed very different from the museum
in Israel. Heike Roms, in her analysis of the performance, fails to
realize this, calling the performance *Arbeit macht frei* in *Deathland*
Europe (suggesting that the work is done *in* Europe) and arguing that
in all of the places where the performance has been shown "the museums' principles of representing the past and constructing a collective memory are exposed in the provocative irony of the commentary."[28] The differences between the site of a concentration camp
or the Wannsee Villa, no matter what kind of exhibition they contain,
and a museum commemorating the Shoah in Israel, however, are not
a matter which can be muddled over. This distinction between *in* and
from is actually one of the most important subjects of the performance,
transforming what may seem like a "provocative irony" into a burning plea for a serious and critical reconsideration of the Zionist myth,
showing that a new form of exile has actually been created in the new
"homeland."[29]

When the group arrived at the museum the first time I saw the performance, we were greeted by an elderly woman called Sarah, a Shoah
survivor and a member of the kibbutz. She pointed out the major
landmarks surrounding the museum and proudly announced that the
kibbutz itself as well as the museum had been built without any repa-
ration payment (*Wiedergutmachung*) whatsoever from the German government. They rather constitute an act of liberation *from* it and from
Europe. Only after this specific performance, which she joined until
the very end, did I learn that this was the first time she had "participated" as the "guide" outside the museum, a role which was "performed" by one of the regular actors (the actor who served as the bus-
guide) the second time I saw the production. It also became clear
after this specific performance that Sarah had not even seen it before
(something which greatly surprised me considering that she was a participant in the actual performance), because after it was over she
openly, in a highly emotional protest, expressed how provoked and
even angered she had become by what she had seen, in particular by
what she felt was the completely unjust comparison between the sufferings of the Palestinians today and the fate of the Jews during the
Shoah. When exposed to the theatrical rendering of her own experiences, Sarah protested. *Arbeit macht frei vom Toitland Europa* is a production that constantly questions what it means to be a survivor and
a victim, contesting in different ways the exclusivity of the histori-

cal victims of the Shoah: here an actress can play a survivor and a Palestinian can be perceived as a victim. The theatre clearly gives much more freedom to the concept of what it means to be a survivor than the reality of which Sarah is a part. This difference between the "real" survivor and an actress playing a survivor lies at the very heart of *Arbeit macht frei vom Toitland Europa*, and the production privileges the latter.

When the group enters the museum, an elderly woman slowly and somewhat insecurely descends the stairs, facing the spectator-participants below her. She comes from some unidentified elevated region and introduces herself as Selma. She is played by the actress Semadar Yaron-Ma'ayan. Selma, who wears an elegant but rather old-fashioned long-sleeved dress with a handkerchief tucked under her wristwatch, says she is a survivor, adding in broken Hebrew (which is later often mixed with expressions in German and in English), "Anahno na'ase avoda beyahad," which means, "We will do *work* together." Because of the museum setting and the way Selma introduces herself, it even takes a while to realize that she is a fictional character played by an actress. From Selma's constant mixture of languages we get the impression of an older woman who has not been able to learn Hebrew properly, an Israeli who has remained an immigrant, still marked by the European languages she has brought with her to her new homeland.

The Zionist slogan *Avoda hi hayenu*—"work is our life"—no doubt functions as an ironic backdrop: in the concentration camps the kind of "work" referred to by the slogan over the gates is not life but death, while in the Israeli context the concept of Avoda was considered to be the collective national emancipatory and redemptive act to build the new country. The performance in different ways explores the possibility that the theatre as a "work" of art is an act or process of "*working* through," which may lead to some form of liberation from the degradations of the Galut. The title of the performance refers directly to this potential act of liberation by adding the words "Toitland Europa" in Yiddish, the language almost extinguished by the Nazis together with the six million Jews. The performance thus raises the possibility of reversing the Nazi inscription so that the "*work*" of the theatre will make it possible to become liberated *from* the country of death. The Hebrew word "Avoda" (work) is also used to designate religious rituals. Thus the work of art also carries a ritual function aimed at the liberation from this continent of death.

Selma starts the tour of the museum by explaining how the ghettos were established during the Nazi period. In a consciously exaggerated educational manner she asks the spectators if we know about other periods in history when such ghettos have been built. Someone mentions South Africa; then there is hesitation. When the name of the Palestinian refugee camp Dehaishe on the West Bank is mentioned, Selma instantly approves, asking if we really believe that what transformed Europe into what she terms a "puddle of blood" can be repeated. She does not develop this subject any further at this point. It is, however, the first time a connection between this specific past and the Israeli present is made. As the performance develops, this interrelation is repeatedly interwoven with other central themes like survival, bodily inscription, and possible liberation from the humiliations of the past.

Selma points out various pictures and objects in the museum, the public arena of documents and memorabilia from the past, which she claims still have a special meaning for her, implying that her own personal fate not only was shaped by them in the past, but still is in the present. Her intimacy with the images and objects of this past in the public memorial space becomes quite uncanny as she points them out and talks about them with us. We have now become participants not only in the tour of the museum but in her personal memories from the past. Sometimes she leans on the wall as if to rest from her physical as well as spiritual exhaustion, and sometimes she touches the face of a Nazi officer on a photograph as if he were an old aquaintance. Pointing at a yellow star of David which the Nazis forced the Jews to wear, which has been "rescued" and brought to the museum, she says that for her it has now become a "work of art." The transformation of the Shoah into a *work* of art is a central theme which the production gradually develops in distinct ways, first giving small hints which suddenly connect to the major themes, the *Arbeit*, the "work" of mourning we are actually participating in, which finally becomes the performance *work* itself.

Selma repeatedly stresses that in order to survive the Shoah a special form of creativity was needed. Her understanding of survival is quite different from the notion presented in *Ghetto*, where it was based on a strategy of deceptive cooperation with the Nazis, while for Selma it is apparently a kind of miracle. Pointing at a photograph of two young women in a ghetto, Selma speculates that they must be hiding a secret under the many layers of their clothes. She says that it is this

Selma (Semadar Yaron-Ma'ayan) in Arbeit macht frei vom Toitland Europa, *1991, explaining the rise of Nazism in Germany in the museum. Photo by and courtesy of Zion Cohen.*

hidden secret which will enable them to survive — adding with emphasis, if they have enough luck. Every human being, Selma explains, has a kind of black hole inside where the key to this person's individual survival has been hidden. Selma points at photographs showing that the ghetto itself also contains such black holes where Jews hid in order to save themselves: the sewage systems, the cellars, and the attics of the almost destroyed buildings. In all these cases of survival, she claims, a special kind of human creativity under extreme pressure was needed to bring about what to many seemed like a miracle. And as we will see much later Selma is also hiding such a secret — a black hole — which on a very fundamental level defines the character Semadar Yaron-Ma'ayan is playing as well as the actress herself as an artist, creating her "work." Her performance as an actress raises the issue of whether it is at all possible to "play" a survivor. This, I think, is the most intricate metatheatrical issue which *Arbeit macht frei vom Toitland Europa* raises.

During the tour Selma emphasizes that she does not feel that all the exhibits in the museum are of the same interest. Leaving the documentary sections of the museum, she leads us to the room where statues and other art objects made by survivors are exhibited. To reach this gallery Selma asks us to climb a staircase, which, as she expresses it, leads to heaven, meaningfully adding: "Don't be afraid, the work must be done." The performance is gradually building up the movement on the vertical axis, representing the earthly and the heavenly spheres, preparing for its final climax. Entering the upstairs gallery, Selma suddenly says that this part of the tour will be very brief because, she repeats, she feels no particular attraction to these art objects and there is also not enough time — a phrase she repeats several times, stressing the urgency of her own testimony and also that there is too much to tell. There are many important exhibits she still wants us to see "before our time is up." This is no doubt said with a complex irony, because the actress playing Selma is, as we will see much later in the performance, gradually becoming exactly such a work of art.

Before we leave this section, however, Selma asks us to pay attention to a statue of a Muselman, a person who is about to die from starvation. The term itself probably refers to the fact that before their death these starving people felt as fatalistic as they assumed the Muslims are when facing death. She points at a statue of a figure who is lying down; "since he is naked," Selma says, "he is so thin that his skin is glued to his bones, [and] he has no place to hide his bread." Then she adds with emphasis: "I would give a fortune to know where this Muselmanchik hides his bread; millions to know where the scream comes out, the Bat-Kol." The Bat-Kol, the mystical heavenly female voice emerging from heaven, to bring redemption, is also the voice of Hanan speaking through Leah's mouth in *The Dybbuk*, bringing "redemption" to her through some form of madness.

Only much later in the performance, in the barrack-structure situated in the theatre in the Akko Crusader fortress, does Selma provide a partial answer to her enigmatic question about "where this Muselmanchik hides the bread." This structure with its barbed wire and low ceiling gives the feeling of a barrack in a concentration camp, and this is where Selma's "home" (the private sphere as opposed to the public sphere of the museum) in today's Israel is situated. But since the performance is constructed on the basis of loosely connected thematic fragments which can only gradually be pieced together into a comprehensive narrative, like the life-story of an individual working through her life analytically, it is necessary to mention here that when Selma raises the question in the museum it is more or less left in the air. Only much later, after the ritual meal in her home, will this question be picked up again, and then her unexpected answer becomes the climax of the whole performance.

The fact that the performance returns to these central themes of survival and the miracle which makes survival possible is usually not pointed out directly. It is rather up to the spectator to make the connections between the fragments of Selma's life, if he or she wishes to do so. And since for Selma the pieces of her life are disconnected fragments, it is finally up to the spectator to create some kind of comprehensive whole. The museum tour and the visit to Selma's home are clearly structured in time and space, moving from one place to another. It is, however, not necessary to make any thematic connections between different fragments in order to participate in the performance as a whole. Each small individual section contains its own narrative structure, which is placed in the context of the whole performance through the character of Selma. This form of fragmentation also reflects the incomprehensibility of the Shoah: no single individual will ever be able to grasp the "whole," but each spectator-participant can construct his or her own specific script.

At this specific moment Selma's questions about survival and in which black hole the Muselman hides the bread remain unanswered; the museum-tour continues. Another fragmented "scene" in the museum which will only gradually fit into a larger thematic pattern is the screening of a section from the Polish postwar film *Ambulance*. This film-sequence develops the theme of *inscription*, showing how children are exterminated after they have entered what they believe is an ambulance. The fumes from the exhaust pipe are directed into the ambulance where the children are sitting. While the film is shown, Selma sometimes appears in front of the screen, slowly pointing out the exact shape of the exhaust pipe and other technical details of the extermination, as if she has been and still in a way actually is present during the event itself, as a kind of omniscient narrator. In this way she actually inscribes herself in the scene from the past on the screen while the movie projector projects the images of the past on her body, in turn inscribing them on her. She becomes totally engulfed by the past, and it seems extremely difficult for her to distinguish between this past, which is literally projected on her body, and the present in which she is now living.

The notion of inscription, which is another unifying concept of the performance, also contains a strong metatheatrical dimension, because acting itself is an art where signs and meanings are inscribed on, and even in, the body of the actor. As the performance continues, this notion will also be gradually developed in order to find out where the secret of survival has been hidden. These inscriptions actually write Selma's history, as well as that of the actress playing her, in their almost desperate attempts to reinterpret and bring new meanings to the ominous inscription on the gates of Auschwitz, which is the most complex and multivalent inscription of the whole performance. Finally, it is that very inscription —*Arbeit macht frei* —which is in fact *unsuccessfully* enacted in this performance. It seems to be impossible to become radically liberated from this past. Selma is even possessed by it. That may be the uncanny price of survival. It is perhaps possible to understand already at this point that Selma's liberation from the past and from *Toitland Europa*, having been irreversibly wounded by that beast, the European bull, will inevitably fail. Paradoxically, what makes the whole performance so interesting is that Selma's struggle to ovecome this past is performed by an actress who in many ways is successful as an artist. The performance of the actress Semadar Yaron-Ma'ayan's in *Arbeit macht frei vom Toitland Europa* is both extreme and exciting: in spite of the view expressed by Celan (in his poem quoted as the epigraph to this chapter) that no one can witness for the witnesses, she is actually able to "perform" the survivor. She shows that a successful performance is one of the ways to confront what is no doubt one of the most extreme failures of human history.

As the tour continues, Selma says she wants us to understand that the concentration camps — which, as she puts it, "were the most effective way to exterminate Jews"— were only gradually "invented" and "perfected." What we today call the Shoah began with small and seemingly insignificant incidents and methods like *Kristallnacht*, the ghettos, and the yellow star. But there is an inner deterministic evolutionary process in oppression and discrimination; as she expresses it, once the exact goals have become more clearly defined, this inevitably leads to a gradual sophistication of the methods used. In the museum, functioning as both a guide and a witness, Selma sums up her own experience as a victim in a tone combining a strange mixture of pride, despair, and exhaustion; she says that "our contribution to this century was the death-camp," echoing the view of the Jewish historian Emil Fackenheim that the Muselman was perhaps the most significant creation of the Nazis. In spite of Celan's pronouncement, Selma gradually becomes a witness for the witnesses. The strange unreality of such a fictional witness was perhaps one of the reasons why the woman called Sarah, who introduced the kibbutz and the museum the first time I saw the performance, became so provoked by it. A survivor can apparently not accept this form of testimony.

Selma's implied message is, however, quite clear in the contemporary Israeli context: such things can happen again, here and now, in the Israel of the 1990s — the first stages of oppression of the Palestinians are already behind us. As the tour continues, Selma repeatedly regrets that the time to discuss these problems in any depth is too short, because she is eager to show us the model of Treblinka which one of the survivors, a carpenter living in the kibbutz, has built from his own memory. This, she says, is his "work of art" commemorating the Shoah. Arriving at the wooden model, she takes a pointer and begins to explain how the death-camp was conceived and developed. In the middle of her explanation of how the small camp was gradually developed into a factory of death, however, she introduces Haled, an Israeli-Palestinian, who plays himself and whose full name is Haled Abu Ali. Haled, as he will tell us later in the performance, lives in a village close to Akko, but his traditional Palestinian family has no idea whatsoever of what he does in the theatre.

After a while Selma passes the pointer over to him so that he, as she emphasizes, can "complete" the explanation of the history of Treblinka. Haled begins by explaining in a quiet voice that he has studied the Shoah for several years in order to become a guide in the museum. He stresses how important it is to tell young Arab Palestinians about the Shoah, because "they do not believe that these things were possible." It remains unclear, however, if he implies that "they" deny that such things existed or that they have to prepare themselves for the next stages of the Israeli discrimination against them. Haled explains how the commander of the death-camp gradually "improved the methods" to exterminate the Jews, from what he calls the "most primitive stage," when the Jews were "simply shot and buried in mass-graves," to the invention of the gas-chambers by what Haled terms the "new ingenious commander."

These comments by Haled immediately created a kind of unease among many Jewish spectators, who are not used to an Arab/Palestinian explaining the developments of the extermination procedures or any other detail connected to the Shoah. How can "they" appropriate "our" Shoah? What does it actually mean when a Palestinian explains to Israelis about the Shoah? One of the uncanny aspects of Haled's explanation is no doubt that he is talking from the perspective of the victims, which in Israeli discourses is almost exclusively ascribed to Jews (and certainly not to Arabs), while the rhetorical position usually ascribed to Arabs in Israel, as a real or imagined extension of the Shoah, is that of the perpetrator and the enemy who may continue the extermination of the Jews.

During this part of the performance in the museum, the relations between Selma and Haled are presented as an almost formal working relationship between two individuals giving guided tours in the museum about the Shoah, implicitly showing that their own lives in quite different ways have become "guided" or even formed by it. Their meeting in the public sphere of the museum is very brief, consisting of Selma's passing over the pointer to Haled and her short, formal introduction of him. The museum as the official monument or arena commemorating the Shoah merely serves as the public cover for the confrontation with their inner private sufferings and pain, which will gradually be exposed during the second part of the performance. The museum is a public memorial, a site for commemoration, with official inscriptions, a model of the camp, pieces of art, photographs, exhibits, and official texts which the performance will gradually uncover in order to expose the much more intimate, unconscious regions of its two protagonists — Selma and Haled — as well as their mutual nakedness and even madness. This confrontation with what is hidden under the surface is shown in the second part of the performance, after the group has returned by bus from the museum to the Crusader fortress.

This second section starts out in one of the most private spaces possible, in what is probably Selma's recurring obsession or her nightmare. The spectators are gently ushered into a completely dark room, where the tickets were collected the first time I saw the performance, indirectly implying that *now* the theatre performance will begin. What we have seen so far was "simply" a guided tour, an approach to history based on the museum experience, which the production constantly subverted. The rest of the performance would provide a more intense and more personal embodiment of history, signaled by the transportation from the public to the private sphere. In this section the spectators are also asked to say something about their own experiences of the Shoah.

When everybody has entered the dark room, standing close to the walls, Selma, now wearing rags instead of her outward elegance during the museum tour, gradually becomes visible in the dim light. She stoops down and, while lying stretched out on the floor, she tries to wipe out the numbers on her arm with the handkerchief she wore under the strap of her wristwatch during the museum tour. These numbers, inscribed into her body, cannot be wiped out. Instead she obsessively takes the piece of cloth, similar to the ones she wears on her legs, and begins to wipe the floor. Then she disappears into the darkness again. This is like a photographic image, literally a writing in light, which gradually dissolves, leaving the spectators in darkness.

The spectators are now shown into another room, where a parody of the official Shoah day ceremony in an Israeli school is presented. It is an obviously theatrical and exaggerated representation of such a ceremony, very different from the more solemn guided tour in the previous section. Selma is now the teacher supervising the ceremony and the other actors, including Haled, are playing small children, while one of the three video monitors in the room shows how the actress Semadar Yaron-Ma'ayan is tattooing a number on her arm preparing for the production of *Arbeit macht frei vom Toitland Europa*. This is documentary footage filmed by Asher T'lalim, and it is a real tattoo, just like those which can still be seen on the arms of the survivors from the death-camps. The number on her arm is in fact the death date of her father, who escaped from Europe before the war, but many members of his family were killed by the Nazis. The inscription on her body constitutes the paradoxical dialectics of life and death; of her life-giver and his death; of the Shoah and survival from the "Deathland" behind the gates of Auschwitz marked by the numerical insignia of death, stigmata of suffering and survival. But at the same time this is no doubt also a theatrical sign, not just temporary theatrical makeup, but a permanent inscription which, unless she removes it through surgery, will remain there for the rest of her life. By making this tatoo on her arm the actress Semadar Yaron-Ma'ayan is in a way undermining what has been considered a kind of ultimate form of testimony of the Shoah, appropriating the tattooed numbers as her own.

Before being let into Selma's present-day home in Israel, we were led through a narrow corridor with barbed wire. Groups of three to four spectators were stopped in front of several windows which were suddenly opened by the individual actors, each with a writing pad and a pencil. The actors asked the spectators when was the first time we had heard about the Shoah and if we had any direct personal relationship to it. I experienced this section of the performance as a moment of embarrassment, a kind of transgression: from primarily having been a passive participant in the guided tour of the museum, once in a while asked general questions, I was now asked to open up experiences which were private. In a way each one of us was asked to become a witness, not just a spectator.

This is perhaps the most private and intimate part of the whole performance, because it is impossible to hear even what the people at the closest window are saying. Secrets are told here, and the actors are taking notes, writing down the personal testimony of each spectator in their notebooks. This is at the same time a form of inscription, as text, and witnessing. This transition scene does not last for very long, however — as Selma has repeatedly stressed during the museum tour, the time is too short to exhaust the subject. It can probably never really be fully exhausted. This is quite an effective transition, suddenly bringing the spectators much closer to the privacy and inner madness, primarily of Selma and Haled, but also of the other characters in the performance.

After we were led into Selma's home and asked to be seated on uncomfortable benches in this claustrophobic space, with its low wooden ceiling, scenes from her daily life (including her relations with her husband, her son, and Haled) were presented. Selma's home is not only a physical replica of a barrack in the concentration camps, like the model of the camp shown in the museum, but a psychological one as well, where all her fears and anxieties from the past are constantly remembered and reenacted. One of the peaks of our "visit" in Selma's home is her *tour de force* concert: accompanying herself on the piano and singing in a strong and vigorous voice, she meticulously compares Nazi and Israeli songs, showing that they actually have the same melodic basis and the same themes, valorizing the earth of the homeland and the home.

Another high point in this section of the production is the ceremonial Friday night Sabbath meal which the spectators are invited to share. The roof of the wooden structure suddenly descends into the midst of the spectators with a full meal served on it, like manna falling from heaven, a kind of theatrical *deus ex machina*. This draws attention to the vertical axis of the performance, as when Selma came down the stairway in the very beginning or when she stooped on the floor when trying to wipe out the number on her arm. During the meal itself a

Selma (Semadar Yaron-Ma'ayan) in Arbeit macht frei vom Toitland Europa *hanging down from the roof of her narrow "home" with the piano in the background. Photo by and courtesy of Olivia Heussler.*

macho Israeli army officer, who is played by Moni Yussuf, a Sephardi actor (whose family, as he says in one of the documentary films, had no direct connection with the Shoah), engages the spectators in a lively improvised conversation, telling provocative, mostly political jokes and constantly embarrassing his wife, who is a kind of transformation of Selma. When the meal is over, the remains of the food are suddenly lifted on the table, closing the roof of the narrow space again.

This performance with its very strong sense of enabling the spectators to participate in something "real," being guided in the museum and visiting Selma's home, fits very well into Una Chaudhuri's diagnosis: "naturalism rested on a fantasy of total visibility, of the impossible translation of private experience into public expression. This problematic of a public privacy survives long after naturalism, persisting into environmental theatre, where its presence is occluded by new spatial arrangements designed to create 'shared experiences' (shared, that is, between the audience and the actors)."[30] Chaudhuri's understanding of the connection between naturalism and environmental theatre can also be applied in this case. The Holocaust museum at the

Kibbutz Lochamei Haghettaot stands for such a fantasy of total visibility in *Arbeit macht frei vom Toitland Europa*, of something which is shared by all Israelis and in this case even by the Palestinians from the neighboring villages. At the same time, however, the Shoah can never be viewed in its totality. The "visit" in Selma's home and the sharing of the meal, where the husband almost ritually humiliates his wife and where Haled is presented as the even more humiliated servant accused of everything that goes wrong, represents another aspect of this shared neighborhood experience. It is a presentation of the "total visibility" by focusing in depth on the life of a single individual. Furthermore, if the theatrical experience is indeed a "public form of privacy" (as I have tried to show in a different context),[31] the Akko performance has created a number of transgressions of the sensitive borderlines between them, involving the spectator in a publicly performed, more or less private working through of the Shoah traumas — and the most striking transgressions are still to come. Before coming to that moment, though, I want to stress that if these forms of total visibility (most evident in the museum section) give the performance a documentary dimension, the uncanny twists of this public space give rise to a fantastic dimension.

A short while after the table with the remains of the food has ascended, it suddenly comes down again: now the thin, almost anorexic body of Selma is lying completely naked on it, wearing only a few rags. She is outstretched on her back, lying in exactly the same position as the statue of the Muselman that she pointed out to us earlier in the museum. She is slowly fondling her vulva and in a strange mixture of pain and ecstasy takes out the piece of bread that has been hidden inside her body. This, finally, is the answer to the enigmatic question of where the Muselman hides the bread and where the scream of the Bat-Kol comes from. This, she seems to say, is the dark hole where the key to *her* survival lies. At this point Selma/Semadar Yaron-Ma'ayan is also showing us where the energies and the nutrition for her survival have been hidden, the source of her own life, as opposed to the inscription on her arm which she has "inherited" from her father as well as her own "labor," the *work* and the *birth* (which is also a form of labor), through which the actress playing Selma transforms herself into a work of art. This is also the point at which Yaron-Ma'ayan shows us where her own creativity comes from, the creativity which has transformed her into Selma, the living replica of the Muselman statue. Here, in short, the borders between character and actress break down,

Selma (Semadar Yaron-Ma'ayan) in Arbeit macht frei vom Toitland Europa *lying on the table showing where the "Muselmanchik" has hidden the bread. Photo by and courtesy of Olivia Heussler.*

and she seems to be completely transformed into a "hyper-historian," the actor who is at the same time also a historian.

Selma, or rather the actress Semadar Yaron-Ma'ayan, places herself in a position where she even transforms herself into what Primo Levi has termed a "true" or "complete" witness. In his book *The Drowned and the Saved*, Levi writes that "we the survivors, are not the true witnesses. . . . We survivors are not only an exiguous but also an anomalous minority: we are those who by their prevarications or good luck did not touch bottom. Those who did so, those who saw the Gorgon, have not returned to tell about it or have returned mute, but they are the 'Muselmans,' the submerged, the complete witnesses, the ones whose depositions would have a general significance."[32] What makes Yaron-Ma'ayan's performance so remarkable is the gradual progression into this kind of muteness, where she becomes what Levi termed a "complete" witness.[33]

The sequence of the meal and Selma's exhibition of herself as the Muselman statue, however, refers in multivalent ways to the Christian martyrology of Jesus, ironically reversing many of the culturally potent symbols of this narrative. First, we have been sitting around the table, as "disciples," sharing a meal with the macho Israeli officer. On this same table the suffering figure of the living statue descends from the "upper," heavenly spheres, but she too cannot bring redemption as a *deus ex machina* is supposed to do. What Selma shows us as she takes the bread from her vulva is not the bread which is a substantiation of the flesh for the disciples to witness, as Jesus did before his death, but rather the bread of survival (which, when it was hidden inside her body during the Shoah, saved the Muselman, which she was, from dying). This bread is no miracle in the Christian sense — it is the scream, the Bat-Kol, the mystical female voice which comes out of her secret black hole. Instead of turning to the suffering of the male figure, which Christianity has done, even if Christ is frequently depicted with very strongly emphasized female characteristics, the Akko performance has placed the suffering female body in the center. Selma is the witness-actress who at this point also transforms the spectators of the performance itself into the witnesses of human suffering.

When this short scene with Selma concludes, the table with the Muselman/Selma on it ascends again and Haled suddenly becomes visible under it, inviting the spectator/guests for coffee and telling the story of his life and his family. It is significant that Haled has been hiding under the table with Selma's artistic representation of the Muselman on it. This is literally an image of the repression he suffers in today's Israeli society, which is represented by the self-absorbed figure of the Shoah survivor involved in telling her painful story of the magic survival while the Palestinian literally has to carry this heavy burden on his back.

Gradually the sounds of popular Israeli songs can be heard from all directions. At the same time the ceiling, from which the meal and Selma previously descended, opens in several places. We are now asked to leave our ("secret") underground hiding place through these openings and emerge into a cacophonic space where the patriotic Israeli songs coming from the loudspeakers and the energetic drumming of the director Dudu Ma'ayan himself become almost deafening. This space above — the Igra Rama, the "heavenly" sphere of popular Israeli culture and life, to paraphrase the division in *The Dybbuk*— also contains different human installations, each of which presents a total "acting-out" of different Shoah traumas, like constant eating. On the walls mementos from the Shoah and from today's Israel are exhibited. Haled, dancing naked on a pedestal with a bottle opener tied with a string around his neck, is surrounded by several beer bottles, which,

Selma (Semadar Yaron-Ma'ayan) with her back to the camera and Haled (Haled Abu Ali) lying in her arms in the final scene of Arbeit macht frei vom Toitland Europa. *The lit-up text in reverse on the gate says* Arbeit macht frei. *Photo by and courtesy of Olivia Heussler.*

through his body language, he urges the spectators to open and drink from. After a while Selma, who is still naked, joins him on the pedestal, where they become unified in a pietà-like configuration, as she holds him gently in her arms. At this point Selma has been transformed from the suffering Muselman into the mother-figure who is weeping over her suffering son, the young Palestinian man.

This is a completely different kind of museum than the one we visited in the first part of the performance. Here the total dislocation of Selma's and Haled's lives, where the subconscious regions of madness are exposed and exhibited in their nakedness, is commemorated. The inscription *Arbeit macht frei* on a replica of the Auschwitz gate can be seen from behind, and the ominous text has been lit by colored lamps, as if we were participating in a carnival. In an evocative way we are now behind the gates of the concentration camp, although we are also in the cellars of the old Crusader castle. The drumming director gently signals that the performance is over. Obeying him, we leave the noise behind, entering the courtyard of the Crusader compound; it is finally possible to feel the cool Mediterranean evening breeze.

There is no applause, there are no bows, only a sense that perhaps the *work* has only just begun.

But it is a work with a very high price, not overcoming Galut or the Toitland but creating instead a new form of spiritual exile expressing the forms of pain and suffering through which Selma and Haled have become possessed by each other in their pietà. As opposed to the possession and the madness in *The Dybbuk*, where the young couple supposedly become unified in a spiritual Igra Rama after their death, initially at least as an expression of a hope leading the way from the Galut to the homeland, in *Arbeit macht frei vom Toitland Europa* we have to leave the possessed couple on the pedestal with their collapsed hopes behind us in the museum of madness.

Hanoch Levin, The Boy Dreams

In Hanoch Levin's production of *The Boy Dreams*, the Shoah itself is not represented on the stage. Instead, we are witnessing an allegorical spectacle about the never-ending cyclical patterns of suffering in history, in this case focusing on the "dreaming" boy and his parents, in particular his mother. This performance has almost completely abandoned the documentary techniques which dominated the two productions examined so far; instead it focuses on the fantastic in Todorov's sense, where the dreamer himself, without really understanding what happens, becomes a witness of different kinds of atrocities that are representative or symbolic of the historical past. Since the events have already been filtered by the dreamer, who in this play is a more potent realization of the fantastic, the events are not presented as specific historical events from that past. The performance rather presents what could even be termed a "generic" representation of history, thus relying strongly on various allegorical features. The names of the characters are also largely allegorical designations of types or functions.

The Boy Dreams was published in 1991 and premiered in 1993 at the Habima National Theatre, where it was directed by Levin himself. The design was done by the Israeli scenographer Roni Toren. This stage production has also been recorded for Israeli television in a film directed by Ram Levy. Levin, who died in 1999 at the age of fifty-six, was a remarkable playwright and director. He published fifty plays, almost thirty of which have been performed on Israeli stages, most of them directed by Levin himself. After his death six more plays have been published. So far his plays have very rarely been performed outside Israel.[34]

Levin's stage career began in the late sixties with a number of satirical reviews that strongly criticized the Israeli euphoria after the Six-Day War in 1967. In the seventies he wrote and directed several plays about family life, marriage, and friendship, all of which presented these institutions in a grotesque light. In the eighties he expanded his thematic sphere, introducing mythical themes and characters such as Job, who is now forced to face the same existential issues as those from the lower echelons of society. In his productions in the nineties, to which *The Boy Dreams* belongs, he constantly developed the mythical themes and allegorical techniques, creating a whole series of plays that confront different aspects of the inevitability of death. The last one just before his own death was called *Ashkava* (Requiem).[35]

In order to introduce Levin's understanding of history as it is expressed in *The Boy Dreams*, it is first necessary to examine the narrative pattern which he has most frequently employed not only in this play but in most of his other plays and performances as well. This narrative pattern can even be seen as a kind of ideological blueprint for Levin's understanding of historical processes. His earlier plays as a rule present the story of an interpersonal relationship, while in the more recent ones it has been integrated within more comprehensive contexts, showing how the individual characters are blindly following the cruel fatalism of these historical processes. Levin's dramatic narratives begin with an explicitly formulated threat. Usually one of the characters is planning to carry out some form of cruelty or violence toward another character. As a rule this intended threat seems to be completely arbitrary and totally unexpected, coming without any previous preparations on the level of plot or characterization.

From a strictly formal-logical point of view threats can be viewed as speech-acts which can be formulated as a conditional statement: "If x, then y." In fact most forms of "education" are based on this kind of logical structure, where the "y" is the reward or the punishment, depending on how the "x" is carried out by the person (or the "victim") being educated. Parents and teachers make young people do certain things, like finishing the main course of a meal or doing their homework, by extending such threats. In Levin's theatre, however, this seemingly logical structure is completely disrupted; instead a perpetrator threatens another character with some form of punishment for reasons which seem totally irrelevant to the situation or without revealing what the reasons for the threat are. Thus the first part of the threat ("If x"), which supposedly creates a rational basis for the threat, is usually lacking. Levin presents situations with threats which are completely illogical or contain only their "then y" part. Furthermore, because of their cruelty the threats seem to be totally unmotivated by the situation. In most cases the spectators have to supply the reasons for this cruelty. The spectators have to justify the threat according to some norm which they do not at all identify with. Since the threat is so cruel it challenges the accepted moral norms and thus becomes problematic not only for the prospective victim but for the sensibilities of the spectators as well; less frequently, it is also based on some form of absurd or black humor.

One typical example of such a threat is Ya'akobi's parodic opening speech in Levin's 1972 play *Ya'akobi and Leidental*:

> I, Itamar Ya'akobi, 40 years old, hereby declare that I have suddenly discovered that I was born to live. Already this evening I will destroy my friendship with my good friend Leidental. I won't drink tea with him anymore and I won't play dominoes with him. I will hurt him and pierce him; I will kick at his friendship and I will make him feel lonely so that he will learn where he is — and where I am. I will hurt him and pierce him. I will pierce him and hurt him. And with hearty greetings I kiss myself warmly, I, Itamar Ya'akobi.[36]

On the basis of such a threat, which also parodies the text of the torchlighters in the traditional ceremony celebrating the Israeli day of Independence, Levin is quickly able to establish a dramatic conflict in which the victim tries to defend herself or himself against the humiliations of the perpetrator. Already in this early drama the antidote to this initial threat is the introduction of an even bigger threat, which in Levin's plays frequently is a female character. In this 1972 play she is called Shachash.

In addition to presenting a threat, the perpetrator — the person who on the basis of an irrational whim has stated that he or she will be cruel — after a short moment usually declares that the threat has been canceled, that it was not really serious. This change of attitude gives the victim as well as the spectators the impression that the initial threat has been transformed into some form of extreme benevolence. The speech-act of threatening has been transformed into another speech-act, promising in some way that the threat will not be carried out. The reason for this sudden change is also usually not directly revealed; it is based on another irrational whim. The change of attitude on the part of the former perpetrator turns out to be nothing but a temporary postponement of the initial threat, however, a tactic to ease the tension. When the victim believes the danger has really passed, the initial threat is finally carried out.

This change usually comes as a great surprise to both the victim and the spectators. The temporary postponement has created the impression that since the perpetrator has realized how cruel and even illogical the initial threat was, the threat could perhaps have been avoided altogether. But when the cruel deed is finally carried out, it seems as if the initial threat had somehow been inevitable; that it was an expression of a scheme of fate which even the perpetrator, who initiated this cruel chain of events (from the threat to the postponement and to its final realization), was somehow unable to control. This narrative scheme, which is the basis for most of Levin's plays and performances, frequently also serves as a transparent allegorical veil through which he examines fundamental issues of human agency in history, without having to assign a specific identity in the performance to the perpetrator or to the victim. These are allegorical figures, who carry out their preassigned sadomasochistic roles on the stage. As a result of this open-ended allegorical dimension, the recurring narrative scheme also makes it possible for Levin to confront his Israeli audiences with their own role not only as victims of cruelty but also as perpetrators of suffering on others. It is quite obvious how this narrative pattern can be applied to concrete historical situations, in particular to the Shoah.

This basic pattern is embedded on both the micro- and the macro-levels in the 1993 Habima production of *The Boy Dreams*. This performance begins with a female voice singing a sentimental melody, which as we will discover much later is the music from the country of the dead children. As we listen to the evocative song, we observe an idyllic scene with two parents proudly leaning over the bed of their sleeping child. There is something quite familiar, even stereotypically pure, about this scene, which perhaps evokes not only one's own family experiences but even religious connotations of the Christmas manger scene of Mary, Joseph, and baby Jesus. The very first lines of the play, however, spoken by the father, immediately introduce the possibility that the boy who is sleeping innocently in his bed, in spite of his purity, or perhaps because of it, is subject to some undefined threat and will somehow inevitably become a victim:

Upon falling asleep, the child becomes infinitely cherished.
Tranquil, his mouth open in helplessness,
This reminds us: how he would look should he die.[37]

At this point we do not know when or by whom this threat will be realized, but its realization and the victimization of the boy constitute the narrative curve of the whole performance: the question it addresses is what this young boy will look like when he dies and arrives in the country of the dead children in the last scene. If the threat in *Ya'akobi and Leidental* is expressed by one of the characters who wishes to break a friendship, in *The Boy Dreams* it is based on the very existence of the child, on his mortality: he is threatened by being born into this world.

The mother is also aware of this danger and wants the initial idyllic tableau to freeze eternally:

Let time stop now, at the peak of happiness,
Because better than this it will never be;
Let the three of us turn into still life:
"Parents gazing at a sleeping child." (p. 1)

Only by stopping the time of history can this threat be alleviated. This is paradoxically also what will happen in the last scene, after the death of the child. In the very first lines of this play Levin already draws attention to the relationship between the idyllic family scene and the potentials of its aesthetic representation, the performance itself, introducing a metatheatrical dimension — a painted still-life. Once the performance has begun, however, it is impossible to halt the inner dynamic development of the cruel events.

The anxieties and the implicit threat triggered by this "peak of happiness" almost immediately serve as a self-fulfilling prophecy through the commotion suddenly interrupting the idyllic scene. In his stage directions Levin has described what happens, which is also very close to what happened during the performance itself:

Strange sounds increasingly becoming louder begin to infiltrate from outside. A man bursts into the room, followed by other people, families, everyone is frightened . . . The Father and Mother are hovering over the child who continues to sleep peacefully. A wounded, bleeding man bursts in, stops, looks with utter amazement at the blood streaming from him. (p. 1)

At first sight these frightened refugees, and primarily the bleeding man himself, who was played by a quite young actor in the performance, seem to be a materialization of the unconscious fears of the parents. The wounded man, a talented musician, mourns his now violently ending artistic career — "Forty years of violin playing / are collecting in a small puddle by my shoes" (p. 2) — and falls down. This is the parents' future vision of their boy, who is now sleeping quietly in his bed, a premonition that his death will not be as peaceful and tranquil as his present sleep is.

At the same time the group of refugees gathering around the family can also be understood as the dream of the sleeping boy himself; what we see is his own nightmare foreboding his death taking shape around his bed. This understanding of the sudden interruption is also based on the fact that the name of the play is *The Boy Dreams*. At the same time, the concrete individuality of the refugees also makes it possible to understand this scene as a theatrical documentation of an event in the world, where the group of refugees and the wounded violinist are "really" appearing in the same fictional world as the child sleeping in his bed. This understanding is reinforced by the ensuing conversation. The bleeding violinist somewhat ironically adds that "the serious approach to music / is being delivered a serious blow here" (p. 2), finishing his speech with a declaration that he will protest.

The character called "A Frightened Observer of Death," however, goes on to ask:

> But to whom? To whom
> will you protest your death?!
> This really is the big question:
> To whom will you protest? (p. 2)

And as the violinist grows weaker and loses consciousness, A Frightened Observer of Death continues:

> This is a great man, this dead man,
> The most important thing of all, he already underwent,
> Whatever casts a shadow on our lives —
> He is now free from it, light and happy,
> A great philosopher, he solved the riddle,
> He knows something that even King Solomon
> didn't know in his life. (p. 3)

The fact that these words are said while the violinist is struggling with death creates a concrete situation on the stage, something that as a norm takes place in the so-called objective fictional world of the performance, established in the beginning by the family scene.

Since the performance has also created such a strong pattern of foreboding — moments after the father says that in death his son will look as if he was asleep we see the young violinist dying from his wounds — both these possibilities begin to exist simultaneously, each confronting the threat of the young boy's future death from a different perspective. The psychological anxieties of the parents, reinforced by the "objective" events themselves, on the one hand, and the nightmare of the boy, on the other, become ambiguously intermingled on the stage. No one of these interpretations necessarily seems to become dominant. A spectator may chose one at a particular point in the production, but, because of its allegorical qualities, is also free to change the dominant mode at any point. *The Boy Dreams* is not like Strindberg's *A Dream Play* in this respect, where the basic mode of presentation is the dream, within which there are fragments of reality. The important point in this context, however, is that both of the interpretative keys are based on a slightly different kind of threat which gradually becomes reinforced as the narrative structure I am examining here is constantly repeated. The monumental, abstract set, with only a bed and the groups of people visible on the stage, reinforces this complex theatrical situation with its double coding.

Before examining this performance further I want to draw attention to an additional aspect of the narrative pattern of threat and realization as it is generally realized in Levin's theatre. As the events are actually presented on the stage, one of the characters, usually (but not necessarily) the perpetrator, points at the victim, summarizing what we have just seen. In this particular sequence it is A Frightened Observer of Death, pointing at the dying violinist, who draws the seemingly obvious conclusion that this man has already become liberated from that which constantly (as Hamlet also knew) casts a shadow on our life — the fear of death. Now that he is dead he has paradoxically become both "light and happy." Without spelling out the words, the Observer — another form of witness — implies that the death of the violinist has actually freed him from the fear of this inevitable end. When the Observer points at the dead violinist as a "memento mori," the obvious moral is that this will eventually be the fate of all human beings. In the context of the multivalence of this situation these lines

The soldiers are threatening the quiet of the sleeping boy in the first act of Hanoch Levin's The Boy Dreams, *Habima Theatre, 1993. Photo by Pesi Girsch. Courtesy of the Habima Theatre.*

also open up the narrative possibility, which becomes more and more prominent as the performance develops, that the wounded violinist forebodes the death of the boy.

While the Frightened Observer of Death talks about the riddle the young violinist has solved through his death, some soldiers suddenly enter the stage. They, too, can at the same time be understood as a realization of the parents' fears and a nightmare dreamt by the boy. The soldiers have long black, Nazi-looking coats; they are somewhat stylized, and it is not absolutely necessary, I believe, to conclude that the performance depicts only that specific historical period. It also contains a more general allegorical dimension. Now everything shown on the stage spells out the notion of threat, totally overwhelming the parents, who are not given any possibility whatsoever to control and understand the situation rationally. The situation is in itself a threat, which they have apparently triggered by formulating their own fears. Threats are not only speech-acts, formulated in words; the words can also give rise to threats which have not yet been clearly formulated. At this stage, the parents also have no chance to question who the invading refugees and soldiers are. They just arrive in the room, which in the beginning was the most private and most sacred part of the home.

The emblematic tableaux-situations in the opening scenes of the performance immediately evoke a broad range of historical and cultural associations: the adoration of the sleeping child with its Christian connotations, which in Israel also carries a mythic quality of the Jewish parents admiring their child; the frightened refugees with their worn clothes carrying suitcases; the reference to the wisdom of King Solomon; and the sudden appearance of the soldiers. The associations with specific historical events are triggered by well-known representations of Shoah refugees and victims as well as by televised images of Israeli soldiers entering Palestinian homes in the middle of the night and boat refugees in Asia. Together with the multivalence regarding the status of these theatrical signs themselves, these vague and fragmented cultural and historical references create the basis for an open-ended theatrical allegory which cannot be given any one concrete, specific interpretation. It is a fragmentary allegory with several references. The ambiguities no doubt also create a kind of hermeneutic anxiety for the spectators, thus reproducing or mimicking the threat experienced by the fictional characters in the production itself.

At the same time, reinforcing this hermeneutic anxiety, it seems that for Israeli spectators the primary interpretative "key" for understanding these multivalent theatrical situations and images is a collective composite "Gestalt" of the Second World War and the Shoah and their possible repetitions and complex present-day reflections. In the performance itself Levin never totally fixes or stabilizes this "Gestalt" as a specific historical reality. But the implicit fragmentary allusive strategy of pointing at the Jewish experience during the Shoah is sustained throughout the whole performance. In the second act ("The Mother") the mother tries to flee with her child on a ship after the father has been killed at the end of the first act ("The Father"). In the third act ("The Child") they arrive in a country which refuses to accept refugees; and finally, in the last act ("The Messiah") the mother, carrying her dead child in her arms, arrives in the country of the dead children. The names of the acts also create associations with the Christian intertext. As a narrative it is, however, closer to a story about the Shoah.

Visually, as a concrete stage-image, this fragmented Shoah-Gestalt is most obviously present in the last act, in the country of the dead children, where a railroad track leads directly from the darkness of the backstage area, ending at the middle of the stage with slightly upward-bent tracks, indirectly signaling that this is the last station. Both the railroad tracks, which are not mentioned in the stage directions of the printed version of the play, and the gold watches which the figure of the Messiah shows the children as he opens his suitcase are clear visual references to the historical Shoah realities. But unlike Sobol's *Ghetto*, which used the testimonial statements of characters to reconstruct a specific historical place and time through a flashback, Levin's play and production do not make any effort to create a complete or coherent representation of a specific reality. His strategy rather implies that it is impossible to create any kind of documentary image of the Shoah on the stage.

The claim I want to make here, however, is that in *The Boy Dreams* these fragmented images, enabling the spectators to associate with the more or less stereotypic Israeli Shoah-Gestalt, create an aesthetic effect which reproduces a certain aspect of the Shoah experience itself as it has been analyzed by the historian Dan Diner.[38] From the point of view of the victims, Diner has argued, their day-to-day experiences of persecution and humiliation never enabled them to create a total image of the threat they faced, and thus they were unable to figure out a viable strategy for survival. Since from the point of view of the victims the methods of persecution were irrational, they were unable to identify by rational means the conditional structures of the threat that they were exposed to. This experience of the irrational threat during the Shoah itself, making it impossible for the victims to create a coherent narrative about the situation, clearly coincides with and reflects the narrative structures and strategies employed by Levin that I am analyzing here, and it is also closely related to Todorov's notion of the fantastic.

Arbeit macht frei vom Toitland Europa demonstrated that there are alternative ways to experience history (and the Shoah) and that these other methods of performing history may open up — for some people (but understandably not for Sarah, the survivor from the Shoah who "participated" in this production when I saw it the first time) — a new way of understanding aspects of the suffering. This production attempts to demonstrate that such suffering is not only the possession of the survivors and Jews. In that sense it even begins to generate a new narrative about the possibilities of contemporary

Israeli-Palestinian relations, while in *The Boy Dreams* the narrative structures generated by the threat create an overdetermination, what Michael Bernstein has termed a "foregone conclusion,"[39] because we very soon understand that, for Levin, the worst fears will inevitably be realized.

How these narrative strategies are activated by the text and the production of *The Boy Dreams* is very clearly illustrated by the behavior of the character called "Woman Born for Love," who makes her entry together with the soldiers in the first act. In the performance she wears a red dress, bringing out her pure erotic sensuality. As she sees the bleeding violinist, she exclaims:

> Dead? Really? Almighty God,
> the first corpse in my life!
> So what they talk
> so much about — happens!
> And this is how he'll lie, cold,
> ascetic, the bulb of his testicles tight
> for all eternity like a dead rat?
> What a terrible world!

And as she sees the group of refugees gathered around the dying violinist she continues:

> Dear God, you can smell the discharge
> of their fear!
>
> How their eyes are glued on me!
> I give them the finger — meaning.
> I'm taking a step — interpretation.
> What a vibration there is in the air,
> I'm almost tempted to say, electricity
> of wild love. (p. 3)

After this speech the violinist suddenly awakens from his unconscious state. According to the Levin formula Woman Born for Love first seems to take pity on him, trying to alleviate his pain:

> Almighty God, he's alive!
> The first dying man in my life!
> Let's have some water!
> Will there also be convulsion?

The death of the violin player in Hanoch Levin's The Boy Dreams, *Habima Theatre, 1993. Photo by Pesi Girsch. Courtesy of the Habima Theatre.*

The violinist pleads:

> Stop please . . . the blood
> I'm a violinist . . . ask . . . (p. 4)

But at this point the Commander is not willing to postpone the threat any more and brutally stomps on the wound of the bleeding youth so that he dies. The Commander sardonically adds: "Violinist? And here's a shoe, / sewn by a shoemaker." "Almighty God, Real military cruelty! / You enjoy shocking?" the woman exclaims. The Commander curtly answers: "You enjoy being shocked?" (p. 4) Violinist and shoemaker, art and power, are the basis for Levin's fearful, constantly repeated dialectics of threat and action.

I also want to draw attention to the fragmentary metatheatrical dimension in this passage. Two enigmatic lines of Woman Born for Love address the fear of the refugees:

> I give them the finger — meaning.
> I'm taking a step — interpretation. (p. 3)

These lines draw our attention to this dimension of the spectacle of cruelty as it is gradually tested and perfected by the woman and the Commander, and through them by the playwright-director Levin himself. As mentioned before, the mother also wants the "peak of happiness" to become a still-life painting. Her finger points out the meaning, as A Frightened Observer before her has done while looking at the wounded violinist. The Woman Born for Love points with her finger and takes a step, to interpret, thus laying the basis for the kind of hermeneutic activity through which she will understand what death means. Immediately after the woman talks about taking this step, the Commander steps on the bleeding man's wound, thus interpreting the riddle of life by creating death with the lethal touch of his shoe. Through their cruel cooperation the Commander and the Woman Born for Love create a "wisdom" which is obviously quite different from King Solomon's. These situations create metatheatrical spectacles which, in constantly changing constellations, are witnessed by the other characters on the stage.

When the Commander asks them all to leave this place, "The Wailing Woman"— who has obviously understood that this act of cruelty is in turn a new threat— cries out: "They'll kill us all" (p. 4). But the mother says she cannot run away because her son is sleeping:

Yes. He's a child. He must
sleep at night. He dreams.
They say that they grow at night.
Their personality is being shaped
at night, the soul opens. (p. 5)

The Commander reacts with a mixture of cynical admiration and resentment, now taking on the role of the oral interpreter, pointing at the sleeping boy:

Child. The essence of our lives. The crystal.
Sleeping, eh? Worlds are crashing down around him
and he is immersed, folded within the bubble of his dreams,
breathing steadily, as if with his breath, he is giving some
semblance of order and meaning to the chaos of our lives.

This threatening chaos is of course something which the Commander himself has created.

After making an invocation to all children, asking how it is pos-

sible to sleep like this, "as if / the world is a place to sleep?" (p. 6), the
Commander decides to wake the child.

Shhh, softly, gently,
we'll peel his sleep off him
like peeling the wrapper
off a valuable gift.

We'll turn the world
into a continuation of the dream. (p. 6)

In order to make this waking dream more attractive for the boy he
asks the soldiers to hide their guns as they and the refugees transform
themselves into a circus company.

The mother cooperates; as she gently wakes the child, she says:

A big circus, full of clowns and magicians,
has come to our town. They've come to you,
my little prince, to entertain you. (p. 7)

She is willingly submitting herself to the idea that the threatening
reality can be dismissed or postponed by escaping into a world of
glamour, another level of metatheatrical fantasies. The boy, however,
wakes up into a world where reality and fantasy are mixed in a different way. For the boy, completely ignorant of the dangers that lie
hidden under the alluring surface of the circus, this situation instills
security, even leading to ecstatic exaltation. For the spectators, however, it gradually becomes more and more ironic, and even uncanny,
as the boy is gradually drawn into his fantasies:

I love to get up at night sometimes
from a deep sleep and to discover that everything
is in its place, that Mother and Father and the room
and all the books and toys — that everything is there,
and that life is normal. The smell of cooked fish
from the kitchen, and the radio still playing,
and the simple tranquillity on my mother's face
is stronger than the web of dreams.

But I especially love surprises.
Oh, surprises — my living soul,
the first snow on the tree by my window,
or a new toy on my chair, or

for example, like now, guests at a ball
that fill all the rooms in the house.
And who are these guests, who? Oh my soul
is bursting with joy! — Circus clowns and magicians
that have come to our town, bringing with them
colors and lights, and the flavor of wonderful adventures.

Oh, I am bursting with delight, I must
roll around a bit to calm down.
The world is a good and happy place,
I recommend it to everyone
I recommend it to those who haven't been born
to hurry up and be born: you won't regret it! (pp. 7–8)

In the Habimah performance, the boy is bursting with delight as the
Commander joins him in his childish enthusiasm.

But the boy's idyllic dream-fantasy gradually becomes transformed
into a nightmare where the cruel realities which the parents and the
refugees have just experienced and the pleasant circus dream begin to
mingle. The Woman Born for Love begins to court the boy, making
a date with him in ten years' time, postponing the threat which the violinist has just experienced. But she immediately goes on, saying that:

. . . [d]eep in our hearts
we feel that this sweetness is not
really life, that there's something else . . .
Nightmares — maybe they'll
tell us the truth.
Do you remember me? Certainly you must have dreamt about me.
The dreams were right. Everything
was in the dreams.
And there is one dream
from which you don't awake. (pp. 8–9)

Her desire for the young boy is immediately transformed into a threat:
there is a dream called death, from which it is impossible to wake up.
Within the narrative curve of the whole performance the realization
of this existential threat is postponed until the last act, when the boy
arrives in the country of the dead children.

The central focus of this sequence, however, is the transformation
of a situation where desires and lustful fantasies can be directly expressed in a state of threat. The boy recommends this world to the

unborn children, but is immediately shown what dangers it holds. As the Woman Born for Love sees the father, she wraps her arms around his neck, saying:

Dear God, this is a man to converse
with on art until the morning light,
and even a bit more!
. . . I love
the first times most.
Ahh, if only I could live the first times only! (p. 9)

But when the father responds to her sexual invitation, she grabs the Commander's gun and points it at him; when the child asks for mercy on behalf of his father, she puts the barrel of the gun into the father's mouth. Female desire is immediately transformed into a threat.

This kind of transformation of a woman's desires into threats to a man is a recurring motif in Levin's plays. Here the threat also develops when the mother asks her child to beg for his father's life by singing a song:

Here come the sweet summer days,
Awash with happiness we wait,
The day is long, the night longer still,
But already we are beginning to worry,
Will the summer last? Will life last? (p. 11)

This song is interesting for several reasons. First, it is repeated several times during the performance. It is heard when the performance begins and is heard for the last time in the final scene, when the expectations for the coming of the Messiah and the resurrection of the dead children have been finally frustrated. Second, the song is an attempt to drive away evil, to postpone a verdict which seems inevitable. This kind of scene, where singing a song and entertaining is a way to postpone an inevitable death, has been used in many plays about the Shoah, including Sobol's *Ghetto*, where Chaya's song for Kittel saves her life.

Here the song has the same effect. The Woman Born for Love takes the gun from the father's mouth and hugs the boy as she says: "Ahaa, Childhood, childhood that cannot be resisted!" (p. 11). But as the father gets up on his feet, thinking that the danger has passed, she suddenly points the gun at him again, shooting him in the face, saying: "Dear God, it really happens!" (p. 11). And the father falls down dead.

This time the Commander is given the opportunity to comment, not only on what we have just seen, but also on the narrative technique used by Levin:

That was good. And that was right.
After you drained the fear
from this man, you had to restore
the belief that he would live, and then
just as he believes —
Boom! Smack in the face! All the slime!
He didn't manage to digest that he would live,
and again — he won't live!
How right! How cunning! Woman! (p. 11)

This metacomment again points directly at the female figure as the most suitable agency to carry out the threat.

Before analyzing the last act of *The Boy Dreams* I want to point out that in the Habima production (the only one so far) the boy was played by the actress Dina Blay, who is small and slim and frequently has an androgynous charisma on the stage. She is often cast in roles with a strong metaphysical or other worldly component (e.g., the Moon in Federico García Lorca's *The Blood Wedding*, a satanic doctor in Büchner's *Woyzeck*). Also, in a deconstructive production of *The Dybbuk*, she played the ghost of Channa Rovina, the legendary actress who played the role of Leah for more than forty years in the famous Habima production of that play. It is worth noting that in all of these roles, including the Boy in the Levin production, Dina Blay was wearing a white dress. Furthermore, in spite of the fact that the witness-function in *The Boy Dreams* was fragmented into several characters on the stage, including even the soldier-perpetrators, it was finally the child played by a female actress who served as the most comprehensive witness, who was marked as a victim in the very first lines of the play, and whose dream the whole performance actually presented.

In the last act of the play, called "The Messiah," the narrative structure presents a threat which is temporarily postponed but in spite of this is realized. Again it seems to become reversed for a moment, but this time this reversal is based on the supernatural forces of redemption. Instead of a threat there is now a promise. From the very beginning of the performance the future death of the child has been the most comprehensive and terrifying threat; but when it has actually taken place it paradoxically seems to bring new hope to the other dead children:

> In the midst of our courtyard games, at the height
> of our joy and exhilaration,
> we were taken and thrown into the pit. (p. 44)

To the question "When will we arise?" the Visionary Dead Child replies:

> I saw an angel, sailing in the sun;
> he dove slowly as into a sea
> of honey and descended and whispered to me:
> "Rest a bit longer, until the full quota
> of your friends and brothers
> who are destined to die like you." (p. 44)

When asked when this will happen the messenger angel answers that only one more child is needed for the quota of dead children to be filled. This brings great excitement to all the children:

> One more dead child! One more!
> Soon we'll awake, the light of resurrection
> will shine upon us, we'll rise, brush our teeth,
> wash our faces — and to the sun! To the sea!
> To splash water and laugh about
> the entire time that we waited in darkness! (p. 45)

When the mother is carrying her dead son to the country of the dead children, the initial threat that he will die now instead bears the potential to bring salvation not only to him, but also to the other dead children. At this point in the narrative pattern, there is a potential for total reversal, whereby the threat can paradoxically become a blessing.

For this dead child, who will be the last one to die, death will be very short:

> How happy he who dies a moment
> before the resurrection of the dead!
> He didn't miss anything! He didn't have
> time to lie in the grave and turn to dust.
> Perhaps he only missed tea at four,
> perhaps a piece of candy, and again he arises,
> like following a short afternoon nap
> after which his entire life stretches out ahead of him! (p. 46)

After the mother has parted from her dead child, the Messiah, looking like a peddler with two suitcases, enters. The dead children, trem-
bling with expectation, ask the old man to take out the magic oint-
ment which will finally bring about the miracle of their resurrection.
But the Messiah, who does not seem to be in a hurry, is fumbling
with his suitcases. Again the soldiers followed by the Commander
and the Woman Born for Love enter, while the Messiah tries to hide
among the children. When the soldiers discover him, the children first
believe that he will overcome them:

> Now, now! The string is about to snap;
> The Heavens — are about to open; it'll happen now!
> Yes, yes, that's how it happens in the movies,
> the hero hits rock bottom, it looks like
> everything is lost, and then at the last minute . . .
> at the very last minute . . . (p. 57)

Instead, after a short postponement the Commander shoots the Messiah in his head, just as the father was previously killed.

The Messiah has just been killed in the last act of Hanoch Levin's The Boy Dreams, *Habima Theatre, 1993.
Photo by Pesi Girsch. Courtesy of the Habima Theatre.*

The dead children are preparing for the last dance around the tree after the death of the Messiah in Hanoch Levin's The Boy Dreams, *Habima Theatre, 1993. Photo by Pesi Girsch. Courtesy of the Habima Theatre.*

Now it becomes clear that the Messianic hopes and expectations have also been nothing but a postponement of the realization of the inevitable finality of death. By presenting the possibility that the state of death can be reversed through resurrection Levin has shown how impossible the dreams and fantasies of such a state are. What for a moment seemed to represent some form of redemption, whereby the death of an individual will miraculously bring salvation to the whole community, proves to be just another temporary postponement of that finality, which everyone knows is inevitable.

There are many kinds of witnesses in *The Boy Dreams*, reinforcing the metatheatrical, self-reflexive dimension constantly hovering over this production, as in most of Levin's work. At the end of the third act, after the Lame Boy who is a poet and therefore also a witness has torn up his notebook of poems and thrown the pieces into the sea, the Bum says:

You wrote your poems to make an impression
and now you try to impress
by tearing them up.

It's too dramatic, uncalled for, unnecessary,
you give them more importance
than they deserve.

To the same degree you could have
published them in a book, even
gained a modest reputation;
The world would have looked the same.

You will still learn to despair
more quietly, more modestly,
in silence. As is proper. (p. 43)

In all of his work Levin has constantly provided a searching critique of the Israeli victim cult, revealing its ritual and mythical sources and examining the forms of cruelty by which it is nurtured. Such forms of cruelty, as we know them from the history books, are constantly evoked in *The Boy Dreams*, which examines the complex psychological and social processes that fostered Nazism or any kind of oppression. Levin has almost completely abandoned the documentary aspects of theatre dealing with the past and has created an allegorical framework within which the fantastic aspects of the individual situations have completely taken over, causing us to consider in a deep, dark manner the human desire and need for fantasy.

The words of the Bum in *The Boy Dreams* can also be read as Levin's own testament, his attempt to confront his inability to change the world by writing beautiful poetry. This is in many ways an image of the same magnitude as that which Walter Benjamin evoked in his reflections on Paul Klee's now famous 1920 painting *Angelus Novus*. In one of the frequently quoted passages from his fragmentary essay "Theses on the Philosophy of History" (Über den Begriff des Geschichte, 1941), Benjamin provided a concrete image of how historical realities are mediated:

A Klee painting named "Angelus Novus" shows an angel looking as though he is about to move away from something he is fixedly contemplating. His eyes are staring, his mouth is open, his wings are spread. This is how one pictures the angel of history. His face is turned toward the past. Where we perceive a chain of events, he sees one single catastrophe which keeps piling wreckage upon wreckage and hurls it in front of his feet. The angel would like to stay, awaken the dead, and make whole what has been smashed. But a storm is blowing from Paradise; it has got caught in his wings with such violence that the angel can no longer close them. This storm irresistibly propels him into the future to which his back is turned, while the pile of debris before him grows skyward. This storm is what we call progress.[40]

This is the angel of history, who is at the same time historian, dramatist, and actor and is caught by the destructive energies of the constant failures of history, which it perceives as one single catastrophe. In its attempts to tap the creative energies, to awaken the dead and to enable them to become alive again, which is actually only possible on the theatrical stage, the angel is hurled into the gradually evolving future by the storm "we call progress."

This is a very complex image, which has been given a constantly growing number of interpretations. In Klee's own painting of the *Angelus Novus*, however, the angel is facing the viewer; we do not see its back. This means, if we interpret this painting in theatrical terms, as a stage, that the viewer's back is turned toward the past, and we are looking into the future, toward which the angel has turned its back. Hanoch Levin's performance *The Boy Dreams* is filled with such angelic figures who are looking at the wreckages of the past: the dreaming boy himself, the other dead children, the lame poet, and, ironically, the figure of the Messiah. When the gaze of the spectators of such a performance, or the viewers of Klee's painting, meets the eyes of such angelic figures, their helplessness meets our hopes. This is a moment when the theatre can create a utopian dimension, a way of reading and performing the failures of the past through a possible completion of history. Benjamin also confirms such a utopian possibility in his 1941 essay on the philosophy of history, claiming that "[i]n every era the attempt must be made anew to wrest tradition away from a conformism that is about to overpower it. The Messiah comes not only as the redeemer, he comes as the subduer of Antichrist. Only that historian will have the gift of fanning the spark of hope in the past who is firmly convinced that *even the dead* will not be safe from the enemy if he wins. And this enemy has not ceased to be victorious."[41] The theatre constantly strives to reaffirm such impulses for liberation expressed by the actors, who through their creative energies are able to stand up for the dead. This is at least one of the reasons why the theatre can have such an exciting and deep effect on us and can even, in some cases, become restorative.

Three European Productions about the French Revolution

*A spectacle, by definition, can never coincide
with either the inwardness of consciousness or the
opacity of the flesh. Still less can it reconcile them.
Once they have been dissociated, these two moments
of human reality are in opposition to each other;
and as soon as we pursue one of them, the other
disappears.*
— Simone de Beauvoir

In this chapter (and in chapter 3) I want to examine performances about historical events that are not as close to us in time as the Shoah. The French Revolution today gives rise to associations that are radically different from those triggered by the Shoah. But that more distant series of events, which undoubtedly has been formative for our modern consciousness, is also saturated with contradictions which the theatre after the Second World War has attempted to integrate into its aesthetic vocabulary. These theatricalized "confrontations" with the French Revolution have given rise to many innovative productions, some of which have become canonized by critics, researchers, and the collective theatrical memory, like the productions by Brook and Mnouchkine. Many plays and productions about the events from this period, however, have been completely forgotten. In his introduction to the two plays by the Polish playwright Stanislawa Przybyszewska about the French Revolution — one of which served as the basis for the script for Andre Wajda's film *The Danton Affair*— Daniel Gerould lists more than two hundred plays about the French Revolution.[1] Most of them are not performed anymore.

The events of the French Revolution were immediately turned into spectacle, so anyone who tries to represent the Revolution as a theatre performance is already contending with a theatricalized, performed history. The French Revolution also gave rise to a very broad range of practices as well as intellectual perceptions which most historians agree signaled a critical turning point in European history. Among the many exceptional individuals during this period the Marquis de Sade no doubt stands out for having created a unique combination of his excessive sexual practices and his extensive reflections on these practices. One way to formulate de Sade's "contribution" is in terms of a radical repositioning of the borders between the public and the private spheres. The issue is not whether this was historically "true," in the academic sense; but the "rediscovery" of de Sade indicates how the post–World War II theatre positioned itself in relation to the dialectics between the private and the public spheres. One of the common features of theatre and historiography — at least the history of mentality — is that in different ways both strive to expose or disclose something in the public sphere that has previously been perceived as private.

In two of the three European examples of performances about the French Revolution examined here, de Sade is one of the central characters. In one of them, *Marat/Sade* by Peter Weiss, he appears as a character on the stage: he is the dramatist-director and himself an inmate, working with the mental patients in the Charenton hospital. In the other, *Madame de Sade* by Yuko Mishima, de Sade is in a sense the central character around whom the whole plot of the play moves, but he does not appear on the stage at all. In Ingmar Bergman's production of this play, this nonappearance can even be given a metatheatrical interpretation, which (at least indirectly) also says something very important about Bergman himself as a director.

Simone de Beauvoir's essay, "Must We Burn de Sade?"— from which the epigraph to this chapter comes — is one of the possible starting points to reflect on theatre performances about the French Revolution. De Beauvoir examines the character and the writings of de Sade from a post–World War II perspective; one of the central points she makes is that there is an irreconcilable opposition between "the inwardness of consciousness" and "the opacity of the flesh." The spectacle, in the theatrical sense of de Sade's own excessive fantasies and practices, belongs to a different ontological sphere than both consciousness and the body. The spectacle can neither coincide with nor reconcile them. Instead de Beauvoir emphasizes the fact that the fantasies in de Sade's *The One Hundred Twenty Days of Sodom* were narrated before they were carried out: they have been imaginatively "witnessed" before they take place or are "performed." They are a prescription for a performance. This actually stands in opposition to the notion of performing history, where the events on the stage are a means to look back at the atrocities as debris from the past. For de Sade, the practices gain their meaning, de Beauvoir argues, "by means of . . . a duplication [whereby] the act becomes a spectacle which one observes from a distance at the same time that one is performing it."[2] The fantasies are for de Sade a kind of *prospective* for the spectacle, while the performances of history are as a rule *retrospective*, just like Benjamin's angel looking back in time (to the place where the spectators are standing) at the catastrophes that have already taken place, trying to confront the rubble.

The theatre, as opposed to de Beauvoir's analysis of de Sade, is — it seems — always based on an attempt to reconcile "the inwardness of consciousness" with the "opacity of the flesh." The theatre creates signs whereby the text literally becomes *embodied* through the actor on the stage, thus creating what Erika Fischer-Lichte has termed a "body-text."[3] From the playwright's point of view, however, in writing a play which is to be performed on the stage, a fantasy is created; as de Beauvoir observes concerning de Sade, it is narrated or told before actually being carried out. From the theatrical perspective, though, when historical events are dramatized and performed on the stage something is shown again which has already taken its course. The processes of the theatre, including the preparations and rehearsals for the performance, have been created in order to confront and reconcile these contradictions. The dialectics between these retrospective and prospective perspectives is even more complex when the theatre is performing history. The historical figures who are presented on the stage act in their own time "as if" their deeds are being done in the present, while on the stage their actions are determined by the fact that they represent historical figures who are appearing again. Repeating the past by theatrical means creates interesting tensions that draw attention not only to the theatrical medium itself, but also to the deeper thematic concerns of such performances.

Such tensions are of course not unique to cases when the theatre is performing history. The realistic theatre as well as Stanislavsky's system of acting, based on emotional memory, certainly drew attention to such complex time-schemes. But theatrical performances presenting historical events on the stage strive to create a particular kind of intensity through which the actor becomes what I have termed a hyper-historian, functioning as a witness of the depicted event. The theatre performing history summons a certain kind of energy, which validates the authenticity of the events that are depicted on the stage as historical events. These energies are in particular expressed through the acting. This analysis of the three European performances about the French Revolution attempts to isolate and examine such energies of acting.

Peter Brook, Marat/Sade

Since these energies of acting no doubt are already created through the process of the rehearsals of a specific production it would be useful to examine the rehearsals too, not only the final result presented on the stage. It is, however, not always possible to find out in detail how the different workshops and more goal-oriented rehearsals for a particular performance have affected the creation of its specific "body-texts." Since the production of *Marat/Sade* was preceded by a fairly famous and well-documented workshop held in 1963–1964 called "The Theatre of Cruelty," with an obvious reference to Antonin Artaud, led by Peter Brook and Charles Marowitz, we know at least something about these preperformance processes.

In an interview with Simon Trussler, published in *Plays and Players* in February 1964, Marowitz said that for him Artaud's notion of "cruelty" has "to do with a certain kind of rigor in expression and a certain kind of formality which, when it connects with a certain kind of experience, produces a result which is *more true* than the conventional ways of expressing that experience could be."[4] This in effect also means that the actor, according to Marowitz, can actually become what I previously termed a hyper-historian; on the basis of Fischer-Lichte's reading of Julia Kristeva, this term can be expanded to include the interpretive praxis of the actor as what she terms a "Subject-in-process." Fischer-Lichte wishes to consider how it is "possible for the different Subjects participating in the production of a theatrical text to constitute themselves as Subjects in that production?"[5] Fischer-Lichte quotes directly from Kristeva, who has formulated how the instinctual drives of an individual are articulated: "[d]iscrete quantities of energy move through the body of the subject who is not yet constituted as such and in the course of his development, they are arranged according to the various constraints imposed on his body—always already involved in a semiotic process—by family and social structures."[6] Performances about historical events in several ways also confront different possibilities of understanding the past, as an extended aspect of the social structures or traditions that Kristeva discusses. This past is an established body of knowledge, something commonly known, which by being presented on a theatrical stage is constantly reinterpreted in theatrical or aesthetic terms.

By taking Artaud as a point of departure for the workshop it was possible to create a "body-text," which according to Marowitz is actually even more true than the conventional images of a particular experience are. This idea of "added truth" which the theatrical images contain *vis-à-vis* the historical documents is crucial for the notion of performing history, where conventional, sometimes even clichéd, images of the past become integrated within a work of art and the historical accuracy of the representations is as a rule not questioned. Since the notion of performing history implies that some kind of authenticity will always be necessary, the actors have to function as historians on the stage. This means that whatever else they are doing, they are also telling us something about the French Revolution as a historical event through the energies of their bodies. At the same time they become the medium through which Brook and Weiss interpreted the French Revolution.

In the same interview Brook himself also referred to these issues from a slightly different perspective: "[w]hat we are *trying* to bring about is for the actor, in making his choice, to make it as an independent, responsible creative artist. Instead of turning his impulses into one of the many forms that are already there (so that his choice fits into the form that he has learnt to appreciate and assimilate), here his responsibility is to transcend his first naturalistic impulse, and then he has to manifest the best expressive choice, in a way that he can afterwards defend as being to the limit of his consciousness."[7] And he added that "[b]y *asking* the questions, we hope to weld the group of actors into a special fighting force. Our main hope in this particular experiment is that it will have the right sort of provocative *professional* effect — and this is different from what Artaud was doing. His aim was infinitely larger, and would relate to something that we can't attempt to get to at once, which was to have an effect on *life*."[8]

The goal of this workshop, at least as formulated by Brook, was primarily to create a professional "difference," while for Artaud the goal of the theatre had been infinitely more ambitious, to have a direct effect on life. But this more limited goal is also related to the creation of a "subject-in-process" as a kind of revolutionary fighting force in the theatre of that time. Brook's aim was to form a collective of actors, "to weld the group of actors into a special fighting force." Their individual energies can become transformed into a collective energy through which the work in the theatre can also become revolutionized. He was trying to find a way to bring about — if not a revolution — at least some significant changes in theatrical performance at the time.

In his descriptions of the rehearsals for *Marat/Sade* in his book *The Empty Space*, which can no doubt also be read as a blueprint for much of his subsequent work as a director, Brook emphasized how the documentation and research of the actors were aimed at finding a bridge between what de Certeau terms the "real" and "discourse":

> In early rehearsals, improvisation, exchange of associations and memories, reading of written material, reading of period documents, looking at films and at paintings can all serve to stimulate the material relevant to the theme of a play inside each individual. None of these methods means much in itself — each is a stimulus. In the *Marat/Sade*, as kinetic images of insanity rose up and possessed the actor and as he yielded to them in improvisation, the others observed and criticized. So a true form was gradually detached from the standardized clichés that are part of an actor's equipment for mad scenes. Then as he produced an imitation of madness that convinced his fellows by its seeming reality, he had to come up against a new problem. He may have used an image from observation, from life, but the play is about madness as it was in 1808 — before drugs, before treatment, when a different social attitude to the insane made them behave differently, and so on. For this the actor had no outside model — he looked at faces in Goya not as models to imitate but as prods to encourage his confidence in following the stronger and more worrying of his inner impulses. He had to allow himself to serve these voices completely; and in parting from outside models, he was taking greater risks. He had to cultivate an act of possession. As he did so, he faced a new difficulty, his responsibility to the play. All the shaking, juddering and roaring, all the sincerity in the world can still get the play nowhere. He has lines to speak — if he invents a character incapable of speaking them he will be doing his job badly. So the actor has to face two opposite requirements. The temptation is to compromise — to tone down the impulses of the character to suit the stage needs. But his real

task lies in the opposite direction. Make the character vivid and functional. How? It is just here that the need for intelligence arises.[9]

Marat/Sade is no doubt an intelligent production in this sense. The two poles Brook is speaking about, the uncontrolled inner impulses and the need to communicate with the spectators from the stage, can already be found in the original Weiss playscript. This description also fits in very well with Kristeva's depiction of how "[d]iscrete quantities of energy move through the body of the subject."

During large parts of the ·performance, the actors are in effect asked to present two roles simultaneously: the mad inmates of the Charenton hospital and the actors playing the characters in the performance which was written and directed by de Sade. The many outbursts of madness, when the characters so to speak "lose" their fictional roles in de Sade's performance and become both incomprehensible and violent as lunatics, are dialectically opposed to the self-control which is demanded not only by de Sade's performance in the hospital, but also by the new social order which has replaced the previous revolutionary one. Thus the process of confronting the two contradictory forces or interests that Brook considered to be an integral aspect of the rehearsals for the production is also clearly present in the play itself. This is an example of how the thematic concerns and the structure of the play are transformed into a metatheatrical dimension in the performance, expressing a dialectics between the uncontrollable energies of "shaking, juddering and roaring," on the one hand, and those which can be mastered, speaking the lines comprehensibly, on the other, in order to make sense in spite of the madness they experience as fictive actors in the mental hospital as well as the madness called the Revolution. There is a constant struggle between the fictional actors in the Weiss play and the actors Brook is directing in his production of the Weiss play.

The Weiss play itself already superimposes two historical situations: the assassination of Marat, which took place in 1793, and the performance in the Charenton mental hospital in 1808. The simple fact that the "historians" of 1808, as they are performing history within the Weiss play, are mental patients is of course also an ironic comment on the role of the present-day actor-historians as they are performing their version of the historical double-exposure which the play itself prescribes. When the Herald introduces the actress who plays

Charlotte Corday in de Sade's play, for example, he gives her the following description:

Here's Charlotte Corday waiting for her entry
She comes from Caen her family landed gentry
Her dress is pretty shoes chic and you'll note
she readjusts the cloth around her throat
Historians agree so it's not lewd in us
to say she's phenomenally pulchritudinous
Unfortunately the girl who plays the role here
has sleeping sickness also melancholia
Our hope must be for this afflicted soul
that she does not forget her role[10]

Charlotte Corday, who is the most active character in carrying out the assassination of Marat, frequently falls asleep and has to be woken up. It looks as if she lacks the energies to carry out the counterrevolutionary act that she believes will redeem the people from the new form of oppression. Also, like most of the characters in the performance presented at the mental hospital, beyond the general description of her ailment Corday has neither a name nor a private identity as a mental patient. She is thus a nameless actress in de Sade's play about the historical events of the assassination. Glenda Jackson, who plays this anonymous patient at Charenton, who in turn plays Charlotte Corday, shows on two levels what it means to perform history, presenting a complex and multilayered image of an actor-historian.

The contradictions and tensions between the mental patients and the historical characters they perform can also be clearly perceived in the theatrical language developed by Brook in the performance itself. This language is based on the creation of composite stage images with a very strong connection between the different levels of events on the stage. This kind of stage image generally has a very clear central focus to which everything on the stage is connected. In some cases it has the qualities of expressionistic theatre, as in scene 21, where Marat is shown suffering from a fever, which in Brook's production, with the help of steam (at least in the film), has been designed as a kind of nightmare. All the other characters appearing on the stage in this scene are therefore the figments of Marat's feverish imagination, which on the level of the fictional world of the Charenton hospital is the expression of the paranoia from which the patient (who is also anonymous) playing the role of Marat suffers. The Weiss text does not make any specific demands of this kind concerning the theatrical images to be used in this scene. By emphasizing the expressionistic potentials of this scene, however, Brook seems to be focusing on Marat's mental energies.

The whipping scene (scene 20) likewise presents a strong center of consciousness on the stage. At the same time it also activates all the fictional levels of the performance. In his speech in this scene the Marquis de Sade tells Marat

> what I think of this revolution
> which I helped to make. (p. 46)

At this point Charlotte Corday is asked to whip him. In Brook's version of this scene, de Sade, stripped to the waist, bends down on his knees; Corday, standing behind him, uses her own hair to do the whipping, not an actual whip as the stage-directions indicate. As she rhythmically moves her floating hair over his shoulders from one side to the other, the inmates gather behind them and join in a chorus of hissing. And when Corday lifts her head to give him a blow with her hair, they all groan and move in a kind of collective pain as an accompanying chorus. The central consciousness or the subject of this scene is de Sade, the writer and the director of the play performed by the inmates at Charenton. All the other characters on the stage are the "tools" which he has "directed" for the purpose of giving a theatrical expression to himself and his ideas.

While the whipping gradually reaches a crescendo of self-inflicted suffering, a reenactment of his own "pleasures," de Sade attacks the revolution for transforming its own initial desire for reform into bloody acts of meaningless terror and sensationalism:

> all the meaning drained out of this revenge
> It had become mechanical
> It was inhuman it was dull
> and curiously technocratic. (p. 49)

Corday and the chorus accompanying her have all become integrated in this mechanized expression of violence on the Charenton stage which de Sade, formerly one of the active participants in the Revolution and now also one of the inmates at the Charenton hospital, has created to illustrate what happened when the Revolution turned against itself and became the tool for its own destruction. Interestingly, de Sade does not deviate at any time from his firm role as the "historian" who totally controls the performance, while all the other characters in different ways become deranged and totally carried away by their ailments.

Corday's hair whipping the shoulders of de Sade can also be seen as a metaphorical guillotine teasing his neck, showing us where its sharp blade can cut off his head. While Corday whips his shoulders and neck, de Sade tells how

> . . . the tumbrels ran regularly to the scaffolds
> and the blade dropped and was winched up and dropped
> again. (p. 49)

This he calls the "mechanical," "dull," and "technocratic" aspect of the newly developed death-industry which the Revolution, and de Sade himself as one of its agents, has "helped to make." De Sade presents himself as both victim and victimizer, as the precursor and the agent as well as the cause of the Revolution. The whole performance-within-the performance in the Weiss play can be seen as de Sade's witnessing of the French Revolution, as a play performing history. The scene with the self-inflicted whipping that de Sade (as the creator of the performance in the hospital) has directed Corday to carry out while the crowd behind them illustrates the whipping vocally is much more specific. Here de Sade becomes transformed into a complex theatrical image of his own transgressive eroticism, illustrating the origins of his transgressive energies for us on the stage. In this scene de Sade not only is the former victim who has become a witness, the central consciousness of the performance at Charenton; he is also staging his own revictimization in the performance of the inmates, of which he is both the author and the director.

For a critic like David Richard Jones, this scene does not carry the multiple layers of meaning which I have tried to point out here. Jones argues instead that "Brook aestheticized the whipping" and that the whole scene was "arty, even phony, given the circumstances" of Charenton in 1808. As a result, "Brook's image conflicted with the scene's point, which I have already stated as a demand to make life personal and real, not aestheticized, abstracted, or distanced . . . Played realistically, the scene can be traumatic — unquestionably the play's most gripping scene — and an experience that literally embodies Sade's beliefs."[11] It seems, however, that the whole point of

Brook's production is to show how a personal life, and in particular that of the Marquise de Sade, is based on and finds its energies in such forms of aestheticization. This process of aestheticization in it- self is actually an important aspect of that historical past which the contemporary performances of the Weiss play are presenting; or to put it differently — the Marquise de Sade is the theatrical historian of the gradual processes of the aestheticization of the assassination of Marat, starting with David's painting.

Beyond this dialectic interaction between the different layers of the past events and their aestheticizations through performance are the spectators. Darko Suvin has made an interesting observation in this respect: "In Weiss's Theatre-As-World, the world is — as the encom- passing stage metaphor shows — a madhouse and a torture place, in which the most alienated and least conscious, politically the most in- sane, are the Coulmiers who do not even know that as the indispen- sable jailer of the jailed they too are inside, not outside the space of madness and torture." [12] The ending of the Brook production clearly recofirms this idea, when the Coulmiers are attacked and his wife and daughter are even raped by the actors. In Weiss' own script this fea- ture is not clearly indicated. But it transforms the Coulmiers — in par- ticular his wife and his daughter, who are apparently unaware of the deeper significance of the performance they have watched — into vic- timized spectators. This ending shows that the energies of the Revo- lution, which supposedly have been contained and repressed by the in- stitution of the mental hospital, cannot be controlled anymore. In her text for an exhibition of her work as a scenographer in Stockholm 1995, Gunilla Palmstierna-Weiss, the widow of Peter Weiss, who de- signed the costumes for the Brook production (the set for this pro- duction was designed by Sally Jacobs), writes:

> The final scene in the film is radically different from the one of the stage production. In the film bars have been lowered as a curtain in order to separate the inmates from the audience. The visible audience is from the beginning of the 19th century, while there also are spectators from our own time. This audience con- sisted of us, Peter Weiss, Peter Brook, myself and all the other participants in the film-team.
>
> I thank God that there were bars between us and the actors. Since there had been dissatisfaction among the actors Peter Brook had invited all of them to vodka and champagne before

the last shooting. He said this was the last day and therefore they could do what they wanted in the last scene. On stage they had been threatening the audience as the curtain went down.

Having played mad and repressed more or less every evening and sometimes also in the afternoons for almost two years, being constantly present on the stage wearing heavy costumes, and carrying out ideas that in the beginning had seemed quite bizarre, they had really become tormented . . . The musicians who had been chained to the floor were gradually really turning mad. An aggression had been built up which now in the final scene was released in an explosion which was directed straight at us. The bars, which separated us from the actors, held sway against their threatening approach and attacks. In anger and intoxication the actors burned the scenography, the costumes were ripped, some were fighting, which resulted in broken legs and a concussion. Everything was filmed.

It was impossible to shoot this scene again. The ending was a documentary and Peter Brook was very pleased. Theatre of cruelty, life.[13]

This clearly shows that the energies of the historical events and those of the performance are (or could become) closely related — the outburst on the stage is a parody of the Revolution.

In this last scene the actors in de Sade's performance attack the three spectators, who, sitting just under the proscenium arch, belong to the play's fictional world. Their liminal presence both as participants in the performance and as spectators mediates between the spectators in the auditorium and the violent action on the stage. During this revolutionary upheaval, which is actually a mock version of the "real" Revolution, the wife and the daughter of the hospital director Coulmier are (in the filmed version) raped by the furious inmates. This is a Revolution transformed into pure sexual violence, no doubt deeply affecting the spectators in the auditorium. Even if we dismiss the Coulmiers for their dumb rationalism and blindness, the audience is at least symbolically also attacked after having witnessed the performance in the Charenton hospital. The series of events from the whipping scene to this violent outburst at the end of the performance of *Marat/Sade* has also shown just how closely the acts of witnessing and victimization are related.

In *Ghetto* (Srulik), *Arbeit macht frei vom Toitland Europa* (Selma), *The*

Boy Dreams (the Boy), and many other performances about the Shoah, the former victim, the survivor, as a rule takes on the function of a witness in the performance itself. The witness tells the spectators of the performance about their own victimization, thus also, at least indirectly, turning them into witnesses through identification. *Marat/ Sade*, in contrast, ends by showing how the spectator-witnesses on the stage become victimized through the rape. But as a dialectical counterpart to the Coulmiers, the victims we can hardly identify with, de Sade holds a position which is similar to that of a Shoah victim like Srulik or Selma. He is a victim of the Revolution who has written a play in which he serves as a witness for the next generation. This generation has been confined to a mental institution, like many of the Shoah victims, who in different ways have had to surrender their sanity to the failures of history. And, finally, in the whipping-scene in *Marat/Sade*, just as in the scene in which Selma comes down on the table as a Muselman, de Sade restages his own victimization as part of the performance at Charenton, creating a metatheatrical dimension which opens up a dark window directly onto history. The victimization of Marat and de Sade thus becomes emblematic of a much more inclusive conception of history, including the horrors of the twentieth century as well. The French Revolution is of course not the cause of these later developments, but it now derives part of its meaning, retrospectively, in the light of our subsequent understanding.

Ariane Mnouchkine, 1789

Mnouchkine's renowned production *1789*, which premiered in 1970, has also become an important landmark in the contemporary theatre for its ideological commitment and its use of unconventional aesthetic means. The point of departure for the creators of this production, which was a collective work, was to dramatize events from the year 1789. But Mnouchkine and the actors wished to go beyond official histories about that year, while they also wanted to examine the crucial year of the French Revolution in the light of 1968. In order to avoid the old traps of historical antiquarianism, the

> answer, provided by Mnouchkine, came with the suggestion to
> play the historical events as if they were being re-enacted by a
> troupe of fairground performers or "*bateleurs*" as a living contem-
> porary agitprop newspaper, using their theatrical skills to pass

on what they knew and thought to the people in a fairground setting. This meant that the familiar events could be shown in a new light which came from below — it was a version of the uprising seen from the point of view of the ordinary people, where the famous figures appeared on stage only as puppets or in extremely caricatured street-theatre portraits but never in mimetic representations.[14]

1789 can be seen as a kind of subjective Brechtian demonstration of certain episodes from that year presented retrospectively.

Mnouchkine privileges the point of view of the common people performing at the fairground, making it obvious who has the authority to tell the stories about the failures of the past and also perhaps to change the present. It is the common people who are the witnesses of this past as well as the hope for the future. Judith Graves Miller summarizes this position, claiming in somewhat general terms that "[t]he Théâtre du Soleil confronts the problem of theater and revolution by questioning the conditions necessary for theater and by producing political plays. Inspired by the concept of revolution both as aesthetic change and as government overthrow, the theatre challenges traditional notions about the theatrical institution."[15] The performance of *1789* was to a large extent based on improvisations, and it is considered the most collective work in the history of the Théâtre du Soleil. Mnouchkine has described the interaction between herself and the actors after they presented their improvisations during the rehearsals in the following way:

> I never had to make a selection: the selection was made of its own accord, on the evidence. It might occur to me to say to someone "That is not good," but I do not say anything because I realize that the actor is going to realize very quickly. In fact it is difficult for me to say exactly what my role is; we work in a totally empirical way. When the production is under way I cannot tell any more which was my idea initially. I may think I had a particular idea, when it actually came from the actors and vice versa. I think I am there to encourage, to *energise*.[16]

The interaction between the director and the actors, at least as described by Mnouchkine herself, seems to have been very flexible and open. But at the same time it is clear that she is there, as she explicitly stated, to energize and to empower the actors.

The production of *1789* not only went through its developmental stages in workshop and rehearsal; it also continued to change during its run. So there is no one version of the production to refer to.
The video version and the printed English translation, however, can serve as a reference for my purposes here. The production started with the flight of King Louis XVI and Marie Antoinette to Varenne. The King and the Queen move as shadow-figures, miming their flight into the darkness, while a voice on the loudspeaker, accompanied by the funeral-march from Gustav Mahler's First Symphony, tells the story of their discovery in a very neutral, matter-of-fact voice: "They've left, the king disguised as a lackey, the queen as a chambermaid and their family. They flee. They passed through the sleeping towns and villages: Villparisis, Meaux, Ferte-sous-Jouarre, Chaulieu, Chalon . . . At Sainte-Merchauld they stopped at a posting house. It was opened for them. The postmaster recognized them. He let them start off again, but they stopped at Varenne and [were] forced to turn back."[17] The King and the Queen, now performed by two other actors, are led back to Paris, while the funeral-march picks up the more popular melodies of the Mahler symphony, and the speaker continues: "The afternoon was warm, the king had lunched well and dozed off. Some kilometers from Paris, a delegation of the National Assembly, led by Barnave, came to meet them and escort them as far as the capital" (p. 12). Upon the return of the King and Queen to Paris, he invites the Queen to dance, which they proceed to do before the spectators, who are situated on tiered platforms on all four sides of the small stage spaces distributed throughout the large performance space. This arrangement is in accord with the fairground idea of the whole production.

This formal, quite nondramatic opening comes to a sudden close when the speaker makes the following somewhat unexpected announcement: "Ladies and gentlemen, that was one way of telling the story, but we have chosen another, here it is" (p.12). Immediately, the hardships of the common people are directly represented. Now a much more excited voice is heard: "In that particular year through the kingdom the most terrible famine was raging: the women were too weakened to nourish their children and throughout the day the men set out to search for food and returned empty handed" (p. 17).[18] Four similarly dressed couples enter simultaneously. They situate themselves on four stages. Each of the four women holds up a similar baby-bundle. As opposed to the announcer in the first scene, whose voice came from the loudspeakers, all four men speak with their own voices in this scene, repeating the same text, which describes their inability to find fire and food for their families. Thus begins the revisionist history of the year 1789, featuring the poor instead of the plight of the King and Queen. Now the fathers, who are in despair, take the children from their mothers, telling them:

> Give him to me, my wife,
> Let me nurse him, my wife,
> Let me fondle him, my wife,
> And send him to sleep. (p. 17)

But instead they take the bundles and strangle their children. The staged formality of the opening scene is clearly opposed to the despair of the four exactly similar families. Here performing history not only repeats the past; it is presented as a fourfold repetition of exactly the same event, which through the repetition is presented as something universal.

Yet despite the somberness of this particular scene, what stands out very clearly in the performance of *1789* is its carnivalesque quality. Perhaps the best-known scene, the storming and the fall of the Bastille, is an interesting example of this. It begins with each actor gathering a smaller crowd of spectators, at first almost whispering the account of the events as someone who witnessed them in person. ". . . Come a little closer, that's right, come on . . . I'm going to tell you how we, the people of Paris, took the Bastille" (p. 32). This chorus of whispering voices, similar to the scene with the four families, can be seen at first as discrete groups of people repeating the same action, which gradually increases to excited shouting. Their gestures also gradually increase in a synchronized manner, together with the drumming accompanying the whole scene. As the narration reaches its climax, the dispersed voices become a totally unified force. When the storytellers, after more than ten minutes of describing the details of the preparations, announce that the Bastille has been captured, the whole performance is transformed into a wild carnival at the fairground, which remains the basic locus of the performance. This is not only a description of the first critical event of the Revolution itself, but also an attempt to make the spectators feel that they become a part of it by listening to the story, almost witnessing it. This is the point at which it seems the performance reaches its highest level of intensity.

Michael Kustow has described this scene in the following way, commenting on its more general significance:

And then, in one of the show's most riveting episodes, the lights dim, all goes quiet, and we gradually hear whispers. "Approchez, approchez," whispers an actor, and we cluster round. With rising excitement, as if he'd just come panting from the event itself, he gives a blow-by-blow account of how he and his comrades took the Bastille. All round the theatre actors are whispering this precious story to little groups of listeners in the dark. Their voices weave together, mount into a triumphant crescendo of victory, the lights blaze on, and the whole place explodes into a carnival, here and now, and we become the people of Paris celebrating "la fête la Bastille." [19]

Here the spectators of the performance are apparently not just passive witnesses, but are listening to a direct eyewitness account of the storming of the Bastille, which triggered the Revolution, and which in turn incorporates the spectators into the crowd celebrating the victory. But the initial pleasures of the carnivalesque energies are soon perceived as dangerous by the leaders of the Revolution. So the liberal aristocrats, represented in the performance by the Marquis de La Fayette, attempt to restrain the crowd. As the music grows louder and the demands of La Fayette remain unheeded, he begins to shout: "I hereby ban all celebrations, all festivities, all public merry-making, and all manifestations of happiness which could, in one way or another, trouble the order of the proprietors, and understand one thing well: *the revolution is over and done with!*" (p. 37).

For Kustow, as a spectator, "[t]his theatrical marketplace also recalls irresistibly the ecstatic debates and feverish all-night meetings of May 1968, and the analogy is no accident. Both revolutions, the production seems to say, had to be contained and repressed by authority because the 'fête revolutionaire,' if allowed to reach its ultimate conclusion, would have brought about absolute change." [20] Kustow was perhaps overly idealistic when he wrote down his reactions to the performance in 1972. The question his reaction raises in retrospect is not only how the sensibilities regarding such "absolute change" have altered, but also the extent to which, as Klossowski formulates this issue, "the existing state of things has eliminated the possibility of another form of existence." [21]

The contrapuntal strategy of the *1789* production, placing opposite points of view against each other, is the basis for such different forms of existence. But the basic question — whether the Revolution brought about change and radically new forms of social behavior — is no doubt answered negatively. No matter what the intentions behind this change are, the notion of dialectical oppositions reflects both the historical situation of the French Revolution and the relationship to revolutionary situations at the time of the performance. It is also interesting to note that the opposition between the stormers of the Bastille and La Fayette, which was stressed by Kustow as well as by the English translation of the text, does not appear in the video version of the performance. This perhaps reflects another historical sensitivity at the time when the video was edited.

The double perspective is reflected in the basic form of the production, having a fairground-within-the-performance as the basic locus where the events from the past are retold by those who "actually" witnessed them. The actors in this production have thus already taken on the role of historians, just as *Marat/Sade* is based on a performance situation at the Charenton hospital, where the past is retold. But most of the characters in de Sade's performance have not witnessed the historical events themselves — or at least they do not show it. The characters in *1789*, however, are presenting themselves as the witnesses of the events described. The actors who took part in the performance also apparently used their historical research directly in the performance, and the audience could no doubt see this. In spite of the fact that the mass-scenes in this production gave expression to social and revolutionary energies that at least theatrically are much stronger and in many ways even more "effective" than in any of the other performances examined in this book, Mnouchkine's approach to history raises many questions. Does the carnivalesque atmosphere of the fairground (where the spectators had to be much more active, moving between the different areas of the action, than is usually the case in the theatre) turn them into witnesses in the sense developed above?

Obviously *1789* did not aspire to achieve what *Arbeit macht frei vom Toitland Europa*, for example, aimed at. What the Israeli productions about the Shoah have in common with *Marat/Sade* and with Bergman's production of *Madame de Sade*, but seems to be lacking in *1789*, is the awareness that ultimately it is impossible to represent the horrors of history on the stage. The other two productions about the French Revolution, but not *1789*, are in different ways trying to negotiate our

horrible new knowledge of human behavior in the Second World War. This again does not mean that the French Revolution was like the Shoah or even led up to it, even if it was in some sense a preview, in-
troducing a new form of industrialization of death. But it means that looking at or "performing" the French Revolution after the Shoah apparently necessitates some kind of awareness that history, like the theatre (but in very different ways) is a form of repetition — of things that appear again. Repetition in history and in the theatre is always a repetition with a difference, and this raises the dilemma of recognition and of taking responsibility. The form of repetition employed in *1789* was based on doing exactly the *same* thing in many different areas of the huge performance space simultaneously, like the fathers taking their children from the mothers or telling of the storming of the Bastille, not on creating a *sameness* or *similarity* through an implied temporal repetition. The repetition does not necessarily have to be explicitly spelled out, as in *Arbeit macht frei vom Toitland Europa*. But it is apparently not sufficient merely to transform the past into a narrative in order for a production to perform history in the sense I am developing here.

1789 does not seem to acknowledge how difficult and complex the task of performing history — representing the past and bearing witness about it — is. It does not perform history; it theatricalizes the past, and its carnivalesque mode has been filtered through the political ideas of the 1968 revolution, rather than a darker and much more complex confrontation with history, both recent and past. It is in a way a production not very dissimilar from the street events of the 1968 era themselves, when so many aspects of the political and social events became spectacle and street-theatre. Mnouchkine and her company, who undoubtedly have made an important contribution to the contemporary theatre, actually seem to have become entrapped within the very discourse they were trying to critique in *1789*.

Ingmar Bergman, Madame de Sade

Ingmar Bergman's production of Yukio Mishima's play *Madame de Sade* premiered at the Royal Dramatic Theatre in Stockholm in 1989 and ran for several seasons. It has also been performed at different festival venues all over the world. This production belongs to a very different form of theatre (in terms of both the dramatic text and the mode of production) from the two productions about the French Revolution examined so far. They depicted public events from the

French Revolution which had very clearly defined effects on the public sphere. The Mishima play, in contrast, brings us to the much more private realm of a specific family. Only the echoes from the streets can be seen and heard. Bergman's approach to this text is much more private too.

The Brook and Mnouchkine productions are also much more clearly experimental than Bergman's and in many ways (even if I have not dealt with this issue here) became crucial for the subsequent directorial work of both Brook and Mnouchkine. In contrast, when Ingmar Bergman directed Mishima's *Madame de Sade* in 1989, he was already a well-known and recognized director. The Mishima production, like several of Bergman's more recent theatre productions and his later films, can be seen as a summing up, a comment on his own personal role as a director. This summing up, which frequently was very direct and even personal in this work, became an important subtext of the performance; it can even be seen as a kind of tongue-in-cheek self-irony on Bergman's part as the director of this performance. Bergman has actually inscribed himself in his production of Mishima's play in several ways.

In the program for the Mishima production there is a photograph, probably taken during the rehearsals. It shows a hand horizontally stretched out from behind the stage, symbolically inviting us to enter or showing us the way "into" the performance. Behind this image of the hand a slightly tilted vertical wall can be seen, crossing just behind the open palm. It is a dynamic image, creating tensions not only between the horizontal and the vertical lines of the photographic composition, but also between the image of somebody presenting himself through an open hand (which like a fingerprint is unique) and the fact that this person is not exposing his identity, that he is hiding. This hand, Bergman's own — as shown in another photograph in the archives of the theatre from the rehearsals, where he is wearing exactly the same shirt — is perhaps the hand of creation, evoking the famous painting by Michelangelo. But the photo of the hand does not show us the traditional object of creation: Adam. Instead Bergman's unidentified hand is directed toward his own creation, represented by the portrait of the actress Stina Ekblad on the opposite page of the program.[22] In contrast to the anonymous image of the outstretched hand, this actress is identified; her name is written on the bottom of the page. This is a facial portrait of the *actress* Stina Ekblad, without the makeup or the wig for her role as Madame de Sade in the perfor-

RENÉE – STINA EKBLAD

The hand of Ingmar Bergman and the photo-portrait of Stina Ekblad in the program for Madame de Sade *at the Royal Dramatic Theatre in Stockholm, 1989. The negative was turned around to achieve this effect, because in the original photo the hand was pointing in the opposite direction. Photo by Bengt Wanselius. Courtesy of the Royal Dramatic Theatre.*

mance. The portrait is shown with her face "floating" against the black background of the photo. Bergman's open directorial hand also indirectly presents the portraits of the five other actresses in the performance, who are shown on the subsequent pages of the program with the same kind of floating faces: Marie Richardson (Anne, the sister of Madame de Sade), Anita Björk (their mother, Madame de Montreuil), Margareta Byström (the Baroness de Simaine), Agneta Ekmanner (the Countess de Saint-Fond), and Helena Brodin (Charlotte, the servant in the mother's house, where the action takes place).

Bergman's gesture depicted in the program can be understood from a number of different perspectives. Besides extending an invitation and alluding to the famous painting of the creation, it also indirectly draws attention to one of the major themes of this performance. Mishima's play, taking place before and just after the French

Revolution, depicts the complex influences of the Marquis de Sade on his wife, her sister, and their mother, as well as the servant in the house and two other acquaintances, all women. The Marquis himself, who in several ways is the central focus in the lives of all these women, never appears on the stage during the performance, just as the theatre director Ingmar Bergman is physically absent from his own work. The photo of the hand in the program reinforces such an interpretation. The production of Mishima's play can thus be seen as an indirect representation of the director, who, from his position of hiding behind the scene, has secretly influenced his work of art, just as de Sade, in quite different ways, has influenced the lives of the six women in Mishima's play. Only Madame de Montreuil and her two daughters, de Sade's wife and her sister, are historical figures, while the other three are Mishima's own literary invention.

The plot of *Madame de Sade* begins in 1772; the second act takes place in 1778; and the third act takes place in 1790, exactly nine months after the storming of the Bastille. It is a narrative about creation and procreation. During all of this time, approximately seventeen years, de Sade is in exile or is imprisoned because of his sexual transgressions. Accordingly, although he is the main character around whom everything on the stage revolves, he has not seen his wife during all this time. He has had an affair with his wife's sister, Anne, but their meetings are not shown on the stage. The complex relations between the women and de Sade, and in particular Renée's longing to become united with him again, are the main focus of the play.

When the Marquis knocks on the door in the final scene, though, his wife, who has become religious, asks the servant Charlotte to tell him to go away. Her previous longing for him is now denied. Mishima's play can thus be seen as a *tour de force* of dramatic writing, wherein the "main" character is anticipated and discussed, but does not enter the stage during the whole performance; only his influence and the expectation of his return are represented. This is no doubt a variation on the theological thematics of Beckett's *Waiting for Godot*.

In his postscript to *Madame de Sade*, which was also published in the program for the Bergman production, Mishima claims that the main reason for writing this play was to explore the reasons for this nonappearance: how did it become possible for Renée to refuse to see her husband in the very last scene of the play? In this text Mishima writes:

When I read *The Life of the Marquis de Sade* by Tatsuhiko Shibusawa I was captivated, as a writer, by the enigmatic fact that Madame de Sade after having shown such inviolable loyalty to her husband during his long years of imprisonment deserted him the moment he was finally released. This riddle served as the point of departure for my drama, which is an attempt to give it a logical solution. I realized that behind this riddle it is possible to find something very difficult to understand, but which at the same time is very true about human nature. I wanted to explore de Sade and keep the whole thing within this frame of reference. This play can thus be characterized as "de Sade seen by women's eyes."[23]

The female characters on the stage reject the return of de Sade and his "penetration" of the female space that the play/performance has established. Paradoxically, while the play expresses Mishima's fascination with the riddle of femininity, rejecting the entrance of the male into the space the women have established, it also expresses in Bergman's production the powerful masculine desire of the director's vision, which controls the actresses who play the roles in Mishima's play. Bergman directing Mishima thus establishes a metatheatrical correspondence and transformation, which says something about the art of directing, which operates as the art of manipulation and empowerment by absence. The characters in the performance react to de Sade in a way that is similar, metaphorically, to the way in which the actresses on the stage "react" to the absent presence and influence of the director.

How poignantly aware Bergman is of this issue can be seen in an interview he gave in 1979, when he discussed a performance of Jean-Paul Sartre's *The Unburied Dead* (*The Condemned of Altona*), staged by another Swedish director. In the torture scene, which "takes place before the eyes of the audience . . . the actor cried and screamed — and it looked just like an actor crying and screaming." One day the director asked the actor "whether he could do it in some other way. So he piled up the chairs and desks for the school children in a straight line, and behind this mountain of tables and chairs the torturing was done. You didn't see it, you only saw some of the movements and heard the screams. And it was so terrifying that people couldn't take it." "That," Bergman adds, "is one of the secrets of our business — not to show everything."[24] The Mishima production is structured on the basis of the same principle of not showing what is apparently most painful, the relations between de Sade and his wife.

Bergman no doubt maintains much more responsibility as well as authority over a production and the performers than Brook and Mnouchkine in *Marat/Sade* and *1789*, at least according to their own reports. Such a generalization is of course also a simplification, but in the 1979 interview Bergman presented his understanding of theatrical energies and empowerment, claiming that every particular stage has some kind of "magic" or focal point of energy, and it is up to the director to find it. He even claimed that he actually models the performance around that particular point, "where the actor is best and most effectively located. Approach and withdrawal effects are all created in relation to this point."[25] Thus, Bergman continued, it is necessary "to locate, very consciously, the point on the stage where the actors are strongest."[26] Later in the same interview, with regard to film directing, he stated:

> When I work together with the actors in the studio, in front of the
> camera, I always place the actors in relation to the camera so that
> they feel they are at their best. They feel — not that they are beau-
> tiful, but that the magic of their faces and their movements will
> be registered by the camera. And they like that. They sense that,
> because I like them, I wish them to be as powerful and multidi-
> mensional as personalities and actors as possible. On the stage
> I do exactly the same thing. I position them . . . according to the
> principle of the magic point. I place them on the stage, in relation
> to each other and in relation to the audience, so that they feel
> they are effective — that their charisma will work on the audi-
> ence . . . I must always function as a kind of radar, you see; I
> can tell whether an actor feels well, whether he feels secure, or
> whether he feels tense and unhappy. And I feel it faster than he
> feels it, I can tell before he says so, because my intuition is always
> at work and tells me at all times what is going on inside this man
> or this woman.[27]

In spite of this authoritarian approach, which in many ways is similar to that of Robert Wilson in his U.S. production of *Danton's Death* (analyzed in the next chapter), the concrete results on the stage seem to be very different. One of the reasons for this is that the production of *Madame de Sade* implicitly refers to the omniscient intuition of directing in the theatre as well as being about the authority and invisible influence of an unseen male figure. In this respect the production can also be seen as a metatheatrical "analysis" of directing.

At the same time, however, there are moments when it is possible to perceive a kind of tension between the directed role, on the one hand, and the work of the actresses, on the other. At these moments the performance seems, for a moment, to fall apart or to disintegrate. This may in a way be my perception projected on the production and may have nothing to do with the actual facts of the rehearsals themselves; it may even be a moment which Bergman has very meticulously directed. But it is a moment where one of the actresses seems to revolt against something she has been instructed to do on the stage. One such point occurs in the second act, when the Countess de Saint-Fond, who is socially and intimately connected to the other women as well as to the Marquis, tells them about the black mass in which she has participated, functioning as a "table." This act takes place in 1788, the year before the Revolution. As we watch the actress Agneta Ekmanner, who plays the role of the Countess de Saint-Fond, we suddenly realize that her hands and arms are marked with bloody stigmata. In terms of her entry and the position she takes she probably very closely followed the directorial instructions, in order to gain as much energy as possible on the stage. The stigmata themselves are no doubt also a directorial invention.

But as she tells her story about the details of the black mass, she also uses a complex sign language, gesticulating in a ritual way, giving her body a very strong presence. This is after all a story about giving meaning to her body and about ritualizing her sexuality in ways which are very similar to those employed by the Marquis himself — because, as she says, "he and I are members of the same coterie."[28] At the high point in her narrative, the Countess de Saint-Fond talks about how, before the mass itself began, a silver crucifix was placed between her breasts and a silver chalice between her legs. Just before going into further details, when she announces that "the time of the mass was approaching,"[29] Agneta Ekmanner/the Countess de Saint-Fond slowly raises her right arm, exposing the stigmata on the palm of her hand, as if she has been hiding a secret and now wishes to reveal it for a short moment. And while she slowly begins to describe the black mass, she covers the sign of blood with her left hand again, as she lowers her head in a gesture which signals reverence.

These gestures function as an enigmatic reinforcement of the tale of suffering, torture, and degradation, as well as redemption. Being a

The Countess de Saint-Fond (Agneta Ekmanner) in Bergman's production of Madame
de Sade *at the Royal Dramatic Theatre in Stockholm, 1989. Photo by Bengt Wanselius.
Courtesy of the Royal Dramatic Theatre.*

feminine transformation of Christ, the Countess de Saint-Fond also
identifies herself with the Marquis de Sade, implying that her suffering is in fact a form of erotic pleasure, which can also be seen as a
kind of premonition of the French Revolution itself. This aspect is
perhaps most clearly expressed in the description of the Countess de
Saint-Fond's violent death, which Anne, the sister of Madame de Sade,

provides at the beginning of the third act, implying that the Revolution was a sexual act which resulted in a kind of "birth." According to Mishima's own stage directions, this act takes place exactly nine months after the outburst of the Revolution, in April 1790.

Anne describes how the Countess de Saint-Fond left for Marseille, where she earned some money through whoring which she wanted to spend on a dress inlaid with precious stones. One evening during a riot the Countess was trampled to death. Anne goes on:

> And when the morning came the crowd found her body. They placed her on a window, which had been taken out, and went crying through the streets and mourned her as the goddess of the people, a sublime victim. Poets wrote songs about the "pathetic whore" and everybody sang these songs. Nobody knew who she was.
>
> Well, in the morning light the dead body of the Countess de Saint-Fond looked like a slaughtered hen. It had the same colors as the tricolor — the red blood, the white skin, and all the blue marks on it. The morning sun penetrated the thick layers of her makeup and revealed her aging skin. People became upset when they realized that the young woman whom they were carrying on their shoulders had become transformed into an old hag.
>
> But this did not in any way affect the honors she was shown. When her feathers had been taken away and the wrinkled thighs had been revealed, her corpse continued to be carried on its triumphal march through the city to the sea — the Mediterranean, which gives a deeper hue to the deep blue color of aging and takes away the wrinkles of aging. This, as you know, was the beginning of the French Revolution.[30]

In contrast to the very effective mass-scenes in *Marat/Sade* and *1789*, which were actually presented on the stage, we are here exposed to a completely different understanding of how the Revolution gained its momentum, through the sexually transgressive energies of the Marquis de Sade, with whom the Countess de Saint-Fond was closely associated and identified. In the Mishima play these sexual transgressions are presented as premonitions of the French Revolution.

The French Revolution is "born" when the Countess de Saint-Fond dies. It is de Sade, as Renée says in the last act, just before she rejects him, who has actually created this new world — in fact he is the progenitor of its violence and cruelty. But the Revolution itself

(the outbursts of the subversive energies, the forces aimed at trying to change the social sphere, which were so central for Brook and
Mnouchkine) is not presented theatrically by Bergman in the same
direct fashion. There is no performance within the performance as
in *Marat/Sade*; nor is there a public fairground as in *1789*. In Bergman's
production these aspects of the Revolution have been suppressed. In
spite of this, there are still short moments of extreme theatricality in
this production, little performances within the performance, which
in quite a sophisticated fashion directly confront the spectators with
the kinds of theatrical energy and charisma which Bergman has frequently talked about in interviews.

In the second act, for example, when the Countess de Saint-Fond
is telling how she submitted her body to the black mass, first showing
the spectators the signs of Christ on her palms and then hiding them,
the character and the actress expose how they both serve as the slate
on which the signs of culture become inscribed. With the stigmata
on her hands it is the Agneta Ekmanner, and not the Countess de
Saint-Fond, who provokes us to consider not only the story of the
black mass, but also how the very notion of the transformation of
the human body into a cultural sign has been formulated, in particular by the Christian cultures. The transubstantiation, when the bread
and the wine both constitute and become the body and the blood of
the savior, is the "mystery" on which the Christian belief is based. According to the Christian belief, this mystery is also "history," and it
is a ritual way of performing history. This transformation is perhaps
even one of the most potent cultural metaphors for the energies
embodied in the art of acting and for the notion of a "subject-in-
process."

It is very important to distinguish between the character and the
actress in situations like this. The reason for this is not only that
Agneta Ekmanner is well known to her Swedish audiences, as are all
the actresses in this performance; the Countess de Saint-Fond's tale
about the black mass and the sign language of the actress — in spite
of the fact that they no doubt are coordinated — can actually be perceived as two separate narratives. Agneta Ekmanner's art of acting
knowingly submits itself to a transformation of the body into a cultural locus, the place where signs are generated through the art of
acting, just as the character she is playing submitted herself to the
practices of the Marquis de Sade. The fact that Ekmanner has also

used similar hand movements in other performances (e.g., in Katarina Frostenson's *Traum*, directed by Pia Forsgren), but without the stigmata, reinforces the impression that this gesture is very important for her as an actress. It even exists independently of the roles she has been playing. Most audience-members are probably not aware of this intertextual performance feature, but the confidence with which Ekmanner carries out this particular movement reflects, it seems, such an awareness. No doubt, all actors "have" such features in their repertoire, which they repeat, but usually they do not possess such self-confidence and awareness in employing them.

It is even possible to say of moments like these that the actress serves as a "witness" for what the character is doing on the stage. In a self-reflexive essay about the art of acting, Ekmanner makes the following comments on this production:

> *Madame de Sade* by Mishima is a play which is completely carried by its language. In principle nothing happens on the stage — there are only language and bodies. Five women who hide their bodies, and one who revealed hers, Saint-Fond, the role I played in Bergman's production.
>
> It was a provocation. The tension in my body was enormous — I wanted to please! It was really only when I put on my scene-costume that I realized how welded into one piece the body of the Countess de Saint-Fond was; her total confidence, caused by her social status and old habits. She did not want to please and she did not want to rise — she wanted to go down! Become a whore, be penetrated, divided, involved, opened. This for me on the conscious level completely foreign feeling invaded my body, as if inflating it until it filled every fold of my suede costume, and it pushed out the tips of my breasts like antennae. Total control, slowly with the motor on, and with the whip lightly in my hand.[31]

The oscillation between the exposure and the hiding or repression of the signs on the body creates an interesting tension which clearly activates special kinds of energies in the performing body as well as in the spectator. The split between the actress and her role is not primarily an expression of Brechtian "Verfremdung," but can rather be described as a kind of rupture in the flow of the performance where something enigmatic suddenly appears and for a short moment brings

The Countess de Saint-Fond (Agneta Ekmanner) with whip and Madame de Montreuil (Anita Björk). Bergman's production of Madame de Sade *at the Royal Dramatic Theatre in Stockholm, 1999. Photo by Bengt Wanselius, courtesy of the Royal Dramatic Theatre.*

the spectator into a state of amazement and uncertainty. During the major part of any performance the spectators as a rule are following the performance-narrative as we make connections on a number of levels between the different elements and aspects of the production, interpreting them. Moments like the one I have described here, however, suddenly throw the spectators out of this "focus," and we really do not know or understand what they mean. In a sense they remain enigmatic, even after they have been carefully analyzed.

Another moment in this production which has this enigmatic and surprising quality is connected with Anne, played by the actress Marie Richardson. When the Countess de Saint-Fond has finished telling her story about the black mass and is about to leave, Anne asks to join her. At this point the Countess slowly opens Anne's dress and caresses her breast. This gesture echoes a short moment in the first act when Madame de Montreuil greets Anne with a similar gesture, very briefly touching her breast. Also, during the fight between Renée and her mother (where Renée ironically describes the marriage of her parents, and the mother expresses her disgust over the kinds of pleasures her daughter gets from her husband — with both of them wearing red dresses glowing with energy and sensuality) the physicality of the otherwise quite formal action suddenly becomes apparent. These intensive flashes of female sexuality on the stage are only distant echoes of the expressions of sexuality that are narrated, but not shown, in connection with the Marquis de Sade. They clearly echo Bergman's own pronouncement (cited above) that "one of the secrets of our business [is] not to show everything."

By introducing these physical moments that hide so much more, Bergman gives the spectators an idea of the energies contained in the transgressions, which are actually not shown on the stage. They can also be seen as moments of narcissistic mirroring, like the hand of the director himself in the program, and they are a very important feature of the performance. The social norms of the aristocracy, represented on the stage by the elaborate dresses, the formalized movements, and the fans behind which some of the characters are hiding, however, are moments of suppression where the characters show their resistance as well as their fascination with the practices of de Sade. The social and sexual norms are constantly challenged by the different forms of transgression represented *in absentia* by the Marquis de Sade, and these forces never really become visible on the stage, except at the very end of the performance.

This moment takes place when Renée, after her religious conversion, has finally gathered the courage to refuse her husband entry into the house. The actress Stina Ekblad, who plays Renée, is known to an international audience for her role as Ismael, the niece of the old Jew Isak in Bergman's film *Fanny and Alexander*, among others. In this

Madame de Montreuil (Anita Björk), the mother of Renée, Madame de Sade (Stina Ekblad) hits her daughter. Bergman's production of Madame de Sade *at the Royal Dramatic Theatre in Stockholm, 1989. Photo by Bengt Wanselius. Courtesy of the Royal Dramatic Theatre.*

film it is Ismael who by psychic means helps Alexander to destroy the bishop, representing the evil forces of repression and hatred. In *Madame de Sade* it is also the character played by Stina Ekblad who takes on the role of opposing the forces of evil and destruction. This happens when the Marquis has finally, through the Revolution, been released from prison, just before he asks to be let into the home. At this point Renée says that "the world we are living in now is a creation of the Marquis de Sade."[32] Then she goes on to tell how

Alphonse has spun a thread of light from the evil, he has created something holy on the basis of all the destruction he has collected . . . The anguish, the pain, and the lamentations of humanity rise like towers striving to heaven from his silver helmet, and he presses a sword saturated with blood to his lips to take the solemn oath . . . His breast expands under his suit of armor when he sees the bloody slaughter, the banquet with millions of corpses, the most silent of feasts. His white horse, dirtied by blood . . . is on route to the morning sky where the flashes of lightning are crossing each other. A flood of light rushes down — a holy light which blinds everyone, and Alphonse is the very nuclear heart of that light.[33]

When she has finished this description, there is a moment of silence; on the backdrop there is a projection of the atom-bomb mushroom as the whole stage is brightly lit for about two seconds. This is the true face of Alphonse, which Renée will now reject. There is, however, nothing in Mishima's text which refers directly to such an image, representing the most destructive energies possible in the post–World War II world. What this image of the atom-bomb mushroom says about the director himself, as a possible metaphor for de Sade, is difficult to say. But, as I have tried to show here, this is a performance with many ambiguous and even enigmatic aspects.

When I first saw this performance at the Royal Dramatic Theatre in Stockholm, in 1989, I felt that this moment primarily expressed a personal or private pain on Renée's part after finally having grasped the true nature of her husband, for whom she has sacrificed everything during the long years of his imprisonment, exile, and debauchery. When she understands this, she has to reject him. A few years later, in 1991, when Bergman's *Madame de Sade* was shown at the Israel Festival in Jerusalem, this specific scene suddenly gained an additional dimension of meaning; I learned later that this had not been intended by the director and the actress as a direct comment on a specific political situation, but rather as a more general reflection on the post–World War II world. When Renée says that the world we

live in is the creation of the Marquis de Sade, she stands on a little
stool, not more than 20 centimeters high, speaking directly to the audience. In Jerusalem, the city in which the Israeli-Palestinian conflict
is constantly reflected in daily life, her words suddenly gained a direct
political significance, referring to the world we are also living in, here
and now. Just before one of the performances in Jerusalem, the actresses — who, due to lack of time, were already wearing their makeup
— participated in the weekly demonstration of the so-called Black
Women, who held their weekly vigil protesting against the Israeli occupation of the Palestinian territories at one of the central intersec-
tions in the city, not far from the theatre where the performances took
place. This no doubt inspired this more pointed political significance
of Bergman's production of *Madame de Sade*.

In the performances about the Shoah examined in the previous
chapter I have strongly emphasized the role and position of the witness as the dramatic character who in different ways passes on knowledge of the past to the spectators. In *Marat/Sade* this function, on the
one hand, is ironically filled by the Coulmiers, showing the witness as
a censor, and, on the other, by the passionate play written by de Sade,
in which he also participates himself. In *1789* the task of the storytellers in telling about the storming of the Bastille is to transform the
spectators into "witnesses" of that event. In *Madame de Sade* there are
several witnesses who report what they have seen, like the reports of
the Countess de Saint-Fond. But it is finally the character of the servant Charlotte, played by Helena Brodin, who becomes the most inclusive witness of what has been shown in this performance. Even if
Charlotte's role as the servant is quite limited in the play itself (for example, announcing the arrival of the guests in the home of Madame
de Montreuil), she is a key figure who actually knows almost everything that is taking place in the house. Before her position in the home
of Madame de Montreuil she was the "servant" of the Countess de
Saint-Fond, and Bergman's performance clearly indicates that this was
also an erotic relationship. She has in fact also been a member of the
"coterie" of the Marquis de Sade, but she is a dumb witness who is
never really given a chance to pass her dark knowledge on to the
spectators.

After the French Revolution, in the last act, she takes over some
of the power in the house; but this theme is only implied and not
developed in any greater detail, because it has no textual basis in

Mishima's play. It is rather an aspect of the production itself which Bergman developed independently of the text. In spite of her minor role, she is present on the stage almost throughout the performance, sometimes nearly hiding behind the columns in the set (designed by Charles Koroly), sometimes exposing her presence more openly. But all the time she is very carefully watching what the other characters are saying and doing as a kind of eavesdropper, who will eventually (perhaps) be able to "write" *her* history of these events. In any case, Bergman's performance seems to imply that she in fact has been authorized to do so, but that she does not yet have the language to carry out her mission.

Charlotte has been witnessing the gradual disintegration of the aristocratic society which she has been serving. Moreover, while Bergman is metaphorically watching the action on the stage from his hidden position behind the stage, Charlotte, as a representative of the proletariat, is the more or less totally silent liminal figure situated inside the border of the stage, perhaps a visual representation in the performance itself of Bergman's hand from the program. Charlotte does not tell what she knows in this performance; and it is quite certain from what we know about the consequent history of the proletariat that even if she becomes empowered as the "historian," there is little doubt that she too will eventually become victimized by the forces of history.

All three European productions examined in this chapter raise an issue which is never directly confronted in the productions themselves. The question is who becomes authorized to become a witness-historian and how this authorization is formulated and crystallized. *Ghetto* and *Arbeit macht frei vom Toitland Europa* clearly show how the witness-historians become authorized to carry out their task of telling about the past. The three European productions about the French Revolution also feature such witness-historians: de Sade in *Marat/Sade*, the common people in *1789*, and the Countess de Saint-Fond and Charlotte in *Madame de Sade*. But the question of how they take on that role, and what is implied by the authority they are given, is never directly raised or even confronted. Instead their role as witness-historians is flawed in some radical manner: de Sade, in spite of his ideological agenda, suffers from having too many words to say what he knows; the common people in *1789* are unable to overcome the counterrevolution which emerges at the same time as their hoped-for liberation; and Charlotte has neither the language nor the power to say what she knows. The only character in these plays who

is given the full authority for telling her story is the Countess de Saint-Fond. The others are all historians with too much to tell and lacking the means to express what they know. At the same time, this is perhaps also what makes these productions so powerful and challenging.

Three American Productions of *Danton's Death*

. . . the dramatist is in my view nothing other than a historian, but is superior *to the latter in that he* re-creates *history: instead of offering us a bare narrative, he transports us directly into the life of an age; he gives us characters instead of character portrayals; full-bodied figures instead of mere descriptions. His supreme task is to get as close as possible to history as it actually happened. His play must be neither more* moral *nor more* immoral *than* history itself; *but history was not created by the good Lord to serve as reading material for young ladies, so no one should take it amiss if my drama is just as ill suited for such a purpose. I can't possibly turn Danton and the bandits of the Revolution into heroes of virtue.*
— Georg Büchner

This chapter examines three American productions of Georg Büchner's classic *Danton's Death* (1835), a much earlier play about the French Revolution than the examples analyzed in the previous chapter. This play has been problematic to mount on U.S. stages, even when major directors like Orson Welles, Herbert Blau, and Robert Wilson directed it. The Welles production opened the second and last season of the Mercury Theatre in New York on November 5, 1938, and ran for a mere twenty-one performances. Blau's *Danton's Death*, which premiered in October 1965, was his first and, as things turned out, also his last production at the newly opened Beaumont Theatre at Lincoln Center in New York. For Wilson's production, which premiered at the Alley Theatre in Houston, in November 1992, the stakes were quite different. In this case the internationally renowned director made a "visit" to his home state. But in spite of this homecoming the production was certainly not a success. These three productions of *Danton's Death* are separated by an exact generational gap of twenty-seven years. In the context of research (not criticism) it is much more difficult and even problematic to anatomize artistic failures, rather than to examine performances which have on the whole been aesthetically satisfying, as I have done in the previous chapters.

In this chapter I try to discover why and in what sense these U.S. productions were unsuccessful or even failures. What were the basic ideological assumptions of these productions in relation to Büchner's classic play and in relation to the American context? And why has it been so difficult to create a viable bridge between the play and this context (which has apparently not been the case in Europe)? *Danton's Death* has actually been produced in the German-speaking world more than three hundred times since its first production by the Volksbühne in Berlin in 1902.[1] One of the more recent productions of *Danton's Death* in Germany was actually directed by Robert Wilson at the Berliner Ensemble in 1998, a production that in many ways was very similar to the one produced six years earlier in Texas. The German production was, however, much more positively received by the critics as well as the general audience. The reception of Büchner's play has apparently been very different in the American context than in the European one. The U.S. tour of Max Reinhardt's 1927 production of *Danton's Death*, which was the second time he directed the play,[2] was on the face of it enthusiastically received by American critics. But they did not really bother to investigate what the play was about; their sometimes superficial understanding of the play and its ideas has no doubt been decisive for its reception in the United States. As Herbert Drake, who reviewed Orson Welles' production eleven years later in the *Herald Tribune*, observed, the 1927 Reinhardt production was the first time *Danton's Death* was performed in the United States, while Welles was actually the first American to direct a U.S. production of it.[3]

The European and the Israeli productions dealing with the French Revolution and the Shoah were able to integrate the performances within the more comprehensive social and ideological discourses of their respective "homes." And when these productions were on tour or participated in festivals they were also able to communicate very strongly within these new contexts. The U.S. productions of *Danton's Death*, though, were unable to domesticate this play, to make it fully or even satisfactorily meaningful in its new social and ideological context, nor to create an aesthetically viable bridge between the his-

A mass scene from Max Reinhardt's production of Danton's Death *as it was performed at the Century Theatre in New York, December 20, 1927. Billy Rose Theatre Collection, the New York Public Library for the Performing Arts; Astor, Lennox, and Tilden Foundations.*

torical past and the present. This "foreignness" of *Danton's Death* for American aesthetic and ideological sensibilities has several aspects. The first is related to the different collective self-perceptions or ideological structures that the French and American Revolutions have engendered, respectively. No doubt many important similarities exist between these two decisive historical events, including the fact that they were more or less contemporary and both called for equality and freedom. The American Revolution was also deeply influenced by European ideas. But despite these similarities they have been the basis for different national narratives, each emphasizing its own specific features. Such differences of perception have no doubt also been reflected in the aesthetic representations of revolutionary processes on the two continents. For the Americans, the struggle for freedom was directed against a foreign (i.e., European) colonial power. This battle was conceived as the attempt of the New World to become liberated from the Old World. It was even a struggle between different kinds of worlds, situated in different geographical locations, separated by the Atlantic Ocean. The French Revolution, however, must in the European context first be viewed as an act of liberation from an internal enemy, embodied by the royal and the aristocratic hegemonies which the Revolution by all available means, including violence and terror, sought to bring to an end.

Büchner's play repeats this basic narrative scheme of fighting against such an internal enemy. It depicts Robespierre's successful struggle against his former revolutionary companions, personified by Danton and his friends; just a few years after the 1789 Revolution, Robespierre considered them not only legitimate political contestants within the newly created legal frameworks, but threatening enemies of the Revolution itself. And as everybody who sees Robespierre "triumph" at the end of Büchner's play knows, very soon his head will also roll in the streets, just like Danton's. *Danton's Death* depicts how a citizen with seemingly good intentions becomes castigated and is sacrificed as a scapegoat. American narratives about treason, in contrast, seem to be much more focused on illicit relations with a "foreign" power and with marking an enemy for being aligned with some exterior "other." An early example of such a drama is William Dunlap's *Andre* (1798), based on an actual event in 1780, when a man with that name was hanged by the Continental army on suspicion of having conspired with the British army.[4] More recently, most frequently on film it seems, this "other" has even become an "alien" creature from outer space, reinforcing a narrative pattern which no doubt has been strongly valorized by American culture. This collocation of "alien" and "other" is quite interesting in the context of the Welles production of *Danton's Death*, which premiered only a few days after his famous radio show *The War of the Worlds* had created a major stir. Usually, though, the other is not an alien, but rather an outsider who for some reason, usually on the basis of race or ethnic background, has not been a full companion in the initial struggle for the birth of the new social order. In the U.S. context the enemy is invariably an individual who is marked as alien. This is one of the reasons, I believe, why it has been so problematic, in the American context, to integrate the European revolutionary paradigm presented by *Danton's Death*. The European paradigm of revolutionary upheaval and crisis, which in many ways has been repeated again in its subsequent history, including even the Shoah, has given rise to theatrical expressions that seem to be radically different from the manner in which the U.S. theatre has refigured and represented aesthetically the important traumatic events from its own historical past — or even its present. American culture seems to focus on the problems of integrating the "aliens" from without into a civil society of "sharing"; it features and valorizes the struggles to achieve this goal.[5]

Even if the three U.S. Danton productions were failures, they must still be seen as interesting and important failures that help us to uncover what the stakes are when a theatrical performance takes on the difficult task and responsibilities of performing history. What I think can be "learned" by examining these productions, all of which no doubt were deeply committed both ideologically and aesthetically, is how difficult it has been to find "American" performance strategies for a play like *Danton's Death*. These three productions were not able to communicate successfully with spectators, mainly because there is apparently something in Büchner's dramatic text which could not be appropriated to the U.S. context. In spite of the intentions of the respective directors to create performances in opposition to the prevalent ideological or aesthetic norms, the opposition or even revolt expressed (in particular by the first two productions) clearly did not receive the desired response from critics and audiences. All three productions were also in different ways based on spectacular stage solutions, employing the most advanced and sophisticated technologies available. As a result, they apparently did not focus sufficiently on the work of the actors in order to bring out the ideological and aesthetic messages directly and, through them, to the spectators. In this context, however, the issue for me is not the measure to which these productions were successful or not, but rather how the very notion of failure itself is knit together with history and performance.[6] *Danton's Death*, it seems to me, is about the failure of the Revolution significantly to change the lot of the individuals within the already existing or newly created social frameworks. And in particular it is a play about the gradually growing awareness of this painful failure, about the subjectivity and awareness of the individual in times of social change and upheaval, which becomes so complex that it can hardly be grasped by Danton himself, let alone by others. When he is victimized through Robespierre's manipulations and submits, Danton finally becomes his own enemy, haunted by a lack of will which even breaks down his own desire to live.

The U.S. productions of *Danton's Death* were apparently not able to communicate this primary idea to their audiences. Of course, this does not mean that the American theatre has not been able to perform its own histories and its own internal conflicts on the stage, even if, as

Tom Postlewait has noted,[7] it has basically turned away from the key issues of slavery and the horrors of modern battle and is still struggling to find ways to represent the history of the treatment of Native Americans. In the contemporary era, playwrights like Suzan-Lori Parks, individual performers like Anne Deveare Smith, or performance ensembles like the Wooster Group have no doubt made significant contributions. But since scholars have analyzed them,[8] they are not included here. Moreover, it is gradually becoming clear within the larger framework of this study of performances about such failures in history as the French Revolution (which admittedly, in addition to the violence it generated, also created the notion of a civil society) that by performing history the theatre proposes a delicate balance between the painful destructiveness of these failures, on the one hand, and the restorative creativity of the theatre, on the other. In the performances about the Shoah this dialectic tension has been even more apparent. Such a dialectics between destruction and creativity can perhaps be applied to the arts in general. The three U.S. productions of *Danton's Death*, as I understand them, were not able to establish this complex balance.

The productions of Welles and Blau not only led to economic disasters for the theatres where they were produced, but made it necessary for both these directors to reformulate their careers as well. For Welles, this failure became a turning point which led to Hollywood and eventually to *Citizen Kane* (released in 1941), a film about the dialectics between power and private memories as nostalgia that deals directly with the very notion of narrativity in reconstructing the lifestory of an individual. Welles, who besides directing *Danton's Death* also played Citizen Saint Just, later transformed himself into the newspaper tyrant Citizen Kane in his self-directed film. This became his Hollywood breakthrough.

For Blau, "the experience of Lincoln Center" — where the performance was produced — became what he later in his book *Take Up the Bodies* termed "the rancid preface to the theory."[9] After the KRAKEN experiment, which lasted from 1968 to 1980, Blau became a fulltime academic and a writer not only *about* but also *of* performance. Throughout his practical theatre career Blau did in fact hold different academic positions; his move from practice to theory, where the theory retains something of the practical, retains a balance between the two fields. This interaction between theory and practice in the American context is perhaps related to the difficulties of confronting a European text like *Danton's Death*. The respective "failures" of Welles and Blau with this play led to very different forms of written reflection on the notion of performance as well as history. The case of Wilson, though, seems to be different. His production of *Danton's Death* at the Alley Theatre in Houston in 1992 was certainly not a great success; as far as I know, it was not a significant turning point in his theatre career. But on another level it is also an interesting failure, as a performance almost totally void of history, in a sense not a production about the historical aspects of Büchner's play at all. Six years later, however, in 1998, when Wilson returned to *Danton's Death* with a production in German, which was performed at the Salzburg festival and at the Berliner Ensemble, his production had a very different reception, perhaps because the European audiences brought their own historical perspectives and experiences to the unfamiliar production of a familiar play.

Before examining these three U.S. Danton productions in depth I want to draw attention to the scarcity of archival materials and the subjective nature of the autobiographical accounts on which I rely. The visual records, in particular for the first two productions, are scarce. Of these three productions, only Wilson's has for obvious reasons been recorded on video. This explains the methodology in this chapter, which is quite different from the approach in examining plays and performances in the earlier chapters.

Büchner's Play and Its Beholders

The newspaper critics who write about culture in general and theatre performances in particular are a major source of information about the U.S. productions of *Danton's Death*. As a rule they are not trained as historians or scholarly critics, so their judgments are often directly tied to contemporary values, tastes, and concerns. This is an important key to why the reception of the Danton productions in the United States has been so problematic. But I also want to draw attention to the intentions of the three directors and the theatres where these performances were presented. Each of the three productions was based on an adaptation of Büchner's play. Welles and Blau made their own versions, while the text for the Wilson production was adapted by Robert Auletta, "who streamlined Büchner's epic romantic drama revolving around the passive, existential figure of Danton."[10] In all cases the adaptations were no doubt subordinated to the comprehensive concept of the productions themselves.

The superficiality and often even hostility with which most of the critics responded to Büchner's drama in their reviews is remarkable. They show no reverence whatsoever for this "classic" drama, which in the European context would have been self-evident. This has no doubt been crucial for the problematic receptions of the different productions. In order to broaden the scope of this discussion it is also necessary to refer briefly to the reviews of the Reinhardt tour to New York in 1927, which, as noted above, was very well received by the critics, mainly on the basis of its exciting performance values. This does not mean, however, that the critics who wrote appreciatively about the Reinhardt production really understood what the Büchner play is about.

The problems of understanding Büchner's drama are also intimately linked to the kinds of audiences the three productions were intended for and what the play, regardless of how it was produced on stage, was intended to communicate to these audiences. Orson Welles, in 1938, counted on a significant constituency from radical left-wing spectators, but they found the rumors that there would be a likeness between Robespierre and Stalin uncomfortable and threatened to boycott the performance. It is difficult to say, on the basis of available materials, how threatening the production really was to their views, but the fact that this production closed after a mere twenty-one performances is clear evidence of such a communicative rupture. Herbert Blau, in 1965, apparently misjudged his prospective midtown spectators at Lincoln Center, seeing them as much more radical or wanting them to take more radical positions. He not only opened his New York employment and the new theatre with a play which no doubt caused problems for this audience, but also issued radical statements (even before the performance itself had premiered), which apparently made these initial problems even more severe. The Wilson production in Houston is also different from its two predecessors in this respect. It hardly seems likely that the spectators who watched this production were interested in any significant manner in what Büchner's play says about the French Revolution or about history; they came to watch the virtuosity of their "own" native-born, internationally renowned director. The event was more about Robert Wilson and less about Danton or Robespierre. The reason for including this production, however, is that it no doubt says something important about the manner in which this director is performing history. But more about that later.

The commercial leaflet announcing the Reinhardt tour in 1927 shows how vague the producers of this tour were about the play they were offering to the U.S. audience. It informs prospective spectators that Büchner's play "is a series of almost futuristic pictures thrown onto the stage like flaming blots of color" — whatever such a description might mean. Thomas van Dycke, writing for the *New York Telegraph*, who greatly admired the production itself, wrote in his review that Büchner's play "starts from nothing, builds to nothing and amounts to just that much."[11] Another review is also a striking example of the kind of writing the play triggered:

Briefly the vast pageant relates the downfall of the fiery hero of the Revolution, Danton, at the hands of the scheming, mad Robespierre, who came on the scene with blood lust unsated at the time when Danton was already falling into philosophic discussion with himself as to the relative worth of all this prodigious achievement. One suspects that the drama itself might be a little wearying as read in the library. But as circussed by Dr. Reinhardt, it seems comparable to the original.[12]

One suspects that this critic never reached the library. Or that he thought the play was designed as a new form of melodrama between good and evil.

Percy Hammond's review in the *New York Tribune* even tops this. He dismisses the play as

a rambling pageant of the French Revolution, [which] is but a series of detached episodes, twelve in number, introducing some of the characters and events of the Terror in a limited stage history of the time. As a document Mr. Buechner's tragedy is but a mediocre hearsay, founded on the facts of tradition, but having few if any bases in what Mr. Gilbert Miller, its American producer, would refer to as Art. Nevertheless, as a show, subtly circussed by the great ringmaster from Salzburg, it becomes at the Century a fascinating example of stagecraft.[13]

There is no doubt a considerable amount of cynicism in these remarks, which — together with the idea that Reinhardt was a ringmaster, "circussing" his productions — must have been quite strongly rooted at the time. John Mason Brown, who reviewed the Welles production for the *New York Post* eleven years later, reinforced what no doubt had become a deeply rooted established opinion. For him, that "'Danton's Death' is not much of a play was made clear when Reinhardt staged it here in German. What Orson Welles has done is to make this melancholy fact even clearer by presenting it in English in a whittled form that lasts no more than an hour and a quarter."[14] In all fairness, it is necessary to point out that these remarks, both in 1927 and in 1938, were also matched by more positive remarks which seem to have been copied more or less verbatim from standard handbooks concerning Büchner's importance for modern drama. But as a rule these comments were totally devoid of any serious or intellectually inspired effort to interpret the play itself or its relevance.

As for the Welles production in 1938, the comments were quite dismissive: "What Buechner had to say about revolutions and their theory may have been subtle and arresting in the original German script, but in Mr. Welles version it is all so cloudy in its presentation that it seems of little value or interest."[15] And: "This season Buechner's 'Danton's Death' is Buechner's play reduced to skimmed milk . . . The play thus diluted has a hundred meanings and none at all."[16] As Walter Winchell informed his readers, the play is "dreary literature and one of us wished the hysterical actors in it hadn't taken it so seriously."[17] It even sounds as if Robert Benchley from the *New Yorker Magazine*, who frequently looked at performances with this kind of humorous verve, thought he had been overhearing a series of rambling conversations at a cocktail party:

> mounted on a series of platforms of varying heights, the characters discourse angrily about the destiny of man. There is a troublesome quality about their talk, like a drunken argument in which each remark is only very loosely associated with the one that went before it, although every man separately says astonishing and valuable things. In the beginning, listening to a little group of Septemberists . . . I didn't believe I'd ever be able to make much out of their disjointed conversation, and it wasn't any better a scene or two later, when M. Danton's young woman attempted to explain, if I understood her, how she had come to admire a previous suitor . . . Gradually, however, I began to catch on — much as years ago I learned to read printer's type upside down — and by ten-thirty, when Mr. Welles [who played St. Just] came

out on the stage to announce that since Nature kills off all men in the end anyway, there is no especial harm in Revolution antici-pating her, I was doing fine. Unfortunately, this was the end of the play and it was time to go home.[18]

There were, however, some more serious pronouncements about the Welles production and Büchner's text, as a few reviewers tried to place both play and performance within a contemporary political con-text. In 1938 the world also seemed to be in more serious trouble than eleven years previously, when the Reinhardt production was viewed in New York. Richard Lockridge from the *New York Sun* noted this:

> Mr Buechner did not, for example, say anything which can easily be interpreted as a denunciation of Hitler. He did not warn that Stalin would become another Robespierre. But he said much about how men acted in the French revolution, and in our multi-revolutionary day they may act the same. You may, if you like, re-gard "Danton's Death" as a warning against the ascendancy of the doctrinaire, of the man who is heartless in pursuit of the hu-manitarian ideal. Robespierre, as Buechner pictures him — and as history pictures him for that matter — was such a man. Such men are to be watched out for.[19]

The last sentence alludes to *Julius Caesar*, which Welles had directed the previous season at the Mercury Theatre. For Lockridge, such men as Robespierre seemed "a good deal more frightening than Martians, as well as considerably more imminent."[20] This allusion to Martians refers to the fact that Welles' Danton production premiered on No-vember 5, 1938, only two days after the broadcast of his legendary radio-play *The War of the Worlds* at the Mercury Theatre on the Air. This broadcast convulsed the whole country, something which most of the critics felt his Büchner performance had not been able to do, in-dicating perhaps that aliens from another planet are more engaging for the American public at large than the French revolutionaries in Büchner's play.

This closeness in time between the Welles radio show and his Büch-ner production reveals how hectic his working tempo at the time was. It may also explain something about the failure of the theatre produc-tion. *New York Times* critic Brooks Atkinson, one of the few critics who greatly admired the production, claimed that "Welles' real genius is in the theatricality of his imagination." He ended his review, moreover,

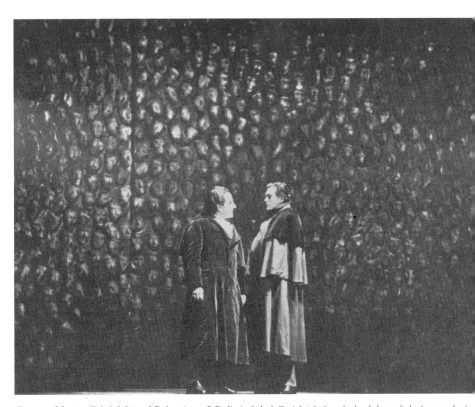

Danton (Martin Gabel, left) and Robespierre (Vladimir Sokoloff, right) before the backdrop of glaring masks in Orson Welles' production of Danton's Death *at the Mercury Theatre in New York, 1938. Billy Rose Theatre Collection, the New York Public Library for the Performing Arts; Astor, Lennox, and Tilden Foundations.*

by jokingly adding in parentheses (directly referring to the radio broadcast): "(Ladies and gentlemen, you have just been reading a review of a performance of 'Danton's Death' at the Mercury Theatre last evening. It is a play of imagination based on history. There is no occasion for alarm.)"[21]

Atkinson went on to claim that Welles, "[u]sing the script as the ground plan of a show, . . . knows how to impregnate it with the awe and tumult of a theatrical performance. 'Danton's Death' is further proof of his power, and endows the Mercury Theatre with the same vitality it had last season."[22]

A week later Brooks Atkinson published an additional article in the *New York Times* further praising the Welles production. He argued that "the revolutionary passions that were inflaming Europe . . . are matters of contemporary pertinence," which for Welles are "congenial to work with," adding:

If Buechner's play continued the chronicle after Danton's murder on the guillotine, it would show Robespierre bending his head to the blade in the next phase of the reign of terror and, after that, a weary, satiated resumption of normal living. For revolutions, like plagues, have to run their course, putting the seal of death on those who blunder in the way. It is not enough to win the program of rights in the first pitched battle. "The ghostly fatalism of history" cannot be rationalized away.[23]

Atkinson's remarks comparing the revolution to a plague clearly place the play in a relevant contemporary context.

To a great extent neither Welles nor his audience was interested in the historical representation of the events of the French Revolution. For Welles and for those who appreciated aspects of the production, the contemporary references to the growing turmoil in Europe proved to be the justification, perhaps the only justification, for staging *Danton's Death*. Just as his production of *Julius Caesar* had served to evoke the Nazi rallies and the dictatorial powers of Hitler and Mussolini, so this production, with its theatrical tricks, was basically understood as a political statement about current events. And for those newspaper reviewers and spectators who did not even see the relevance of these contemporary allusions, the play and production were a waste of time.

It was also this more contemporary aspect of Büchner's play that Herbert Blau chose to emphasize when he began working on *Danton's Death* for his production in 1965. Blau and Jules Irving had been invited from California by the board of directors at the Beaumont Theatre to head the new repertory theatre there. A press release issued on May 5, 1965, by Barry Hyams, who held an administrative position at the theatre, was no doubt intended to draw attention to the aspects of the play Blau wanted to emphasize in his production:

> The Repertory Theatre of Lincoln Center, under the direction of Herbert Blau and Jules Irving, will initiate its new and permanent home, the Vivian Beaumont Theater, with the presentation of *Danton's Death*. The drama by Georg Buechner will be the first in a subscription series of four plays and has been scheduled to open on October 21st.
>
> To be produced in a new version by Mr. Blau, *Danton's Death* was originally performed [*sic*!] in Germany in 1835, two years prior

to its author's decease. Its last two major productions were by Reinhardt in Berlin in 1927, and by Orson Welles in 1938 at New York's now departed Mercury Theatre.

In evaluting the choice of the Season's opener, Mr. Blau who will also direct the drama stated: "*Danton's Death*, written in secrecy during the Romantic period, leaped so audaciously into the twentieth century that it has influenced every major dramatist of the modern theatre. The guillotine cuts through this prophetic drama of the French Revolution to the social revolutions of our own day." [24]

It is worth noting the way in which this press release refers to the American performance tradition of *Danton's Death*, even though it does not mention the fact that the Reinhardt production had also been shown in New York. The expression "now departed Mercury theatre" can even be seen as an implicit reference not just to the previous failure of the Welles production but to the struggle to establish a repertory theatre in New York City. In any case, Blau's more explicit intentions were carefully integrated within the more formal text, even if the last sentence (quoted here) clearly states his understanding of the text (prefiguring "the social revolutions of our day").

This press release also contained a statement, probably written by Blau himself, about the "Historical Background" to *Danton's Death*. This statement does not provide an interpretation of Büchner's drama, but points to some of the complexities of the French revolutionary situation which the planned production apparently wished to evoke and explain. It is worth quoting the last two paragraphs of this one and a half page typewritten document in this context:

> Danton, who had saved the Republic by organizing the armies to check the coalition at the frontier, was taking little part now in the Jacobin debates. His friends — among them Herault and Camille Desmoulins, who had led the crowd to the Bastille — were alarmed. Danton was innocent neither of blood nor of blood money. To allay fear at home, he fomented the September Massacres, wanton slaughter in the prisons. To maintain contact abroad, he apparently engaged in foreign speculations. Robespierre, a bourgeois at heart, was the pattern of public rectitude, Danton was pleasure-loving and extravagant. When a delegation from Lyons came to the Jacobins to complain of counterrevolutionary action there, Robespierre, urged on by St. Just,

seized on these indulgences to wage war against the moderates who followed Danton.

But the machinery of the Revolution eventually superseded all the men who created it. Soon after their triumph, Robespierre and St. Just followed Danton to the Guillotine.

This text emphasized that Danton's "treason" was "apparently" also based on his "foreign speculations," rather than on his being considered an internal enemy, which the play itself quite clearly articulates as the more or less exclusive reason for his being branded a traitor. This shift of emphasis reveals how the play was interpreted in the American context. Danton becomes a corrupt capitalist.

The real troubles at Lincoln Center, however, started when Blau published a program-note, or rather "manifest," before the first previews of his production. He later decided to withdraw several passages from this text because of the effects the controversy had on the actors, and the newspapers began to smell some form of scandal. In his own retrospective account of these events in *Take Up the Bodies*, published in 1982, Blau admits quite candidly that this withdrawal was the most shameful thing he ever did in the theater.[25] His book includes some of the passages removed from the program-note that had angered several newspapers as well as members of the board, giving the performance a scandalous reputation even before it premiered. The typewritten press release (also available in the New York Public Library for the Performing Arts at the Lincoln Center) contains several passages which he later also left out of the book. I quote this archival document in full here because it very clearly reveals what Blau's intentions and his "reading" of Büchner's play were, which he had only summarized by a single sentence in the earlier press release.

Blau's "manifesto" is a radical text from the mid-sixties, which in a sense is self-reflexively also "performing" the play, something which the performance itself apparently was unable to achieve with the same kind of emotional and intellectual intensity as this text:

The French Revolution was a series of small nuclear explosions climaxed by the Reign of Terror. It came at the end of the eighteenth century when Enlightenment looked over the abyss to anarchy and, in our own time, absolute unreason. The Terror was designed by the Committee of Public Safety as an instrument of order. "Terror, but not chaos." The bloodletting seemed required by History. Terror, according to Robespierre, Castro,

Verwoerd, Mao Tse-Tung and President Johnson, is the moral whip of Virtue.

This is not to equalize all aberrations of Power, but to recognize — as Buechner did at twenty-one — that nobody has a premium on tyranny. By fault or default, from whatever good motives, we are all executioners. "What is it in us that whores, lies, steals and kills"? The question may be hard to tack for a new season. But we may as well begin where our world leaves us: with the Balance of Terror. We would hold our peace if we had it.

Buechner wrote *Danton's Death* in 1835, while in hiding from the Hessian police. The drama is clairvoyant, seeing the Reign of Terror from within the Terror, as a pilot project for the more marvellously organized savageries of later generations. Liberty, Equality, and Fraternity may be natural rights, but they are subverted by the equally natural brutality of man to man. The true revolution has never happened. Creation and destruction, arising from a common source, compose a fearful symmetry.

So all factions in the play were once of the same party. When the drama begins, the extremists or anarchists have just been executed. The faction of Danton is becoming increasingly moderate as Danton himself, gorged on blood, is becoming increasingly inert. Robespierre is in charge of the mechanism of the Revolution with its "long slow procedural murders." But Power creates its own vacuum, and as the play proceeds we incline to ask, "Who, really, has power?" The mechanism of the Terror seems to run itself like a natural force. Nightmare become politics, and politics nightmare.

The heroes of the Revolution were responsible for murder, rape, arson, cannibalism, atrocity of every kind, and the horror is that they were no more (or less) sadists than the men responsible today for releasing napalm over the jungles. They were indeed men of intellect, principle, and honor who wanted to wrap the Rights of Man in the lineaments of Beauty. They acted with religious fervor. "In the beginning was the word," says Camille Desmoulins, who led Freedom to the Bastille. "We spoke a new language of ancient power, and this is the translation."

The terror is the mind's revenge on itself. It was conceived by men of romantic temper who thought themselves, depending on the degree of bureaucracy in their nature, classical Greeks or Romans. The Revolution was played out in a landscape of myth and monument, where the monsters of the psyche have been tamed by form: Medusas, Minotaurs, Saturn eating his own children, and the vision of Man as a reborn Adonis. But the earth has a thin crust. The geometry of this world was torn up by the demons of the unconscious. Behind the idealism of politics, bloodlust and blind id. The Revolution, ripped from Liberty's mighty womb, turns into an orgy.

"There's nothing that we build that's not of human flesh," says Danton, anticipating the lampshades of Auschwitz. "It's the curse of our age." But the guillotine is not only to be compared with the incinerators; that would miss its bloodier point. The guillotine, introduced as a humane method of capital punishment, quick and surgical, is the absurd chop-logic of the bureaucratic mind, like the tumblers of the computer that decides how many people are expendable in the next holocaust. People submitted to it as we submit to our own most impossible conceptions, by what psychiatrists have called "selective inattention."

The Revolution may have been a time when, for their little day, the poor were the terror of the earth. But the guillotine was the debraining machine of the bourgeois world. The executioner, like Eichmann, was a respectable man, an obedient part of the mechanism. Revolution comes from oppression, but the price indices rose then as they do now with Viet Nam. Buechner creates a scene where prosperity promenades while murder is laughing in the streets.

The virtue of Robespierre is in its purest form the sexually repressed morality we have come to know. For Danton, worshipper of Eros, sex is the guillotine; for Robespierre, political puritan, the guillotine is his sex. "What is it in me that denies me?" he cries. Their conflict is like that between two incompatible aspects of the psyche. While Robespierre is tormented by Duty, Danton suffers from a disease which knows no name; in another time it might have been called the Sloth, that disorder of the soul which turns back upon itself death-breeding doubt, the boredom of the hyperactive mind which sees unnaturally through life while possessing death.

There is grandeur in Buechner's most pessimistic vision. King Lear never shivers Danton's spine. Where Lear runs when he is cut to the brain, Danton stands still, until he is forced to claim himself from History in all his bloody glory. A bright spume of energy informs this play, whose craft runs recklessly after Imagination. If Imagination gapes on death, it is to open, as Blake said, the doors of perception. If we are crushed by the fatalism of History, we are reminded that "creation is all around us, raging and brightening, born anew in every moment."

Men are bright swords wielded by invisible powers. The deaths of Danton and his friends, in the burnt-out Olympus of their Utopian dream, evoke the waning forms of the dying gods. History — murderous, bloody, and full of shame — passes beyond fact into the eternity of myth. When all is said and done, we realize as in all great drama that History is never the whole story — and the best craft is the deepest vision.[26]

The specific reason for the public outrage concerning this text was the list of names in the first paragraph, placing President Johnson together with Robespierre, Castro, and Verwoerd. By putting the external and the internal enemies on the same level, Blau was apparently posing a difficult challenge to the political and intellectual sensibilities of most of his compatriots. And including Mao Tse-tung in this list of political leaders was no doubt a foresight which even most European leftist intellectuals would not easily have accepted at the time. To what extent this text was the reason why the Broadway audience did not like the performance is difficult to say, but it certainly formed their "horizon of expectations," perceiving it as a politically radical production.

Blau's text is written in an essayistic "performative" style where interpretation, theory, and subjectivity are welded closely together. This is a genre or mode of writing which Blau, since his withdrawal from practical theatre work, has gradually developed in his books. Starting with *The Impossible Theatre: A Manifesto* (1964), but more clearly in more recent works like *Blooded Thought* (1982), *The Eye of Prey* (1987), and *The Audience* (1990) (where this form of writing has become even more extreme, sometimes beyond the comprehensibility of routine reading), Blau has performed his theory in writing. It is perhaps even possible to point to an American "tradition" of writing in this kind of "performtive" vein. Such a tradition would include writers like Susan Sontag, in particular her *Illness as Metaphor* (1978), and more recently Peggy Phelan, who has termed it "performative writing."[27] What these texts have in common is their attempt to integrate the discourses on performance with biography and history as these are re-

Photo from Herbert Blau's production of Danton's Death *at Beaumont Theatre at Lincoln Center in New York, 1965. Billy Rose Theatre Collection, the New York Public Library for the Performing Arts; Astor, Lennox, and Tilden Foundations.*

flected or refracted through memory in art and other forms of creative discourse. This kind of performative writing is in different ways also an invitation to theory, serving as the prism through which the past can be both seen and revisited, through paradoxical and sometimes even elusive theoretical refractions.

Blau's text about *Danton's Death*, in spite of stating that it does not wish to "equalize all aberrations of Power," clearly stresses the universal aspects of different forms of revolutionary violence. On the level of language, which is the medium of this textual "performance," Blau generates a whole set of almost freely floating metaphorical vehicles that constantly interact with each other in extrapolating this universal violence and the kinds of humiliation it leads to. In this respect it is even possible to compare Blau's style and its performativity with that of Allen Ginsberg, a poet from the Beat generation whose work Blau was certainly closely familiar with. Ginsberg's *Howl*

and Other Poems was published in 1956; in 1957 the book was charged
with obscenity and indecency, a charge which was finally not accepted by the judge in the court case. During the trial itself the defense called in a number of expert witnesses, among them Blau, who
at the time was teaching at San Francisco State College and also served
as consulting director of the Actor's Workshop in San Francisco. In
his testimony Blau stated that

> what strikes me most forcefully about "Howl" is that it is worded
> in what appears to be a contemporary tradition, one that did not
> cause me any particular consternation in reading, a tradition, as
> someone previously remarked, most evident in the modern pe-
> riod following the First World War, a tradition that resembles
> [the] European and literary tradition that is defined as "Dada,"
> a kind of art of furious negation. By the intensity of its negation
> it seems to be both resurrective in quality and ultimately a sort of
> paean of possible hope.[28]

This characterization, I think, is also valid for the performative
writing Blau has developed, at least in his later books, which frequently even recalls the incantatory style developed by Ginsberg
in his poetry.

In his program note for *Danton's Death* Blau calls the French Revolution "a series of small nuclear explosions"; Danton's words about
human flesh are an anticipation of "the lampshades of Auschwitz";
and the guillotine is an expression of the "chop-logic of the bureaucratic mind." These, together with the list of political leaders which
caused the big uproar and the mention of the napalm dropped over
the jungles, are only some of the examples in this text which bring different historical periods into a constantly floating interaction with
each other and with the present. As a result of these unexpected metaphorical shifts, which Blau activates through his performative language, the French Revolution, nuclear weaponry, the Shoah, and the
Vietnam War begin to lose their distinctive qualities as discrete events
in history. They become universalized. The dialectics of history, making connections, are constantly activated, almost chaotically, through
these violent metaphorical shifts, expressing the uncontrollable desire
to create connections through language: "For Danton, worshipper of
Eros, sex is the guillotine; for Robespierre, political puritan, the guillotine is his sex." Here Blau's own words in his preface to *Take Up the
Bodies*, looking back at the events surrounding his production of

Danton's Death, could also be applied: "There's nothing like failure to trip the images out of people."[29]

This universalizing strategy disregards the distinctive characteristics of each of these discrete events, which expresses Blau's concern with what was happening in America at the time. But paradoxically, this strategy can also be seen as a form of blurring distinctions, as in the debate called the "Historikerstreit," which featured some prominent historians who put the Nazi atrocities on a par with those committed in other countries and in different historical contexts, thus erasing the uniqueness of the Shoah. This issue can also be seen from a somewhat different perspective — it becomes very difficult to establish a clearly discernible dialectics between the past and the present when the representational strategies in different ways are erasing these differences. Since the past can undoubtedly not be altered, Blau instead argues for a radical change, at least in the perception of the present/now, because of the cruelties it "reminds him of" in the "pile[s] of debris" from the catastrophes of history, to borrow Walter Benjamin's metaphor from his text about the Klee painting *Angelus Novus*.[30]

But the central "gestus" of this section from Benjamin's "Theses on the Philosophy of History" is the gradually growing distance between the angelic observer and the events in the past, because the storm blowing from Paradise "irresistibly propels him into the future."[31] Blau's reflection in his "manifesto" that "[c]reation and destruction, arising from a common source, compose a fearful symmetry" recalls the angelic images in Blake's poetry, to which he frequently returns. Blau also refers directly to Blake in his text. Such images make it very difficult to create the kind of distance which I argue is so central for the notion of performing history. The "diagnosis" of Blau's text presented here also makes it possible to point out what may have been the problem with his production of *Danton's Death*. It was apparently not a primary concern for the critics and the spectators to "read" the French Revolution through Blau's much more immediate concern with the Vietnam War. Nor did they see the world through his perceptions of the universal aspects of the cruelties which have been carried out by humans. Or, in Blau's own words from the last paragraph of this text (quoted above): "History — murderous, bloody, and full of shame — passes beyond fact into the eternity of myth. When all is said and done, we realize as in all great drama that History is never the whole story — and the best craft is the deepest vision." The question in trying to understand and cope with the failures of the past always seems to be to what extent this understanding of history is repressed or not.

These basic issues were also pointed out by several of the critics who reviewed Blau's production. I have selected two voices that seem to be representative here: "Hobe" in *Variety*, who argued that "[t]he play is ostensibly about the self-destroying excesses of the French Revolution and the conflicting attitudes and personalities of two of its leaders, Danton and Robespierre. If, as Blau has been at pains to point out, the work has special application to modern times and particularly to the present domestic and international situation, the analogy is buried under the avalanche of declamation."[32] George Oppenheimer in *Newsday* expressed a similar view, perhaps even more forcefully: "It is possible, maybe probable, that director Blau, in his effort to bring 'Danton's Death' up to date and in order to pin up the theme of dictatorship, in direction and translation, decided to make the play as contemporary as possible in mood and in manner. If so, he made a mammoth error, for Buechner's early 19th Century play has become neither fish nor fowl. It is, in fact, a hybrid with actors attuned and attached to the sounds of today, trying inexpertly to read dialogue of an earlier day."[33] The production no doubt reflected some of the metaphorical strategies of Blau's text for the program note, and several critics were no doubt strongly influenced by it in their own viewing of the performance.

In spite of Blau's efforts to clarify what he believes the play is about, however, it is still possible to hear strong echoes in the reviews of the simplistic remarks triggered by the two previous productions in New York. Louis Chapin in the *Christian Science Monitor*, for example, wrote about Büchner's play, after having seen Blau's production, that "[a]t the beginning George Danton and his friends — sometime radical leaders become moderates — are in danger from Robespierre and the so-called Committee of Public Safety. By the end, after much philosophizing by all and some spurts of heroic self-defense by Danton, they succumb to the guillotine. That is essentially all that happens. It represents, of course, a crucial moment of history, and sharpens it with incisive individual portraits."[34] And Walter Kerr ended his review in the *New York Herald Tribune* with the following remark: "Not a soul at the Beaumont succeeds in telling us what the play is about, emotionally, historically, philosophically. We know only that some ardent youngsters are posturing familiarity in black boots too big for them.

All that is left to us is hope."[35] It is unclear, though, exactly what Kerr had hoped for.

The reviewer who most seriously reflected on the significance of Blau's production of *Danton's Death* for contemporary America and most clearly perceived how much is at stake, ideologically as well as for the arts, was Michael Smith, who wrote:

> The most interesting train of thought the play led me to concerns the relationship between revolutionary ideals — France's took a similar direction to the United States'— and present democratic practice. Buechner shows the leaders of the revolution succumbing to desperate expediency and ruthless power struggles only five years after the Bastille was stormed. More specifically disturbing to me is the change in rhetoric. The revolutionaries were struggling to find words for their ideals — words that would express what they believed, not just sound good — and were only second concerned with feasibility . . . How hollow, by contrast, sound the words of contemporary politicians, whose first aim must be to get elected, whose rhetoric is based on advertising techniques more than deep conviction.[36]

Smith went on to point out what he believed was Blau's role in drawing attention to the processes, which had led such a commercialized, superficial form of leadership in an ideologically shallow society. He also stressed that through the production of *Danton's Death* Blau had paradoxically exposed both the most vulnerable and the most promising aspects of his new position as the artistic director of the Lincoln Center theatre:

> Herbert Blau seems spectacularly out of place at Lincoln Center, and that is his great promise. He is on record opposing most of what Lincoln Center stands for; the Lincoln Center theatre is his Bastille, and he has taken it. Now he has to transform it. The difficulty of simply carrying on must be exhausting; the obstacles against any fundamental change of orientation are immense. If they prove insuperable, we are moved closer to despair. To add a further twist, the ideological battle must be fought in aesthetic terms: Blau must not only maintain his convictions but succeed in expressing them, not only choose the right plays, but find a style to give them force. In "Danton's Death" he has failed.[37]

This critic clearly did not know at the time of writing that Blau had in fact also "failed" at Lincoln Center in his effort to revolutionize the American theatre.

In *Take Up the Bodies*, Blau summed up his own experience:

It is not the best of memories, but I ought to follow it through. For the experience did reflect — from a rare if slippery point of vantage — the social and psychic history of a period which was changing our ideas of performance; and it did cause me to re-think, out of obvious personal necessity, what I was doing, or could continue to do in the theater.[38]

The fact is that we failed at Lincoln Center because we weren't good enough — I mean good enough to do what we proposed to do . . . What we had proposed was a virtual reformation of the American theater at almost every level, aesthetically and po-litically. It was worth the dare, but we were simply not that pow-erful, aside from all excuses we might invoke having to do with the space, the machines, the critics, the knives, the Board.[39]

After that, blackout. We were clobbered. It was humiliating. We never recovered. I wish I could say it knocked some sense into me. But artistically speaking, the most appalling part of the ex-perience is that it left me devastatingly uninstructed. There was nothing to be learned from such a failure (except more about failure), possibly because it wasn't true pathos, which is why it wasn't quite humbling either. The calamity was too abrupt, like an earthquake or a flash flood against which there is no argument at all. If there is something to be said after the split ground settles or the waters subside, it has not so much to do with the justice or meaning of the event, but merely with how one survives it. If I am saying it now, it's because that became the atmosphere, if not the cause, of the ideas that followed after (some of them al-ready latent), infusing my current work.[40]

It was, nevertheless, a considerable fall, and the problem was how, through a growing pathology of failure, to make something out of the nothing that seemed to be left. By increments, later, out of the subtext of my licked bones, the semblance of a method appeared in all the madness.[41]

. . . sometimes — for this happened too — mutual desire striking flame *in* the Idea and (why it happened and why it didn't a mystery, for I have seen things ill-conceived take fire too) taking us all beyond ourselves as, for a while, we thought it might do at Lincoln Center. That may in the end have been the tragic fault of *Danton's Death*, not the paucity of its conception — for say what they would they could never convince me of that — nor a mere failure of the execution, but some unaccountable blindness in the pitch of desire that for all the reach of its conception, let the prize, the astringent grandeur of the play, escape us, escape me, and nearly ruin some of the lives.[42]

Blau had apparently misjudged both the directors of the board and the support of the audiences. His backward glance provides a possible answer for the failure, but the more general problem of the Broadway audience trying to understand the production, probably without agreeing with its ideological as well as aesthetic suppositions, was no doubt crucial for its and Blau's fate.

During the preparations for his production of *Danton's Death*, Welles had also encountered problems in reaching out to his established constituency of spectators at the Mercury Theater. Before the previews and the official opening of his Danton performance there were already serious problems with the most loyal supporters of the theatre. According to Houseman, who was Welles' co-producer, the Mercury Theater "always counted on the solid support of an assured and loyal public — the organized, left-wing semi-intellectual audiences we had brought over with us from the Federal Theatre and which consisted predominantly of the Communist party, its adherents and sympathizers."[43] Mark Blitzstein (the political advisor of the Party) argued that the leaders of the theatre "were all guilty of a serious and dangerous error."[44] After being pressured Blitzstein admitted that this view came straight from the Cultural Bureau of the Party, because, as Houseman recalls,

[w]ith the Moscow trials still fresh in people's minds and the Trotskyite schism growing wider by the day, couldn't I see the inescapable and dangerous parallel?

To the politically uneducated and even to some of the younger emotional members of the party, Danton, the hero of the Revolution, who had raised and commanded the armies of the young republic, would inevitably suggest Trotsky, while his prosecutor, the incorruptible, ruthless Robespierre would, equally inevitably, be equated with Joseph Stalin . . . To placate him, we removed a few of the more obvious Trotsky-and-Stalin parallels. In exchange, the party agreed not to boycott us: they merely withheld their support. When we needed them desperately after our mixed notices in the capitalist press they did nothing to help us survive.[45]

The fact that the Welles production had to close after twenty-one performances can no doubt at least partly be ascribed to these problems.

With Wilson's 1992 production of *Danton's Death* a very different kind of reception strategy can be discerned. Not only did the spectators have to be educated to watch this production, but the actors themselves had to learn how to play in it. Wilson's methods of directing and his visions of this specific performance were based on aesthetic values and expectations that were apparently quite different from the schooling both the spectators and actors had previously received. But because of the unique qualities of Wilson's work as well as his international fame, the production team did everything they could to "sell" the performance. The fall 1992 issue of the Alley Theatre newspaper, typically named *Audience*, which is completely devoted to Wilson's production of *Danton's Death*, provides a key to what the performance is really about: Wilson's work as a director. Several of the articles in this newspaper introduce different aspects of his work and offer panegyrics on its general importance, while others give reports from the rehearsal process. The play by Büchner becomes a mere backdrop, an occasion for Wilson's genius. In his short introduction Gregory Boyd, the artistic director of the theatre, insists that "Wilson is unique": because he "offers a far different theatrical experience than the linear 'cause and effect' dramaturgy of 'Naturalism' . . . with which we are familiar . . . he asks something different from the audience."[46] For Boyd, Büchner's play served merely as an existential vehicle for the Wilson experience, what a critic previously had named the "ground plan" for Wilson's show: "With *Danton's Death*, Wilson looses his imagination on Buechner's brilliant descant on mortality, life, death and ethics . . . Watch and listen with a heightened awareness and I think you will be rewarded with an indelible experience."[47]

Besides a complete list of Wilson's productions and art exhibits, the issue of *Audience* also provides a short introduction to Büchner himself, where *Danton's Death* is characterized as a "sharp indictment of his would-be censors, as well as to provide much-needed income."[48] As far as I know the fact that a play earned the writer an income is very rarely used to describe a play in a program, but perhaps in this specific context it was relevant. In any case, *Audience* also included an interview with Richard Thomas, who played Danton and for whom this was his first time working with Wilson. Thomas said, "Well, one of the chal-lenging things about working for somebody that you want to please is trying to figure out what they want. Now, this can be a terrible problem."[49] A section termed "Notes from the Dramaturg's Jour-nal" includes Christopher Baker's excerpts from his "production di-ary," which describe different aspects of the rehearsal process. These notes, however, hardly say anything about the play and its specific in-terpretation in this performance.

On its front page the newspaper also presents what is termed the "Informances": "There will be an 'informance' discussion on the background of *Danton's Death* and Robert Wilson's work 1 hour prior to every performance of *Danton's Death*. These discussions, led by members of the Alley staff and *Danton's Death* artistic and production team, are free and open to the public."[50] I cannot say anything, of course, about how the regular audiences of the Alley Theatre reacted to these "informance" sessions where the play (which as we know by now did not have a very favorable reception tradition in the United States to rely on) and Wilson's work were introduced. Melanie Kirk-patrick, the *Wall Street Journal* critic, however, commented:

[I]n the information session that precedes every performance, the audience hears about Mr. Wilson's "new theatrical idiom" and is told to look at the stage as art. The production is unen-cumbered by heavy textual interpretation, it's said, the better for the audience to draw its own conclusions.

In other words, if you do not like it, you've only yourself to blame. You just must not be sophisticated enough for such a demanding work.

Well call me a hick, call me a philistine, but to my mind, the Wilson "Danton's Death" falls more in the category of theatri-cal fad than theatrical genius. To be sure, Mr. Wilson has created many striking images, as he has in his other productions. Visually the show is arresting. But he has also turned a powerful play into an inaccessible, even dull, one.[51]

Concerning the play itself, Kirkpatrick understands it as a moral and "political clash between moderation and bloody extremes" which Wilson has interpreted "as a conflict between dark and light — with some stunning lighting that takes the place of sets."[52] In his much more favorable review, in the *New York Times*, John Rockwell also focuses his discussion on the individual fates of the heroes, but disregards completely the social or ideological contexts within which they lived. According to Rockwell, the adaptation of the play "does no violence to its depth of detail or its inner message. Danton is still the faded firebrand, consumed with sensuality, trapped by fatalistic acceptance of his imminent death, yet calmly heroic at the end."[53] But the word "Revolution" does not appear even once in his review of Wilson's *Danton's Death*. It therefore seems no exaggeration to claim that this production, devoid of both history and historical awareness, failed to bridge the gap in any way between the past and the present. It was a production about history which refrained from performing history, reflecting what I believe is still a strong tendency among American intellectuals, though far from the only one. Wilson's production seems to have been a symptom of this, rather than the problem itself.

The Production Qualities

The critic Robert Littel from the *New York Post*, reviewing the 1927 Reinhardt production of *Danton's Death*, was extremely impressed by two of the mob scenes which "blew the audience right out of their upholstered seats last night and filled the theatre with the fickle, lurid, terrifying cyclone of the French Revolution." He added that he felt the two actors playing Robespierre and Danton (Wladimir Sokoloff and Paul Hartmann) were like "great captains on the bridge in a gigantic hurricane, . . . the sort of thing that can be seen in the theatre only once in a very long time."[54] Such stunning memories of Reinhardt's production are no doubt significant for the subsequent reception of *Danton's Death* in the United States, creating very high expectations which the three subsequent productions of the play were apparently not able to fulfill. John Houseman, in his memoirs from the Welles production, also recalls that Büchner's play had previously

been seen in New York in 1927 when Max Reinhardt presented it (in an augmented version with vast crowd effects) as one of the great successes of his American season. This success, far from helping us, made our undertaking more hazardous: it conditioned Orson's approach to the play and influenced the nature of his production. Since Reinhardt had made a mass spectacle of it and Orson himself had already demonstrated his ability to handle a crowd, *Danton's Death* would be performed as a "drama of lonely souls and the mob," with the mob ever-present but rarely visible.[55]

At this time Reinhardt's methods for creating mass scenes, with roots in the German tradition established by the Meiningen Theatre — where "the primary principle of the theatre is to depict movement, the relentless progress of the action"[56] were already well known and had no doubt become absorbed by most forms of theatre. Reinhardt's work had also been seen more recently in New York, where he had directed Franz Werfel's mass pageant *The Eternal Road*, which told the story of the persecution of the Jews in Europe. This production had premiered at the Manhattan Opera House in January 1937, the year just before Welles' Danton production. And in the American context the use of meticulously directed mass scenes was no doubt also decisive.

To achieve the effect of crowds Orson Welles used "a huge, curved wall, formed entirely of human faces, that filled the rear of the stage from the basement to the grid"[57] — a wall of skulls signifying the heavy toll of the Revolution — as the dominant element of the set. When the rehearsals began, however, Welles had no idea how difficult it would be to handle the technicalities of the stage. Houseman's description gives a clear picture of the problems which had to be confronted:

In front of this wall, starting immediately behind the forestage, was a yawning pit forty feet long and twenty deep, hacked out of the center of the stage floor we had so lovingly and proudly rebuilt the year before. Out of this hole, rising in steep steps from the basement, like a miniature Aztec pyramid, was a four-sided structure the center of which was occupied by an elevator shaft through which a small platform traveled up and down, descending to the basement to unload and rising to a maximum height of twelve feet above the stage. This was successively used, at various levels, as a rostrum, a garret, an elegantly furnished salon, a prison cell, and a tumbril until, in the final scene, it rose slowly to its full height to become the raised platform of the guillotine.

It was a brilliant conception but mechanically it was a horror.[58]

This solution almost ended in real tragedy.

The evaluations of the critics were clearly divided. Benchley, the ("cocktail party") critic from the *New Yorker Magazine*, reported that "[t]hese little faces, illuminated with such hellish ingenuity that as death draws nearer for Danton and his friends, they came to look like skulls, have a macabre effect, suggesting the millions grimly watching and waiting all over France. It may be a comment on the thin line that divides New Art from nonsense that, winking and glowing in the darkness, they occasionally made me feel as if I were at the Hayden Planetarium."[59] For Brooks Atkinson, however, who greatly appreciated the production, the "living sound of the footless mob," which actually was not seen on the stage, is symbolized by this wall of "staring faces which gives a strange mottled effect in dim lighting and becomes a rigid dance of death when the lights go up."[60] In *The Director in the Theatre Today* Welles explained his own intentions with the elaborate set and the use of technology: "My conception of the play was such that the elevator seemed to me to represent, when it was raised, the constant threat. It was made like scaffolding, because the republic of France at that time was an impermanent affair, and upon such existed the lives of these people, and it was made to look like a guillotine."[61] But Welles did not know how threatening this elevator would literally become. During one of the last rehearsals, Houseman recalls,

> as the street scene faded, behind it, slowly rising out of darkness into light, the elevator platform came into view, revealing a delicate, civilized, eighteenth-century drawing-room scene, all silk and elegance and laughter — two men and three women drinking tea to the soft playing of the harpsichord. It had just cleared the level of the stage, swaying gently as it was wont, when it was shaken by a slight tremor, barely perceptible from the front but enough to make the actors glance at each other. For a few seconds it continued to rise — a charming sight. It had almost reached its mark when it stopped, shuddered (so that a teacup fell off the table and smashed), and began to sink — slowly at first, but gathering speed as it vanished from sight.[62]

As a result of this technical disaster one of the actresses broke her leg and was replaced. The others were suffering from the shock. Then two previews were canceled, and after one hour's delay the third preview had to be canceled because of technical problems.

Welles' initial intention was that in "the last scene, as Danton and his followers went to their execution, this whole rear wall opened and revealed a narrow slit against a blue sky topped by glittering steel. At the final curtain drums rolled and the blade of the guillotine flashed down through the slit as the lights blacked out."[63] This indeed sounds effective, but it hardly saved the performance from its cool, even hostile reception, summed up by Simon Callow in his biography of Welles. He claims that even if the critics "acknowledged Welles" skill and imagination, there was a widespread sense of a machine operating in a void."[64] These comments clearly show that the technical effects, especially the visual ones, and in particular the execution in the last scene, seem to have been the focal point of the whole performance.

The crowd scenes in Blau's production on the huge stage of the Beaumont theatre were apparently also one of the main challenges of the performance. In *Take Up the Bodies* Blau has provided some detailed descriptions of the production itself as well as the complex process which led up to it:

In recent speculation about the building [of this theatre], there has been talk about demolishing and renovating the stage. That was always premature. For in the history of the Beaumont, there had been to my knowledge no production which, like *Danton's Death*, went head-on at the still-unexplored possibilities of the total space (Foreman's *Threepenny Opera*, from all accounts, coming closest). I mean the whole bastard stage with its botched contours and true dimensions: the long-receding distance to the back wall, the vast see-through wings, the vomitoria with passages below and (usable) airspace above, the vaulting loft so large that Irwing (later) had to prevent them from dividing it into a movie house, and the side ramps with electronic close-in panels — a technological disaster to begin with, used now only as expensive tormentors for the perplexed frontage; that is, the cross-purpose proscenium and pimple thrust . . . Everybody realizes now that the place is so huge that the hundreds of lights in the remote ceiling are like a galaxy of dying stars, and that if you don't take precautions to give the actors amplitude and voice they will look (as we had to learn to our dismay) not only smaller but younger, and acoustically forlorn. Despite all this and my own equivocal feelings, it is still . . . possibly and by accident an exciting space — not the first in theater history to pose a challenge in its faults . . .

If some things were carried too far, some were not carried far enough; for instance, the differential momentum of the moving crowds, whether describing a neoclassical geometry in a promenade or volatilized from the wings in a rush of Terror. (The wings, by the way, still need to be explored — given the ovoid sightlines — with mirror images or dialectically with negative space, using the fact that the audience on each side of the thrust sees a different wing and those in the center see a triangular segment of both.) Sometimes the crowds were splayed out in swift strokes, like paint on a canvas of an Action field; but the unmastered difficulty of the space, particularly the disproportion of the thrust (later built over and extended), may have caused me to hedge the intended randomness of the image and left things looking roughly, I suppose, neither consciously improvised nor designed.

There were other things people didn't like, but plain old well-blocked crowds might have spared us a lot of grief. It was a shame, given all the large productions we had done before, with a lot of complicated movement in good order. I still like the other idea and thought, whatever its faults, it was visibly there . . . That we attempted such things at all may have been part of the overreaching. That we didn't take it any further — I mean a thorough exploration of the huge space — was partly due, after the guillotine fell, to our being too intimidated to try. I did start to think again about those dimensions in preparing *Galileo*, but that was done by another director after I left.[65]

The critics of Blau's performance also commented on the crowd-scenes, which no doubt were central to the performance. Howard Taubman in the *New York Times* was quite reserved, arguing that "[t]he early crowd scenes carry no conviction. There is a commotion caused by people screaming and racing hither and yon, but instead of the illusion of the mobs in bloody, feverish Paris, one has the impression of actors going through their paces."[66]

The critic from *Variety*, however, felt that Blau's "handling of the riotous crowd scenes shows admirable vigor and detail, and a praiseworthy effort to exploit the possibilities of the new stage."[67] In his previous work, Blau had already paid meticulous attention to the significance of crowd scenes. In the performance of *Mother Courage and Her Children* (the first production of this play in the United States) which he directed at the Actor's Workshop in San Francisco in 1956, Blau, according to Peter Thomson, "had come to realize the need to develop stage-groupings that were, in themselves, signs, and the further need for these signs to invite a judgement from the audience."[68] These kinds of groupings, later used also in *Danton's Death*, were an integral aspect of the way Blau conceived the more comprehensive and independent stage narrative.

The general evaluations of Blau's production in the newspapers, however, provide a much less obvious sense of direct failure. They were indeed "mixed," but at the same time they very clearly communicate a hope that the new performance ideas which Blau brought to the grand theatrical space at Lincoln Center will eventually, in the subsequent productions of the new theatre, flourish much more fully. Whitney Bolton, in the *Morning Telegraph*, claims that Blau's *Danton's Death* has given us

> the most spectacular production in New York housed in the most spectacular and beautiful theater in New York, a vivid, magnificently theatrical production filled with life and vigor, with bright colors and extremes of staging, but they also have given us a company not yet mettled and meshed enough to compass the formidable demands that the George Buechner play makes on its actors . . . The cast simply is not up to the enormous demands of the play — but I am willing to wait and hope that in time it will be.[69]

The critic of *Daily News*, John Chapman, ends his review in a similar vein: "Of course, it is too early to judge the company as a repertory company. But last evening offered a brave, noisy, generally exciting start. Good luck, everybody!"[70]

The critics, however, make relatively few comments concerning Blau's ideas and his aesthetic and ideological intentions. When they do say something, it is with a clearly negative note. Louis Chapin, writing in the *Christian Science Monitor*, argued that, "[t]hough this new version of *Danton's Death* does show Mr. Blau's concern with challenging ideas and his effective handling of large forces on the stage, it does not bear out his widely propagated wish to reveal to the American theater its own creative potential."[71] Walter Kerr, in the *New York Herald Tribune*, argues that it is difficult to take the ideas of Blau seriously as theatre: "We are at school again, directed by our teachers to attend tonight's pageant for our own good, and the bright red seats we're sitting in and the bright red carpeting we climb at intermissions are only reminders that history and social tea are sometimes served together."[72] For Howard Taubman in the *New York Times*, however, this production provides "heartening signs of a viewpoint and a commitment. One could not ask for more this early in the game."[73] Clearly, Blau's production, like the ideal challenge Brecht posed for the theatre, divided the audience into different points of view and opinions. In this case, however, such a division could apparently not be handled by all the different parties involved: the board of the theatre, the new directors — Blau and Irving — and the audiences of upper Manhattan. We also have to remember that this was October 1965, just before the radical impulses which became the trademark of the late 1960s had been more clearly formulated by intellectuals and artists, even if they had hardly any effect on Broadway theatregoers. The ideological and aesthetic intentions of Blau's production were, however, no doubt heavily informed by this kind of radicalism. After *Danton's Death* the repertoire Blau had planned for the first year at the Beaumont theatre included plays such as Sartre's *The Condemned* and Brecht's *The Caucasian Chalk Circle*.

In *Take Up the Bodies* (published in 1982 two years after the end of the KRAKEN experiment), Blau sums up his Danton experience more concretely:

> Whether we were inept by nature or circumstance is still a puzzle. I am not using the word as our harshest critics did; they've seen far less talent that they've commended. I mean it historically, *at that moment*. The dimensions of the problem were enormous, or we made it so by trying to do everything at once: change the repertoire, shape up a divided company, avoid the use of stars, alter the economic structure of the theater, renovate the unions, develop a newer audience, protect the actors from sudden firings, open a new theater and test out the machinery, introduce a new and radical music, bring in the blacks, take on the Vietnam War, anticipate the self-defeating excesses of protest, educate the Board, reconcile the Underground and the Establishment — and stay in spirit, 3000 miles off-Broadway.[74]

In a private letter from Copenhagen, dated April 22, 1995, Blau responded to my general question about his Danton production, looking back again at the performance from a distance of thirty years. He begins his letter by commenting that "*Danton's Death* would seem lightyears away," but immediately goes on to clarify some of the issues involved:

But actually it never has been. It may be that the experience at Lincoln Center has suffused my thoughts about the play, or the play seemed at the time to embrace the tortuous calamitous period there. There are some reflections on it here and there in the chapter on "The Power Structure" in *Take up the Bodies*—mostly having to do with the assaults upon us because of the illfated program notes about power, atrocities, + the Vietnam war. (This was before the country had turned against it.) There is also some stuff on how I wanted to use the stage, even its imperfections against itself, splaying out crowds in mirror images as on an abstract expressionist canvas. The original idea for its *mise-en-scène* was, I thought, quite remarkable, although it had to be discarded when, late into rehearsals, Jo Mielziner—a legend then on the Broadway scene—showed up with an empty facsimile of what he had in mind. And we started all over with an inadequate compromise. Even so, people in NY—recalling the production—realize now that there was something unusual in the staging and conception, and very little like it since. Mielziner, who had collaborated with Eero Saarinen on the design of the Beaumont, was a mistake for us; but I thought he deserved a chance to do the first production there, instead of our own designers. But they would have easily picked up on the visual idea: it had occurred to me that the French Revolution had been played out, not only as Marx said in *The Eighteenth Brumaire*, in costume dress (Roman), but against a backdrop of classical imagery or—at least as figured in representations of the period—in a sort of classical *imaginary*. So I wanted projections to start with [of] great winged griffins, or mythological creatures, against which the violence would erupt, with the close-in (electronic) panels of the theater going up and down redefining spaces like the blades of the guillotine. The images were to have been, at first neo-classical in form, but as the action proceeded would mutate, and in a residual history of modernism erupting from the choplogic of the Revolution, would eventually become futurist, surreal, constructivist and, in a final explosive demoralization of the subject, the deject itself would disappear into the expressionist nonobjectivity of action painting. But that was sadly not meant to be.

But besides the practical questions (about who could have done the work more successfully and which images could have been more effective on the stage), the central issue which begins to emerge is how the text and the *possibilities* of performance gradually begin to inform each other. This is where the theory and the theoretical considerations begin to develop, from theatrical practices as well as from the interpretive strategies that can be applied to Büchner's classical text. Before continuing to explore how the text of *Danton's Death* and its performative potentials can serve as a point of departure for examining the theoretical implications of the notion of performing history, I want to take a closer look at Wilson's 1992 production of this play.

The Individualized Crowd

I do not know exactly why Robert Wilson chose *Danton's Death* for the production he had been invited to direct at the Alley Theatre in Houston. Thematically, in many of his previous performances he had already focused on famous historical personalities (Freud, Stalin, Einstein, Queen Victoria, Abraham Lincoln, Rudolf Hess) as well as important historical events like the American Civil War in the series of productions named *the CIVIL warS* (1983–1985). In all of these Wilson had created clusters of private associations and images around these different historical figures, but had not attempted to re-create their "lives" in the historiographic sense, "writing" their lives on the stage. The historical figures and events are rather fragmented. Previous to the 1992 production of *Danton's Death* Wilson had not directed any canonized play that featured the publicly known aspects of historical events. After this Danton production he made a video film, in cooperation with Heiner Müller, called *Death of Molière* (1996), which is also about the death of a historical figure. The Molière video, in which Wilson himself plays the dying playwright, is at the same time an elegiac meditation on the impending death of his longtime friend and creative partner, Heiner Müller (MoLieRe/MüLleR), who died just after the video was completed. Wilson's second production of *Danton's Death*, in 1998 at the Berliner Ensemble (of which Müller was the artistic director at the time of his death), can thus be placed in a more personal context. But these connections probably did not exist in 1992. According to Colin Counsell, in all of Wilson's performances "the events on the stage are governed by logics alien to our usual experience" and "the playing space is to be viewed in a way different from ordinary social space."[75] In view of this general characterization of Wilson's work, his choice of a play like *Danton's Death*, which actually presents a direct confrontation between conflicting personal/ideological goals and aspirations within such a well-known social space, may seem exceptional. It signals a change of direction which can at least partially account for the apparent problems of this production.

Preceding the notes of the dramaturg, Christopher Baker, there is an anonymous note in the issue of *Audience* published for the Wilson production which relates directly to this complex issue, so central for Wilson's performance aesthetics: "[r]ejecting Stanislavski's System or the American Method, Wilson is interested in his actor's presenting, not interpreting the play. Seeking to place the visual life of the stage work in equal standing with the verbal life, he pays particular attention to the physical production and 'choreography.' Often the text, movement and scenic elements contradict each other. Sometimes they reinforce each other. But they always leave room for the audience to draw conclusions and make connections that are wholly their own."[76] This independent "visual life" of Wilson's work has indeed been given a very strong prominence in his *Danton's Death* production. The most striking visual tension created in this performance is between the dynamic, frequently lit backdrop, on the one hand, and the individual, totally isolated characters who are illuminated by spotlights on the usually completely dark front stage, on the other. Only rarely are the characters brought together in smaller groups by the illumination of smaller sections of the otherwise completely dark/black space. But there were definitely no crowd scenes in the traditional sense in Wilson's production. Instead, according to the notes of Christopher Baker, who worked as dramaturg, the aim of Wilson's production was to "steer away from the usual rendering of the play, with its many crowd scenes, and instead suggest the shouting Jacobins with sounds and music."[77] The sound score of these scenes culminates with sounds that are like a blowing wind.

In Wilson's production the black backdrop opens and closes during the performance, creating different-sized square or rectangular "empty spaces" which usually are filled with a "white" light, but sometimes also with a colored light. The black frame of the backdrop around this empty space expands or contracts in different directions. On one level Wilson seems to be challenging the notion of the empty space as articulated by Peter Brook, questioning the idea that such a thing is possible at all in the theatre. For the brand of postmodernism developed by Wilson, as opposed to the modernist theatre heralded by Brook, the theatrical space, whether it is "white" or "black," and even if it seems vacuous, is *a priori* never completely empty or void. There is no totally empty space. Wilson raises the question of what the white and the black signify, as in the classical argument between Goethe and Newton concerning the nature of color and whether it is black or white which contains all the colors of the spectrum. Also, according to Baker, "Wilson describes the scenic elements, the system of shutters upstage that will open and close to create different sized openings, like the iris of a camera."[78]

Wilson has explored this kind of dynamic, seemingly abstract stage image in several of his more recent productions, including *Doctor Faustus Lights the Lights*, based on the play by Gertrude Stein, which was produced in four different theatres in 1992, the same year *Danton's Death* was performed at the Alley Theatre in Texas. In the Stein production at the Hebbel Theater in Berlin, these abstract visual scores, just as in Wilson's production of *Danton's Death*, created heavily charged images combining geometrical forms and lighting. During the last scenes of the performance the place of the stage action gradually "moved" or was transferred into this seemingly abstract locus, which gradually became "filled" with body movement and human action. This process culminated in the execution scene, which took place in this inner space, showing where the crimes of history have been committed. But since the development of moving the *mise-en-scène* to the backstage area came very late in the performance, it does not become contextualized ideologically in Wilson's Texas production of *Danton's Death*. It rather had the characteristics of a *deus ex machina*, suddenly reversing the action through an otherworldly agent, not directly connected to what preceded this event. In Wilson's German production of the play, in 1998, this development of moving the action to the backstage area was initiated during the very first scenes of the performance. This, together with the classical heritage of the play in Germany, created a much stronger ideological contextualization for this production.

The major part of the dramatic action in the Texas version of Wilson's *Danton's Death* takes place on the large front stage, which is usually quite dark. During the long opening sequence, while the spectators are still taking their seats, a character dressed in black—no doubt an impersonation of death and of "Robert Wilson" too, who typically dresses in black—moves around on the half-lit stage where a torch is burning. By changing the lighting, illuminating the back-

The opening image of Robert Wilson's production of Danton's Death *at the Alley Theater in Houston, 1992. Photo by Jim Caldwell.*

drop, or emphasizing the lighting more on the front stage, this opening sequence already achieves striking photographic effects, as if a
photograph suddenly changes from a negative to a positive representation of an abstract human body. Silhouettes thus suddenly become transformed into human figures. Such interactions between

Robert Wilson's production of Danton's Death *at the Alley Theater in Houston, 1992. Photo by Jim Caldwell.*

different perceptions of the abstract human images, represented as shadows or ghosts or even human forms, are continuously "performed" in different variations throughout the whole production. Also, the characters are usually not seen when they enter the space, but appear or just become present when they are suddenly illuminated. By contrast, the characters frequently make their exits by extinguishing the lights.

In the first scene of the play, after a long blackout, where Danton and his wife and the card players are entertaining themselves, each group of characters is lit individually. In other scenes only a face is lit. The characters, as a rule, speak very slowly, pronouncing every single syllable in a declamatory style. The dramaturg of the production reports that Wilson explained to Deborah Kinghorn, the vocal coach, that he wanted the actors to embrace a vocal quality, "a cold, clear manner of speaking, delivered in long sustained lines, rather than short pauses."[79] This mode of presentation, which is reproduced in different variations throughout the performance, creates a strong sense of isolation and fragmentation, even a solipsistic version of the historical situation. And as the performance advances one does not get a sense — at least not from the video-recording — of the tensions or the political arguments between the characters or political factions, so forcefully represented in the play itself, but rather of shadows from the past who literally appear again.

The characters on the stage in Wilson's production of Büchner's play are in a way like those almost abstract "things" referred to in the opening scene of *Hamlet*, when Marcellus/Horatio asks if "this thing," the ghost or perhaps even the performance itself, has "appeared again tonight." They are like shadows returning from the realm of death, formally repeating the very same words and the same lines which once, in some distant, almost forgotten past, no doubt triggered violent passions, but are now, on the stage, only dim recollections of them. Wilson seems to imply, from the very beginning of his performance, that all that is left of history is a ghostly ritual in which the motions and emotions from the past can only be formally repeated, yet again. The individuals on the stage are isolated from each other and the social space is fragmented, or even nonexistent, creating what Counsell in the context of Wilson's work has termed an "other-place."[80] The dramaturg reports that at one of the early rehearsals Wilson said: "We will need to play with time. Some parts are in real time, some parts are in supernatural time, some parts are as if you were in a large room speaking to others, some are inside of your head."[81] At this stage the actors also discussed the exact location of each scene, but the performance itself shows very few traces of this kind of concrete quality.

For Melanie Kirkpatrick of the *Wall Street Journal*, who clearly did not like the performance, this kind of dislocation or double time scheme was quite problematic. She commented, for example, that the "encounter between Danton and Robespierre, when the latter is in his bath, is a good example of how the Wilsonian method of acting willfully undermines the basic theatrical energy of Buechner's play. By rights, this scene ought to be a dramatic highlight of the play, since it's the only time the two antagonists appear together. Instead, the men seem to ignore each other and deliver what might as well be monologues. Danton stands onstage and nearly out of view of Robespierre; in fact, the two men never even look at one another."[82] This meeting in the sixth scene of act I, when Saint Just comes to visit Robespierre after Danton has left, is based on historical evidence, though we do not know what the two contestants really said to each other. According to Büchner's stage direction this scene takes place simply in "A Room."[83] Wilson's choice to situate the scene in Robespierre's bathroom while he is taking a bath can, however, be seen as placing it in a recognizable "social" space, albeit the most private of all such possible spaces.

Wilson's choice can, for example, be compared to Andre Wajda's film based on a much less known play about the struggle between Danton and Robespierre, Stanislawa Przybyszewska's *The Danton Case* (1929).[84] Wajda's 1982 film, in which the French actor Gérard Depardieu performs a remarkable Danton, has had a fairly widespread audience and has been awarded several prizes.[85] Because of the cinematographic medium, in stark contrast to Wilson's theatre production, the social milieu of the time has been meticulously reproduced in Wajda's film. The meeting between Danton and Robespierre takes place over a luscious meal, hosted by Danton in a *chambre séparée* at the Café de Foy, which Robespierre simply refuses to enjoy. In Büchner's play, and consequently in Wilson's production, it is Robespierre who is "hosting" this fatal meeting between the two contestants.

The bathtub in the Wilson production is in its form and function similar to the stylized sofas on which some of the women recline while talking to Danton. These sofas and the bathtub are the only pieces of furniture used in the performance. In his notes the dramaturg emphasizes the care with which the sofas were designed and the small but apparently important adjustments constantly made during the rehearsals, before the "piece" is finally "built," for the production itself: "The furniture and other objects are not only set pieces to be manipulated by actors for the brief run of the production, but also art objects, with a 'life' of their own, on view both in and out of the production. Some will end up in galleries, some may find their ways into future exhibitions of Wilson's work, some even in other productions."[86] But the bathtub probably had an intertextual function as well.

The sight of Robespierre in the bathtub also may recall David's famous painting of Marat after he was assassinated. Peter Weiss even refers directly to this painting in *Marat/Sade*—how the dead Marat is supposed to look after having been stabbed—as a kind of documentary gesture. This scene has frequently also been played in this manner, as in Brook's production. The bathtub, however, is absolutely necessary from the very beginning of the Weiss play. It seems to be no coincidence that Wilson also decided to place his Robespierre in a bathtub, because as Wilson, according to the dramaturg, said, "[a]ctors' faces should look clear, porcelain, reminiscent of the paintings of Jacques Louis David."[87] This image transforms Robespierre into a potential victim, something which he avoids in the Büchner play, while it is Danton who will die. But it does place Robespierre in the larger narrative of victimization connected with the French Revolution. In spite of these contextualizations of Robespierre's bathtub, it remains a free-floating image, which hardly absorbs a more comprehensive significance in the midst of all the disconnected images and characters in this production. But that, indeed, also seems to have been Wilson's explicit intention.

In his review of the production for the *New York Times*, John Rockwell summed up the contradictions between the stylistic formality and the themes of the play in a much more positive manner. Guided by the commentary of the dramaturg, Rockwell claimed that "[a]gain as usual, the essence of Mr Wilson's vision is visual: extraordinary cool, sensuous, elegant stage pictures that he says are inspired by David but look archetypically Wilsonian. What makes this production more potent than some of Mr Wilson's recent work, however, is how the formalism contains and contrasts with the passion of the play and of the actors, and the especially beautiful images Mr Wilson has conjured."[88] It is thus possible to see how the preparations, the "informances," and the program notes have directed the reception and interpretation of this performance. The strongest impression from the video-recording of Wilson's *Danton's Death* (confirmed by having seen other Wilson productions live on the stage as well, including the German version of *Danton's Death*) is that there seems to be an intentional gap between the narrative of the Revolution and the formal stylization of the acting. Even the street-scenes with the common people are very consciously designed according to different genres of musical theatre, with sudden freezes that suspend and nullify the subversive energies of the crowd.

Kirkpatrick in her review also makes the charge that "the Wilsonian method of acting willfully undermines the basic theatrical *energy* of Büchner's play."[89] Wilson's "choreographic" interpretation of the play is based on containment and control of the revolutionary forces instead of letting the actors express them either physically or emotionally. The actors have been integrated within the larger visual scheme rather than being allowed as characters to realize the dramatic situations of conflict with which Büchner's play abounds. The actors seem to be "testing" the words of the characters in a solipsistic space of self-containment which Wilson has created for them. They become his puppets. This is a serious charge, dealt with only briefly here. In the next chapter, however, I attempt to delineate the fields of energies created and passed on by the actors in theatrical performances.

In order for the notion of performing history to become effective and communicative and for the individual actors to become what I call hyper-historians, it is necessary for them to bear a sense of independence and responsibility not only toward the historical events depicted, but also toward the spectators. This, I believe, neither the Wilson production nor the two other American Danton productions were able fully to achieve, as the directorial concepts apparently took over. There were specific problems in each of the individual productions, of course. But finally it seems that each of the three directors for different reasons was unable to pass on this responsibility to the actors who were performing *Danton's Death* on the stage. Alternatively, the actors were perhaps not able to shoulder this responsibility. Because of the nature of the archive materials this aspect can only be examined more closely with regard to the Wilson production.

Wilson, rejecting Method acting, wants the actors to present the play, not to interpret it. But such an approach apparently raised problems not only for the spectators, but for the actors as well. The "Notes from the Dramaturg's Journal" point at a possible cause for these problems. In the middle of an improvisation, Wilson used to stop the actors and say: "Think in lines. It's OK to do something abstract, without meaning, not related to the text . . . Think about it formally — a structure, drawing in space."[90] *Audience* also published an interview with Richard Thomas, who played Danton. The abstract method used by Wilson created problems for Thomas. This mode of rehearsing seems to have been based on what Thomas, in an article published a little less than a year after the production itself, describes as creating abstract movement sequences which have their own life and rhythms, extrapolated independently from the text: "After these movements were created they were numbered and learned, as one would learn a dance. Then we spoke the text while doing the movements. Sometimes the words and gestures reinforced each other, sometimes they had nothing to do with one another, and sometimes the pairings revealed something new and extraordinary — some third idea between gesture and text."[91]

Ellen Halperin-Royer, who followed the rehearsals of Wilson's production of *Danton's Death* with the explicit aim of understanding the role of the actors in his work, clearly wanted to demythologize Wilson's "puppet master" image. But in reading her account it seems that

Wilson's method for rehearsing the play was even more authoritarian than she herself admits or than can be understood from Thomas' recollections. Referring to the three-week workshop, the first stage of preparations for the production, Halperin-Royer points out that

[s]ince the work in the first scene had progressed at a painfully slow rate without satisfactory results, Wilson spent the rest of the workshop using a much more prescriptive method. He began working on scenes by placing the actors in initial positions, dictating to them a series of movements, and assigning a number to each movement. Rommen [Wilson's longtime assistant director] wrote these movements down in shorthand, and the actors then memorized the numbered movements. Once the movements were learned (usually the following day), Wilson rehearsed the scene by having either the dramaturg or a production assistant read the text while the actors executed each movement at the moment Wilson called its number. A few times Wilson mixed up the sequence of the numbered movements, calling out "one, two, three, four, three, four, five. . . ." The stage managers wrote every number Wilson called out into the script. The actors then memorized the word corresponding to each numbered movement. The actors practiced performing the movements at the correct time as the text was read from the director's table until the movement was mastered; finally, the actors spoke their own lines while performing Wilson's movements on cue.[92]

The Execution

Büchner's play ends with the execution of Danton and his companions by the guillotine. This is ultimately the "drama" toward which the play is moving, signifying the failure of history to come to terms with the creativity and freedom of an individual within the context of the revolutionary situation. This is the point in the play when the Revolution and its struggles for freedom, equality, and brotherhood become transformed into a cruel spectacle of death. In all three American productions dealt with here this spectacle was no doubt the high point of the respective performances. In the Welles production, however, for reasons which I have indicated above, the guillotine was perceived as "a machine operating in a void."[93] In Blau's production it was perceived as a crescendo. Norman Nadel, in the *World*

Telegram and Sun, writes that it was not possible to "underestimate the power of a sturdy built guillotine full size and mechanically complete — to execute Danton, Desmoulins and the others. When the blade drops, you hear the swish as the steel slices through gristle. We watched that blade and listened for that sound; nothing the victims said in their final seconds made nearly as much an impression."[94] In Wilson's production the guillotine scene was the only scene in which the characters in the real world, not just in some kind of supernatural world, entered the illuminated area of the back stage. The black floor of the front stage area was opened in the same way as the "camera" of the back stage area had operated previously, exposing a large white square. This seems to indicate that the two worlds have become integrated.

In Wilson's production the guillotine was signified "by a large wooden square into which the victims slowly sank, forlorn jacks-in-the-box. 'The real guillotine,' Wilson noted, 'is the white carpet that unrolls on the floor with the speed of lighting.'"[95] The whole performance builds up to this theatrical ritual. Or as Andrzej Wirth comments: "The guillotine in the last scene is reduced to such a perfect cubistic stage object, that the execution of Danton is perceived more as an aesthetic closure than as a tragic historical event . . . the real protagonist of the evening is the thrust stage itself, poetically transformed by Wilson into a form resembling a giant guillotine that kills with the sharpness and speed of light."[96] Looking at this performance in the context of the performances about the French Revolution examined in this book shows that the aesthetic formality of performing history has taken over completely. The "performance" has been carried to its greatest extreme, almost completely emptied of "history"; in another sense, Wilson substitutes aesthetic history for a social and political history.

The insistent employment of the theatrical machinery in these productions in order to bring out the frustrations and disappointments caused by the difficulties of realizing the high revolutionary ideals is perhaps also indicative of American culture, with its strong valorization of technology. All three U.S. productions in different ways emphasize that the ending is not primarily a human challenge, but rather a technological one. On the ideological level the guillotine is an expression of the failure of the Revolution, and on the theatrical level it is an expression of the failure of technology fully to redeem the performances as works of art. Instead of presenting the theatrical machinery as a machinery of redemption, a *deus ex machina*, through which the state of affairs in this world is put right again by supernatural intervention or by imaginatively showing some kind of utopian option to the cruel conflicts of history, the machineries in these Danton productions are almost exclusively presented as machineries of destruction which are unable, theatrically, to show the spectators any viable alternative to the destructiveness of *this* failed revolution. The three American productions of *Danton's Death* seem to express a wish or longing for redemption through technology, and in Blau's case also a constant struggle with such machineries (those bombing Vietnam with napalm or those of the stage itself). For Blau the focus was on the human agents behind the machineries, who instead of gaining strength actually become powerless through them, while for Welles and Wilson the machineries seem to have been more an end in themselves. This is expressed by striving to redeem the performances through the use of these theatrical machineries.

For Blau his theatrical failure implicitly became a springboard to theorize on the notion of performance itself. In one of his more recent "meditations" on ideology and performance (without specifically referring to Wilson's performance of *Danton's Death*, but drawing his distinctions on the basis of Wilson's production of *King Lear* at the Frankfurt Schauspiel in 1990),[97] Blau claims that when Wilson approaches classical plays, "the texture of the performance is such, its attenuation, that we may think of all appearances as 'the baseless fabric' of a vision in which the actors have melted into air, thin air, even before the revels have ended (*Tempest*, 4.1.148–156), since they have assumed from the beginning — without that fractiousness of will which is a figure of the drama and its paradox of necessity — the function of a sign."[98] Blau considers this kind of "postmodern pastiche" to be "a function of the logic of consumer capitalism."[99] Also in *The Audience*, published in 1990, Blau argued that "the sumptuously decentered productions of Robert Wilson, . . . [could] perhaps [be] best described as masques, presenting another model of the psyche in which, displacing the princely observer, the invisible power of the director is distributed all over stage."[100] This no doubt also holds true for Wilson's production of *Danton's Death*. In the opening chapter of *Take Up the Bodies* from 1982 Blau already argues that Wilson, in spite of his "unusual graphic abilities," has developed an aesthetic: while "he avowedly wants to put the theater back into the mind or the mind back into the theater, his tracing of thought-revealing images is still occurring at a level where no specific idea, *as idea*, has to be thought through."[101] Blau and Wilson no doubt represent two diametrically opposed positions with regard to the place and function of ideas in the contemporary theatre.

While for Wilson it is the "dumb" visual images which carry the performance, for Blau history and theory are worked out in different forms of writing, where performance is mediated by writing, not only by the formal structures in space. Blau has continued to look at the theatre from a perspective which has been clearly influenced not only by his production of *Danton's Death*, but by the issues of revolution and theatre as well. In *The Eye of Prey* (1987), for example, he claims:

> Any way you look at it — which may be the price of looking — the theater is the place where nothing is being transacted except what has been imposed on the disfigured body of thought of an infinite chain of representation. The missing links of this chain, its *structure of disappearance*, wind through the body politic and are strengthened, as Genet suggested in *The Balcony*, by the delusions of revolution, which maintains [*sic*] the chain of servitude intact. We felt something like that after the sixties (when the "whole world" was "watching"), and it appears to be no different after every insurrection around the globe . . . It is against this [vanishing] power that performance continues to struggle, always coming round, with no higher aspiration than another reversal of history in the play of appearances: the liberation of the performer as an *actor* who, laminated with appearance, struggles *to appear*.[102]

The notion of performing history itself is no doubt also based on such a struggle to appear and to create the unique energies of the performance. To quote the Envoy in Genet's own play: "History was lived so that a glorious page might be written, and then read. It's reading that counts"[103]— or in the words of the Chief of Police in the same play: "The rebellion's riding high, it's moving out of this world. If it gives its sectors the names of constellations, it'll evaporate in no time and be metamorphosed into song. Let's hope the songs are beautiful."[104] This is apparently the point at which not only the performer but also the Revolution itself is transformed into a glowing star. This glowing star of artistic creativity and inspiration, at the same time signifying both the individual character and the actor as well as transformative historical events, has in the post–World War II imagination become an angel.

In spite of his directorial "failure" with *Danton's Death* Blau continued to "perform" the Büchner play as part of his more comprehensive theorizing meditations on the theatre, through his writing. In *The Audience*, Blau terms *Danton's Death* "a virtual agenda of postmodern thought,"[105] which at the same time serves as a "kind of prophetic metadrama on the generic futility of poststructuralist thought."[106] Blau primarily focuses on Danton in the prison cell, where he asks, "Will the clock never stop?"[107] This question creates a dialectics for the progress of time framed by Danton's cynical statement in the first scene of the play, saying, "In one hour, sixty minutes will have passed."[108] It is highly questionable whether such a tautological statement says something about the nature of history beyond the mere fact that hours are divided into minutes. This understanding is also echoed by the Officer in Büchner's *Woyzeck*, who, while he is being shaved, says to the play's eponymous hero:

> Steady, Woyzeck, steady; one thing after another. You're making me quite giddy. What on earth am I to do with the spare ten minutes if you finish too early today. Woyzeck, just think, you've still got a good thirty years to live, thirty years! That's 360 months, not to mention the days, the hours, the minutes! What are you going to do with all this vast expanse of time? Pace it, Woyzeck, pace it! . . .

> I get really frightened for the world when I think of eternity. Activity, Woyzeck, activity! Eternal means eternal, it means *eternal*, you must see that; but then again on the other hand it's not eternal, it's a moment, a single moment — Woyzeck, it frightens me when I think that the world revolves in a single day, what a squandering of time, where's it all going to end? Woyzeck, I can't bear to see a millwheel turning any more — it makes me melancholic.[109]

Apparently eternity is tautological; it is a Wilsonian image, while it is the concrete aspects of time which feed writing and ideology and are re-created through them. It is the passage of time which makes the officer melancholic in the mode of self-reflection.

From Danton's own subjective perspective, however, his individual death will terminate both time and history, because then his life can no more be accounted for by exact figures and numbers. For Blau, too, there is "[n]o solace in history, only its end, and only the corruption infinitely mirrored."[110] Commenting on what he apparently considers to be this kind of inevitability, Blau adds that, "[i]n its reflexive and shadowed thought, the scene — in which nothing appears to happen — is like an incipience of theater which reflects upon the thought that it is thought itself that divides. What we have in the division is the future in the instant, which still remains one of the better definitions of theater, as well as the aspect of theater that still remains hardest for the audience to see."[111] The most difficult question, however, it seems to me, is how the theatre can make this future (always eternally present beyond the limited life-span of the individual characters on the stage) visible for the spectators in the auditorium, not as a tautological eternity, but as an idea of utopia — and how, when the theatre is performing history, this future in which the spectators are already situated can be represented on the stage. These questions do not have simple answers, of course. But relying on the metaphysical tradition of the angel, the then and there of the historical past, the here and now of the performance, and Blau's forward flow of "the future in an instant" can perhaps be united.

Writing about *Danton's Death* in *The Audience*, Blau argues that the vision of Camille Desmoulins, Danton's friend and a journalist by profession, which, "in its fearful symmetry, [is] not only a parallel to Blake but a prefiguration of Deleuze: the disintegration of the atom converted by the desiring machine into pure libidinal flow, while the Revolution is already enforcing another kind of repression, he attacks the oedipal dramaturgy of a schizophrenic culture, with its fetishizing institutions and mimetic dependence."[112] It is he who says to Danton and Lucille, Camille's wife:

> I tell you, unless they get everything in stilted imitations, a little bit here and a little bit in concerts, theatres, art exhibitions, they have neither eyes to see nor ears to hear. Cobble up a puppet with conspicuous strings and make it jerk round the stage on iambic feet: "What stunning psychology! How neat and logical!" Take a jaded maxim, a half-baked emotion, a commonplace idea, stuff it into coat and trousers, paint on a face, stick on hands and feet, make it wheeze and puff its way through three acts till it gets itself married or shoots itself dead: "An idyllic ideal!" Scratch out an opera that expresses the ebb and flow of emotion as a cracked tin-whistle conveys the song of the nightingale: "Ah! the power of art!"
>
> Put these people out of the theatre and into the street: "Ugh! miserable reality!" They forget their Maker for his incompetent

copyists. They hear and see nothing of the glow, the hum, the radiance of creation regenerating itself in and around them each second of the day. They visit the theatre, read poems and novels, ape their ridiculous contortions, and dismiss God's creatures as "Oh so ordinary!"[113]

Thus, according to Blau, "What Buechner seemed to know prematurely . . . was that the Imaginary is formed by the subject who, unable yet to listen, *does not see himself seeing* and who — so far as representation is concerned — perpetuates a structure in which one does not see at all *unless* one sees oneself seeing. That, of course, is the condition of alienation (*Entfremdung*) which is the self-observing condition of the Brechtian technique (*Verfremdung*)."[114] The character in Büchner's play who is finally able to do that, to see herself seeing, is Lucille; therefore, I believe, she gradually becomes the emotional center of Büchner's play.

After Lucille kisses Camille and bids him farewell, she says, "These are evil times. It's the way things are. What can anyone do? Be brave and accept it."[115] She starts singing a popular song:

Who had the heart
To make lovers part
And part and part and part.[116]

After the execution, in answer to a comment by an unidentified woman that it is "a good thing dying's so public these days,"[117] it is Lucille who — before she calls out "Long live the king" and is arrested — asks: "Dear Camille! Where do I look for you now!"[118] She exposes the complex semiotic economy of emotions and the flows of energy, where, finally, what we usually call history is after all only one of the signs. This is a moment exploring the vulnerability of the emotions of an individual searching for redemption, striving to end the struggles of the individual in history not through technology, which carries destructive potentials, but on a more private level on which the voice of Lucille can be heard. Admittedly, this is also such a moment in Wilson's production, when a spotlight illuminates Lucille's face as she is leaning on the guillotine which has just destroyed her husband as well as his companions.

When Lucille finally sits down on the steps of the guillotine and says, "Silent angel of death, I sit on your lap,"[119] it seems (as Walter Benjamin was to confirm a little more than a century later) that the image of the angel is in fact both the beginning and the closure as well as a metaphysical option for the never-ending performance of history: the angelic "body" constantly enables that thing from the past to appear again tonight on the stage. For Lucille, however, this again is a failure. But at such a moment, which both Büchner and Benjamin saw as an instance of danger, an *Augenblick* (literally, "eye-glance"), what is at stake for the individual also inevitably becomes history. Such moments can bring the spectator to an awareness of seeing oneself seeing the past, like the ghost in *Hamlet*, appearing again tonight, or like the *Angelus Novus* — the *new* angel.

Theatrical
Energies

The theater like the plague . . . releases conflicts,
disengages powers, liberates possibilities, and if these
possibilities and these powers are dark, it is the fault
not of the plague nor of the theater, but of life.
—Antonin Artaud

When we grow weary of the disorder of the world whose
disorder spreads through our language so that we grow
exhausted, we retreat to or look for energy in the apparent
order of art, its ingrown autonomy.
— Herbert Blau

Lucille's failure, her lonely gesture of despair before submitting herself to the angel of death, is the climax of Wilson's American production of *Danton's Death*. It is a forceful moment, a crystallizing image which even in the video-recording brings focus to a performance
about which the evaluations were otherwise quite divided. There were,
no doubt, forceful moments in each of the productions examined in
the previous chapter, but for different reasons they were not fully integrated within a performance context that allowed the individual
actors to communicate the historical past to the spectators in the present. Wilson's German-speaking 1998 production of *Danton's Death*, in
cooperation with the Salzburg festival and the Berliner Ensemble,
much more clearly, it seems to me, communicated something of the
complexities of the historical past to its audiences. The scenes in the
Assembly, for example, were done differently in the U.S. production,
where Robespierre is standing on a platform that almost invisibly
elevates him more than two meters above the ground or where Saint-
Just raised his fist during his speech reverberates with historical references, which I am sure neither the actors nor the Berlin spectators
failed to perceive.

The aim of this book, however, is not to provide some exact measuring tool for the notion of performing history. The question I wish
to raise is rather how the complex semiotic economy of emotions expressed in the words of Lucille — or moments similar to it, moments where everything seems to be at stake — is transposed, perceived, and experienced in specific performances about history, and in particular how the actors on the stage transmit such moments to the spectators. This question of how theatrical energies are created and communicated is no doubt an issue that concerns all forms of performance and theatre, not only those about the historical past. But by examining the question of theatrical energies — and in particular how the actor commands and communicates these energies — from the specific perspective of performing history, it is possible to focus on certain aspects of theatrical communication that have only rarely been examined in detail. The aim of this chapter is therefore to examine the expressions of theatrical energies connected to the notion of performing history more systematically than in the previous chapters and at the same time to raise some more general issues related to theatrical communication. This chapter thus points out more in detail how the theatrical energies shape a very crucial dimension of the notion of performing history, which I believe also contributes to a more general understanding of the theatre. Therefore, while this last chapter summarizes some of the major issues examined in this book, it also opens up some new issues that are not strictly within the boundaries of performing history.

The notion of theatrical energies and the way they are created on the stage, to be communicated to the audience, is quite frequently employed in discourses about theatre and performance. It is used to depict how an uncompromising engagement on all levels of theatrical communication, but mainly through the art of acting, is achieved. It is indeed surprising to find how many texts about theatre and performance refer directly to energy or draw on concepts closely related to it, usually without indexing them as key concepts. They simply appear as the central ligament around which discourses about the theatre in one way or another have been organized. The notion of energy does not primarily relate to the world of the theatre; today it usually refers to some kind of machinery or technical aid that through physical or chemical changes produces labor. It also defines the ability through human intentions to perform actions with concrete results. Energy thus not only is the outcome of technological achievements, but concerns human will and actions as well. It is a term that in many ways is also closely related to the concept of performance — not only the performance of cars or computers, but a whole range of human actions in all conceivable fields, including the theatre.[1]

In contemporary discourses about theatre and performance the notion of energy has been most frequently employed in the contexts of acting and directing. But it can also be found in discourses about dramatic texts from the distant past, the "vehicles" used by the actors to create their energies on the stage, and how they contain energies which can still make them relevant to us, centuries after they were written and first performed. In these cases the art of acting both transmits and transforms social energies from that past on the present-day stage. The notion of energy has been employed to analyze the different modes of communication in the theatre, drawing on concepts from semiotics, psychoanalysis, and philosophy. This chapter also examines how some contemporary directors have used this term and discusses the important role of catharsis (the emotional, intellectual, moral, or even physical energies that may be experienced by spectators while watching a performance or as a result of it) in theatrical communication.[2] Finally, "returning" to the city of Berlin, I also wish to show how the notion of performing history has incorporated supernatural phenomena as a source or a metaphor for metaphysical energies. To sum up, the concept of energy seems to be situated at the threshold of a number of different discourses related to the theatre, just like the notion of performing history. Its vagueness is at the same time both a weakness — since it is frequently not clearly defined — and a strength, because it joins aspects of human experiences and social practices which are usually separated into distinct categories of description and analysis.

All these aspects of energy have a long and complex history. In the classical world it was, however, a concept primarily used within the field of rhetoric. For Aristotle *energeia* (force) and *enargeia* (shining forth) were the rhetorical expressions through which the speaker made the objects described appear before the eyes of the listener. This was also the way in which Quintilian interpreted the Aristotelian terms, as *evidentia in narratione* (literally "set before the eyes": being able to present the facts, in particular in courtrooms, by being able to create an illusion of reality).[3] This is an idea that is actually closely related to the notion of performing history; just as in the courtroom, on the stage the role of the witness is crucial in bringing back an event from the past to the spectators. The witness (in particular the performance dynamics created through his or her presence on the stage or even outside of it) is of central importance not only in performances about history, but in all kinds of performances.

What I finally want to argue here is that theatrical practices can be seen as a point of convergence or union for these differently constituted energies, which are generally conceived of as belonging to completely different ontological spheres. This kind of convergence of fields was one of the reasons why theatre and the arts in general were so threatening for Plato. In his dialogue "Ion" Socrates explains to Ion, the young "actor" or rhapsodist, the nature of his performative talent:

> The gift which you possess of speaking excellently about Homer is not an art but an inspiration; there is a divinity moving you, like that contained in the stone which Euripides called a magnet, but which is commonly known as the stone of Heraclea. This stone not only attracts iron rings, but also imparts to them a similar power of attracting other rings; and sometimes you may see a number of pieces of irons and rings suspended from one another so as to form quite a long chain: and all of them derive their power of suspension from the original stone. In like manner the Muse first of all inspires men herself; and from these inspired persons a chain of other persons is suspended, who take the inspiration. For all good poets, epic as well as lyric, compose their beautiful poems not by art, but because they are inspired and possessed.[4]

The power-fields through which the magnetic energies of performances are produced, through what Socrates terms *enthusiasmos*, are according to Plato subject to an *a priori* hierarchy; each link in the creative chain refers back to a divine source, creating an integrated totality. Plato totally denied the autonomous nature of the actor's art. The actor is merely the conduit for inspiration and energy that is located elsewhere. When the actor triggers the emotions of the spectators, communicating with something in them, an additional ring is added to the chain. The moment such an autonomy is accepted and mapped out, however (and Plato was no doubt aware that this is possible; otherwise he would not have banned the poets from his ideal state), artistic creativity in general, and acting in particular, seems to carry a strong transgressive potential. Furthermore, as Plato certainly also recognized, such a transgressive potential is not always confined within the field of art, but can also profoundly influence the social and the ideological spheres through the reactions of the spectators.

In trying to understand why the notion of energy appears in such a broad variety of discourses, it seems that the different forms of energies created and constituted by performances are somehow able to bring together diverse ontological spheres. I would even argue that one of the constituent features of theatrical performances, an important aspect of their so-called theatricality, is such a constant mingling of ontological spheres, which as a rule do not coexist to the same extent in other contexts. On the one hand, the theatre is capable of making distinctions between different spheres (the aesthetic and the social sphere, the fictional and the historical, the natural and the supernatural, the static and the dynamic, the "naive" and the metatheatrical, etc.). But at the same time the theatre also seeks to bring all of these spheres together, first to make them interact and in certain cases even, at least for a moment, to unify them completely. It is finally this bringing together of different ontological spheres which creates the unique energies of theatre and performance. This is the point where history becomes fully integrated within a performance.

Thus in the context of theatre performances the concept of energy can at the same time be seen as a unifying and as a separating force. The ability to bring disparate ontological spheres together is no doubt also one of the reasons why it has been so difficult to delineate theatre and performance as aesthetic phenomena, even if this is an issue which basically concerns all the arts. But the presence of live human bodies, both on the stage as actor-performers (presenting characters) and in the auditorium as spectators, has made it much more complex to define the "theatrical" than to delineate the "fictional" in prose fiction. The theatre also has to confront issues of fictionality, of course. But the comprehensibility of the theatre and of performance in bringing a vast number of ontological spheres together is at least one of the reasons why they have become paradigmatic for so many aspects of human action. Finally, returning to the larger argument of this book, this ontological hybridity — giving theatre and performance a dimension of "post-modernity" before the term was even invented — makes the notion of performing history such an interesting test case for what the theatre has always been doing. Performances about a specific historical past contain an added ontological dimension compared to the so-called fictional performances, also integrating historical "facts" into the fictional world.

The theatre activates energies from textual, performative, and metaphysical perspectives. The textual perspective is based on onto-

logical assumptions that differ from the performative one, which as a rule integrates the human presence both on the stage and in the auditorium. And the metaphysical dimensions of the theatre, relying on the presence of supernatural creatures from other worlds, are activated by radically different assumptions from the textual and the performative ones. The fact that the theatre at critical stages of its development has been closely associated with ritual and religious practices has certainly also influenced our perceptions of this art. Finally, however, it is the spectators who create the meanings of a performance, by activating different psychological and social energies. The extent of these reactions depends on our individual perspectives and our abilities to change the world in which we live.

This may perhaps sound overoptimistic, because the complex interaction between performances and life (as Artaud, in the epigraph to this chapter, understood) is actually based on the fact that this world is permeated by destructive energies. But the creative energies of the theatre can in some cases be seen as a force that becomes a dialectical antidote to the destructive energies of history and its painful failures. The Second World War, in particular as a result of the Shoah and the use of the atom-bomb, both of which contain distinct but almost unimaginable destructive energies, has profoundly affected our understanding of all expressions of culture, including the theatre. By examining the notion of energy in the theatre I wish to raise the question to what extent it is possible to view this art — and in particular the theatre performing history — as a form of expressing vital and creative energies. When this happens and when the different spheres of theatrical energies become fully integrated, the individual actor can be perceived as a hyper-historian, a witness presenting testimony for the spectators.

Textual Energies

Energy is a source for socializing as well as revolutionary processes, to bring about a change of social structures and hierarchies. The approach developed by Michel Foucault to deal with the ways in which cultural expression is related to social and historical realities concentrates on power and hegemony as the major forces constituting culture. Instead, I believe, a distinction has to be made between this focalized power structure and a more multidirectional flow of textual and performance energies in the theatre. In his book *Shakespearean Negotiations*, subtitled "The Circulation of Social Energy in Renaissance England," Stephen Greenblatt raises the question why Shakespeare's plays are still so viable and makes an interesting shift between a more hegemonic approach and the nonfocalized understanding of textual and performance energies. Greenblatt relates the notion of energy both to power and hegemony in the social sphere as expressed through different public discourses and social practices and to the literal and metaphorical expressions of these practices in the dramatic texts from the same period.

On the one hand, and this is a position closer to Foucault, Greenblatt argues that Shakespeare's dramas "precipitated out of a sublime confrontation between a total artist and a totalizing society."[5] In order to focus his analysis on the interactions between the completely self-absorbed artist and the surrounding society with its "occult network linking all human, natural, and cosmic powers [which] generates vivid dreams of access to the linked powers and vests control of this access in a religious and state bureaucracy at whose pinnacle is the symbolic figure of the monarch,"[6] Greenblatt introduces the notion of "social energy." This concept, he argues, will enable us to explain why the "aesthetic power of a play like *King Lear*," in spite of the fact that it has been radically refigured since the play was written almost four hundred years ago, still so strongly affects us today.

On the other hand — and this gives rise to less hegemonic strategies of reading — "these refigurations do not cancel history, locking us into a perpetual present," but are, Greenblatt continues,

the signs of the inescapability of a historical process, a structured negotiation and exchange, already evident in the initial moments of empowerment. That there is no direct, unmediated link between ourselves and Shakespeare's plays does not mean that there is no link at all. The "life" that literary works seem to possess long after both the death of the author and the death of the culture for which the author wrote is the historical consequence, however transformed and refashioned, of the *social energy* initially encoded in those works.[7]

The social energies are embedded within a network of intertextual webs that continue to reverberate within these individual plays. According to Greenblatt, the aesthetic modes of these social energies have been so powerfully "encoded in certain works of art [that this energy] continues to generate the illusion of life for centuries."[8] He

closely examines the contemporary textual evidence of specific social practices at the time of Shakespeare and how these texts can serve today as intertexts with the Shakespearean masterpieces. His aim is "to understand the negotiations through which works of art obtain and amplify such powerful energy."[9]

The issue Greenblatt confronts is what enables the transformation of these classical masterpieces into performances on the stage, and in particular how the actors are able to communicate the energies embedded in these texts to today's audiences. In terms of my own study, however, this issue has been expanded to include the sense in which the actors are able to bring the energies of a specific historical event to the audiences of today. Instead of focusing on the way in which a *play* from the past preserves its social energies, the issue that has been raised here is in what sense a *historical event* continues to be present and to reverberate in contemporary plays and performances about this event.

From Textual to Performative Energies

Since most theatrical performances are representations of individual or social change, the theme of the play and the means of representation inevitably reflect upon each other and interact in some way. Michael Goldman has provided some very thought-provoking comments about this issue. On the one hand, "[a]n actor is not simply a man presenting a careful behaviour of other men, or even of his own behaviour. His relation with what he imitates is never that of rough equivalency or representation. Acting is never simply mimetic; it appeals to us because of some other or more inclusive power. We feel an energy present in any good actor's performance that goes beyond the demonstration of what some 'real person' is like."[10] Goldman goes on to define the energy of the actor's art as "'terrific' energy, bearing in mind that word's root suggestion of the awesome and the fearful."[11] This is clearly something that is also related to catharsis.

On the other hand, Goldman claims, there is always something in the drama itself, its plot and its characters, which enables the actors to realize such energy potentials of their art. Most forceful in this respect are different forms of aggression. But

[t]he aggression of the plot is not the result of some dramatic law requiring struggle, debate, event, emphasis — all of which can be quite undramatic. It springs from other aggressions — the aggressions of impersonation and performance. The plot must offer the actor's aggressive energy (and the related aggressive energy of the audience) ample and interesting scope. The effort of the actor to act and the pleasures that acting generates are perceived as part of the action of the play, which forms their field.[12]

It is only when the different energies of acting and those of the drama in combination meet the audience, Goldman argues, that the performance will take its real course. This collocation can in terms of energies — at the same time perceived through the means of representation, the "gestus," and the theme — perhaps be most clearly perceived in performances about violent social upheavals such as the French Revolution.

Since such revolutionary events, in history as well as on the stage, as a rule are intentional and stem from a single individual or collective of individuals (as opposed to earthquakes or volcanoes, which are outbursts of energy caused by nature), they are also closely connected to instinctual drives and their articulation in different social contexts, or what Julia Kristeva has termed the "Subject-in-progress." Erika Fischer-Lichte has formulated this articulation in semiotic terms for the theatre: how is it "possible for the different Subjects participating in the production of a theatrical text to constitute themselves as Subjects in the process of that production?"[13] The function and role of "the Subjects in the process of text constitution" are of utmost importance for "the constitution of the theatrical text."[14] The answer to these questions, she argues, lies partly in the complex process of literally in-corporating the dramatic text through acting. This is the result of an active and intentional effort. Here the "individual physique [of the actor] masters the text by making it an extension of itself. He [the actor] thus creates the text a second time — under his body's own specific conditions — both as something foreign to him and as something integral to his body. In this respect, the actor produces the character as the meaning of the body-text constituted by him."[15] At the same time, however, "the actor's body, which at this point in the process is only semiotized and not yet significant, is raised to the level of a signifier through the reference to the linguistically created role and to the actor's code."[16] In working on a specific role the actor thus has to negotiate as well as confront the different components which make up the fictive character presented on the stage; "[a]s the subject of precisely this process of interpretative praxis, he constitutes himself as that subject-in-process which Kristeva has in mind."[17] According to Fischer-Lichte's reading of Kristeva, the creative psychic energies thus become directly and fully integrated through theatrical processes. The resistance an actor has to overcome to constitute such a subject-in-process — the energies this demands to create the "body-text" when performing history — can even be seen as refractions of the social energies contained within the historical event itself.

Just as the dramatic text which has served as the basis for a specific production literally becomes incorporated (i.e., embodied) through acting, performances about the French Revolution and the Shoah also incorporate these events as open texts. Such a performance becomes historiographic, in the sense articulated by de Certeau, operating "as if" the real and discourse were being joined.[18] Ideally this creatively unifies or dialectically counteracts the energies of these events with the energies expressed through the performance itself. But even for de Certeau himself this joining together is a utopian state: "Never will the gap separating reality from discourse be filled."[19] The theatre can play its role in creating such an "as if" situation.

Performance Energies

The notion of energy, it seems, has been most frequently used in the more theoretically oriented writings and interviews of theatre directors, who sometimes refer to their experiences in working with actors for specific performances or in different workshop contexts. These pronouncements are often formulated from a hegemonic position, summarizing what the directors have been able to "do" to and with the actors, such as liberating different kinds of performance energies from or through them. By examining how the notion of energy has been employed in the writings of three major contemporary directors — Richard Schechner, Eugenio Barba, and Peter Brook — it is possible to distinguish differences of emphasis and attention. Although I have not considered the stage work of Schechner and Barba here, their views put the work of Brook (whose production of *Marat/Sade* I have already examined) in perspective. Brook's position, which

gives the notion of energy a much stronger creative force than do the two other directors, has been formed not only through his interest in the work of Antonin Artaud, but probably also through his experience with historical drama, including not only Peter Weiss, but Shakespeare, Chekhov, and even his production of *The Mahabharata* (1989), which refers to itself as "a history of the world."

According to Schechner, "the sense of being taken over by a role, of being possessed by it in its 'flow' or in the flow of the audience's appetite for illusion, ludus, lila: play,"[20] is of central importance for the understanding of theatre and performance. The transformation which takes place during the performance is what he terms a kind of "absorption into the center." This, he adds, is the point at which "the chief parallel between performance and ritual process" can be discerned.[21] Schechner presents what could be termed a "passive" view of the energies generated in and by the performance: the "surrender to the flow of action is the ritual process"[22] through which the "restored behavior" of acting originates.

Schechner argues that Stanislavsky, who is of major importance for the formulations about energy, regarded this flow in two opposing ways. On the one hand, the actor has to be carried away in a manner which according to Schechner characterizes a number of sports and leisure activities. On the other hand, however, Stanislavsky really "wanted a trained intuition. He wanted the actor to be carried away not into chaos but into the precise score of what had been prepared through rigorous training, workshop, and long rehearsals of often a year or more. Thus the 'Stanislavsky system' is largely devoted to training the actor so that flow can be generated through a conscious process."[23] From these formulations about Stanislavsky, which no doubt also reflect Schechner's own interests, one could even reach the conclusion that acting is a kind of recall of reactions that have been structured almost like intuitions.

Eugenio Barba, by contrast, presents a much more "activist" understanding of the actor's energies. But at the same time these energies of what he terms the "dilated body" are more like a kind of theatrical "trickery." According to Barba, "[t]here are certain performers who attract the spectator with an elementary energy which 'seduces' without mediation. This occurs before the spectator has either deciphered individual actions or understood their meanings."[24] The performer's presence holds a special force and attraction:

But it is not something which *is*, which is *there* in front of us. It is continuous mutation, growth taking place before our very eyes. It is a body-in-life. The flow of energies which characterizes our daily behaviour has been re-routed. The tensions which secretly govern our normal way of being physically present come to the surface in the performer, become visible, unexpectedly.

The dilated body is a hot body, but not in the emotional or sentimental sense. Feeling and emotion are only a consequence, for both the performer and the spectator. The dilated body is above all a glowing body, in the scientific sense of the term: the particles which make up daily behaviour have been excited and produce more energy, they have undergone an increment of motion, they move further apart, attract and oppose each other with more force, in a restricted or expanded space.[25]

In order to describe this dilated body which is glowing with energy, Barba relies on metaphors that tend to reify the processes of acting.

For Barba there is, moreover, an important distinction between the human body in its everyday daily behavior and the aesthetic functions of the human body in the performative, aesthetic context. "While daily behaviour is based on functionality, on economy of power, on the relationship between the energy used and the result obtained, in the performer's extra-daily behaviour each action, no matter how small, is based on waste, on *excess*."[26] And to achieve this kind of "excess," Barba goes on to argue that "[o]ne does not work on the body or the voice, one works on energy. So just as there is no vocal action which is not also a physical action, there is no physical action which is not also mental. If there is physical training, there must also be mental training."[27]

Thus, "the long daily work on physical training, transformed over the years, has slowly become distilled into internal patterns of energy which can be applied to a way of conceiving or composing a dramatic action, a way of speaking in public, a way of writing. Thought has a physical aspect: its way of moving, changing direction, leaping — its 'behaviour,' in fact. This aspect also has a pre-expressive level which can be considered analogous to the performer's pre-expressive work, that work which has to do with presence (energy) and which precedes — logically if not chronologically — real and actual artistic composition."[28]

This aspect of Barba's thinking is summarized by what he calls the "negation principle," which can also easily be applied to the concrete work of the actors both in training and on the stage:

> There is a rule which performers know well: begin an action in the direction opposite to that to which the action will finally be directed.
>
> This rule recreates a condition essential to all those actions which in daily life demand a certain amount of energy: before striking a blow, one draws one's arm back; before jumping, one bends one's knees; before springing forward, one leans backwards: *reculer pour mieux sauter*.
>
> In the performer's extra-daily activity such behaviour is applied even to the smallest actions. It is one of the means which the performer uses to dilate his physical presence.
>
> We could call it the "negation principle": before carrying out an action, the actor negates it by executing its complementary opposite.
>
> The "negation principle" becomes a formalistic void if its soul — that is, its organic quality — is lost. Often in the theatrical and non-theatrical use of trivial declamation, the "negation principle" becomes a way of *inflating* gesture. A parody, in fact, of *dilated* action.[29]

Barba himself has perhaps seen some of the dangers of applying his own principles of energy, dilation, and negation. They can easily become a magic "trick" for the actor to use in order to seduce the spectators rather than inviting them to participate emotionally or intellectually in the theatrical creation. At the same time, though, it is important to note that Barba conceives of this energy as a form of visible tension, not as a flow, as Schechner does.

For Peter Brook, too, energy results from tensions, but his understanding of this notion seems to be based on the fact that it is not always possible to perceive the components of these dialectical tensions. According to Brook, "[w]e know that the world of appearance is a crust [and] under the crust is the boiling matter we see if we peer into a volcano." This leads him to the question: "How can we tap this energy?"[30] In a later interview Brook developed his quasi-scientific metaphors comparing the theatrical event with an "explosion."[31] Sometimes, he claimed, there will be an explosion when mixing exactly the same "elements" for a production, while at other times nothing at all will happen. In this interview Brook also reflects upon how the meeting of the two poles of a carbon-arc lamp leads to the production of light. The crucial difference for the intensity of the light produced depends on the resistance to the flow of energies. Comparing Brook's thinking about the theatre with that of Blau, it seems that there is a difference in the location of the "explosion," where the source of energy is located. For Blau the outburst of energy comes from the inside, in the present moment — or as he expressed it in the controversial program text for *Danton's Death*: "The terror is the mind's revenge on itself." For Brook, in contrast, the energy is located somewhere else, in the volcano or in the intensity of the carbon-lamp — metaphors for the social sphere perhaps — and the aim of the theatre is to tap this energy. It has to be synthesized through the theatrical processes.

For this reason the meeting between the audience and the actors is also crucial, according to Brook:

> At the outset, these two elements are separated. The audience represents multiple sources of energy, as many as there are spectators, but these sources are not concentrated. In itself, the audience is just like the carbon-arc lamp: it has no intensity, each individual's energy is diffuse and dispersed. There is nothing inside any of these individuals which could make them sources of intensity in themselves. An event will only occur if each one of these individual instruments becomes attuned. Then all you need for something to happen is for a single vibration to pass through the auditorium — but it cannot be produced if the thousand harps that represent the audience are not tuned in the same way, to the same tension.
>
> The same thing occurs with the actors. The first step in a performance is a process of gathering and focusing the dispersed energies of the audience, which in turn reflect the dispersed energies of the actors.[32]

The central point in any theatrical event is thus to fine tune the different energy sources of the actors as well as the spectators in order to make them flow within the new collective which has been created. The aim, of course, is to make these energies visible and understandable for the spectators, to make them communicative on the aesthetic as well as emotional and intellectual levels. This, according to Brook, is the task of the director.

The use of metaphors to talk about performances and performance energies creates a mystique about the theatre, an opaqueness which does not necessarily lead to a greater understanding, even if there are mysteries on the stage which cannot be easily explained. The aim of such metaphors, in discourses about theatre as well as in performances, can be seen as an attempt to subordinate the creative energies to an aesthetic code (or a set of such codes), which in turn enables the spectators to experience and interpret the energies that have been codified so that they make sense not merely as expressions of force or pure volcanic energy, but aesthetically as well. Brook's production of *Marat/Sade* viewed on film today is highly charged with such energies, coming from many different sources, and those who still remember the stage performance of this production had the same impression. The outbursts of the mentally deranged actors in de Sade's performance taking place in 1808 in the Charenton hospital — some of whom have not been "cured" of the outdated revolutionary energies from the 1789 revolution — and the erotic energies, which in part, but not exclusively, stem from the mental conditions of the patients — are constantly interlaced as distinct aesthetic codes. But on the stage they were integrated to create what Brook could have termed a "volcanic effect."

Such energies of acting can even be seen as a kind of metaphorical expression of the energies of the French Revolution itself. The energies of acting are the theatrical mode of telling the present-day spectators about these historical or revolutionary energies; the revolutionary energies are conjured up by the energies of acting. And the energies of acting are the aesthetic embodiment of the revolutionary energies, making it possible for the spectators to "read" the energies on the stage metaphorically, as a kind of displacement or transposition of that historical past. By showing these energies on the stage, which are cultural constructions, just like class, race, or gender, the actor becomes a hyper-historian. In presenting or demonstrating the event, this hyper-historian becomes painfully "present" at the event itself, carrying the mimetic force of the theatrical event as it is presented on the stage in a Stanislavskian mode of "as if." This could be seen as a moment when the energies of acting serve as the connecting link between the "real" and "discourse" in de Certeau's sense. And at the same time it will always remain a construction that can never become "real" in the sense that the historical past was.

The Eavesdropper and the Survivor-Witness

The actor as witness and hyper-historian is not only dependent on a specific knowledge about the historical past, the "real," that he or she brings to the spectators. The way in which the witness appears on the stage and communicates with the spectators — the aesthetic dimension of his or her appearance — is also of central importance for the creation of a theatrical discourse performing history. It is hard to make a generalization about all of the actor-witnesses who appear in the productions analyzed in this study; each one, like de Sade in *Marat/Sade* or Selma in *Arbeit macht frei vom Toitland Europa*, carries out this role in a specific way. It is nonetheless possible to formulate some principles for situating the witness within the *mise-en-scène* of a theatrical performance and showing how this positioning can serve as a possible source for catharsis. Why an individual spectator reacts in a specific way to a performance is no doubt very difficult to understand or to examine in detail. By pointing out certain features of the performance and in particular the relations between its thematic focus and its *mise-en-scène*, however, it is possible to comprehend why catharsis, usually translated as "pity and fear," does occur.[33]

Shakespeare's *Hamlet* clarifies how a theatre performance can change and perhaps even challenge the moral and emotional perceptions of the spectators and trigger some form of catharsis. This is of course not a play performing history in the strict sense, but it is a play where the flow of history, the murder of Hamlet's father, becomes transformed into a tragedy. At the end of *Hamlet*, with the arrival of Fortinbras, the new ruler, this tragedy becomes a play about history again. And it is Horatio, the liminal character who reports to Hamlet about the ghost, who becomes the witness-historian. This occurs when Horatio addresses Fortinbras, the character in the play representing historical agency:

You from the Polack wars, and you from England,
Are here arrived, give order that these bodies
High on a stage be placed to view,
And let me speak to th'yet unknowing world
How these things came about. So shall you hear

Of carnal, bloody, and unnatural acts,
Of accidental judgements, casual slaughter,
Of deaths put on by cunning and forced cause,
And in this upshot, purposes mistook
Fallen on th'inventors' heads. All this can I
Truly deliver.[34] (V, 2, 355–364)

These treacherous deeds are the stuff that history is made of. Horatio is already beginning to supervise and even direct his own performance of history, placing the bodies on the stage to view.

Looking more closely at this play, it is also possible to find instances when history is performed. Hamlet's production of *The Mouse-trap* is an allegorical rendering of the murder of his father, as the ghost has told it to him. But can we really, as Hamlet clearly does, assume that "the play's the thing / Wherein I'll catch the conscience of the king" (II, 2, 557–558)? Will this performance make a significant difference, as Hamlet somewhat naively, but with a lot of irony on Shakespeare's behalf, believed? For Hamlet, as the director of this theatrical performance, the question is whether Claudius will experience some form of catharsis when the actors, as Hamlet himself formulates it, "play something like the murder of my father" (II, 2, 548).

Several of the performances about history analyzed in this book, like *Marat/Sade* and *Ghetto*, where theatre companies performing on the stage are depicted within the performance itself, or *1789*, which also depicts the events of the Revolution retrospectively in a market-place setting, contain such performances-within-the-performance. Even if this device is by no means exclusive to the genre of performing history, it often serves a specific purpose when it is used in such performances, as a filter through which the "truth" about the past can be examined and critiqued.

But there are also other compositional devices through which spectators or witnesses can appear on the stage, creating metatheatrical mirroring effects. This happens in what could be termed "screen-scenes," where one of the fictional characters is secretly spying on one or several of the other characters. One of the most well-known instances is the so-called closet scene in *Hamlet*, where Polonius, the eavesdropper, is hiding behind the arras secretly spying on Hamlet, while Gertrud is knowingly participating in this deceit. Since the audience in the auditorium also knows about this arrangement, it creates an obvious dramatic irony. As a rule the eavesdropper intentionally takes a position outside the direct action. By overhearing and secretly witnessing the other characters the eavesdropper presumably will get some hidden knowledge and thus also gain power. This position, which according to Barbara Freedman can be clearly distinguished since the Renaissance, depends on what she has described as "an epistemological model based upon an observer who stands outside of what she sees in a definite position of mastery over it."[35] This arrangement can also serve as a model for spectatorship in the theatre. The audience is also "secretly" watching the action on the stage.

When such a situation of secret witnessing is used in a performance, as an integral aspect of the theatrical apparatus or machinery, the mastery or control it is supposed to bring to a character like Polonius turns out to be an illusion. In most of these screen-scenes the eavesdropper is suddenly and unwillingly drawn back into the action again. While apparently observing the action safely from behind the curtain (another reminder of the metatheatricality of this device, also drawing attention to the liminality of this character), the eavesdropper is usually discovered. Instead of mastering the situation, the eavesdropper becomes a victim: Polonius is killed by Hamlet.

This victimization of the eavesdropper — the character who is "punished" for being a spectator — is a central factor in creating catharsis for the spectators in the auditorium. The emotions that the spectators experience and the insights they consciously or unconsciously arrive at as a result of the victimization of this transgressive character stem from the fact that the spectators are also in a sense "eavesdroppers." Therefore, just like the victimized eavesdropper on the stage, we — the spectators — may, at least potentially, be punished. The eavesdropper on the stage, who secretly eavesdrops on the other characters and who is punished for this, can thus be seen as the scapegoat who is sacrificed during the theatrical "ritual." Instead of the spectators in the auditorium (who are in many respects situated in a similar spectator position, secretly witnessing the action on the stage), it is the eavesdropper hiding behind a curtain on the stage who becomes the victim. The symbolic sacrifice of the eavesdropper activates a number of very complex processes for the spectators. These processes create identification and involvement as well as distance from the eavesdropper, finally releasing the spectator from the "fear" of being punished for having secretly violated the privacy of the characters in the fictional world of the performance. The development from eavesdropping to victimization exists in innumerable variations, in tragedy as well as in comedy. It is enough to point at Orgon in Molière's *Tartuffe* to understand how complex this phenomenon is. Even if the "punishments" of Polonius and Orgon are very different, they both become victimized. But in both cases, the eavesdropping precedes the victimization. My claim is that catharsis is partially based on such a scapegoat "ritual," where the eavesdropper becomes victimized instead of the spectator.

In contrast, when the theatre is performing history, and this is most obvious in theatre about the Shoah, the victimization has preceded the dramatic action. Instead of an eavesdropper who is "punished" for secretly watching the action on the stage, in the theatre about historical events the witness is already a victim who is giving some form of testimony within the framework of the performance of what he or she has seen. Theatre about historical events generally focuses on a character with knowledge (sometimes even too much knowledge), where the victimized survivor is given the position of the witness. This witness is able to tell the spectators something about the experiences previously hidden behind the "veils" of his or her past and now, through the performance, revealed to the spectators. The cathartic processes activated by the theatre performing history are more like a "ritual" of resurrection, a revival of past suffering, where the victim is given the power to speak about the past again.

As I have already mentioned, this reversal of the role of the witness can be most clearly seen in the performances about the Shoah. Srulik, in Sobol's *Ghetto*, is the survivor telling about the theatre the Jews founded in Vilna during the Nazi occupation of the city, bringing the voice of Chaya back to his own "stage" of memory. Selma, in *Arbeit macht frei vom Toitland Europa*, is a guide in a Holocaust museum, who in the second part of this performance brings the spectators into her home to witness the madness hidden behind her organized outer visage. But in the performances about the French Revolution there are also witnesses who have a more poignant authority within the fictional world as well as *vis-à-vis* the spectators concerning the historical events depicted on the stage. De Sade in Weiss' *Marat/Sade* definitely holds such a position, and the performance of Mishima's *Madame de Sade* directed by Ingmar Bergman clearly gives both the Countess de Saint-Fond and the maid Charlotte a privileged position as victimized witnesses.

The presence and intervention of supernatural figures in the theatre is basically an extension of the eavesdropper. The ghost of
Hamlet's father is in many ways an eavesdropper who follows the actions of his son throughout. The ghost is also a victimized witness, belonging to the metaphysical sphere, whose function, just like the
intervention of the gods in the classical theatre through the *deus ex
machina*, is to set things right again. But this device is also strongly
present in the modern theatre, in plays like August Strindberg's *A
Dream Play*, in *The Dybbuk* (which I have referred to frequently as a
central intertext of the Israeli productions), and even, with an ironic
reversal, in Brecht's *Threepenny Opera*.[36]

In the productions examined here this device is realized through
the Marquis de Sade, who is a "divine/satanic" figure in Mishima's
play, a kind of Godot who, just as in Beckett's play, does *not* appear,
because he is not admitted by his wife. At the same time the atom-
bomb mushroom, which is the metaphorical representation of the destructive forces of history, does appear. Instead of a *deus ex machina* of
redemption, Bergman presents the destructive nature of the forces of
history as a metaphysical presence, which has no logical cause. The
atom-bomb mushroom appears in the central area of the backstage
screen, just as the traditional *deus ex machina* did in the Baroque theatre.
The painting of Napoleon hanging on the wall in the Charenton hospital in *Marat/Sade* is also such a "divine" presence,[37] overseeing and
interrupting the performance of the mental patients led by de Sade
by proxy, through Coulmier, the director of the hospital. In Brook's
production the hospital director was even dressed as Napoleon. The
Nazi officer Kittel in Sobol's *Ghetto*, who has the power to take the lives
of the Jews in the ghetto, always appears unannounced and considers
himself to be a God. And Selma in *Arbeit macht frei vom Toitland Europa*
makes a very clear *deus ex machina* appearance, which almost makes
her supernatural as she descends on the dinner table as the Muselman
statue. And, finally, in *The Boy Dreams* the aborted redemption of the
Messiah also represents a failed *deus ex machina*.

The *deus ex machina* in the modern theatre is usually an expression
of a metaphysical rupture, an attempt to fill a void, something that
lacks the redemptive powers it has traditionally had. On the thematic
level it usually represents the destructive forces in the modern world,

which the performances about history have been trying to counter-act by different creative energies. But the use of the *deus ex machina*, at least implicitly, also points to a utopian dimension, the aspect which these metaphysical images have traditionally represented on the stage, but which history itself constantly seems to be challenging.

Epilogue
"Ich habe noch ein Koffer in Berlin . . ."

To articulate the past historically does not mean
to recognize it "the way it really was" (Ranke). It
means to seize hold of a memory as it flashes up
at a moment of danger.
— Walter Benjamin

The issue I have tried to confront in this book is how the flashes of memory from the past can become transformed into theatrical images on the stage. Many questions are still unresolved. And as I have been progressing new ones have appeared which do not have any easy answers. One of the most difficult of these questions is in what sense the actor-witness becomes what I have termed a hyper-historian. Here I return to it one last time, but only to give one more example, this time not from the stage, but from the screen. The two films —*Der Himmel über Berlin* (*Wings of Desire*, 1987) and its sequel, *So Weit und so Nahe* (*So Far and So Close*, 1993), both by Wim Wenders — are also a way to end the journey of this book in Berlin. These two films about Berlin (the first depicting the still divided city, while the second takes place after the wall has been dismantled and the two Germanys have been unified), are also in many ways performances of history. They present one of the possible solutions to the riddle of the actor-witness-historian. According to Wenders, the actor is a fallen angel.

Traditionally the supernatural figure of the angel can be seen both as a servant and a figure of revolt against the divine powers. Through its fall the angel who revolts accumulates a kind of spiritual power, which for Wenders is apparently connected to the art of acting and storytelling, a telling of the historical past in its minutest and sometimes most painful details. This is what Damiel and Cassiel do when they meet at the beginning of the first of the two films. They compare notes about what they have observed during the last hours, reporting the most trivial details about the daily history of the city, such as when the sun rises and sets. The two angels are also able to follow the lives of individuals — the birth of a baby or the death of a motorcyclist. They have the privilege of seeing without being seen, except by the small children who perceive their presence. They are eavesdroppers, who as angels are unable to intervene directly in the lives of the humans.

The crucial scenes in *Der Himmel über Berlin* for understanding that the actor is a fallen angel are Damiel's meetings with Marion and with Peter Falk. Damiel is the angel who falls as a result of his love for Marion, who walks on the tightrope with angel wings glued on to her dress. The American actor Peter Falk, who plays "himself" in Wenders' film, has come to Berlin to make a film about Nazi Germany. It is Damiel's desire for Marion that leads to his "fall," his transformation to a human being who takes on an active role in the flow of history.

This is a love story. But it is Peter Falk who is able to recognize this gradual process. The first meeting between Damiel and Falk takes place outside a coffee bar. Damiel is still an angel and can therefore, according to the conventions established in the film, only be "perceived," not "seen" by Falk, who starts talking into what to the owner of the coffee-bar seems like empty space: "I can't see you, but I know you're here! I wish I could see your face, just look into your eyes and tell you how good it is to be here. Just to touch something! Here that's cold! That feels good." [1] The actor Peter Falk has the same kind of sensitivity to the angelic figures that the children have. The scene outside the coffee-bar ends with Falk stretching out his hand to Damiel, who does not respond. Falk says *"Companero,"* [2] clearly indicating that as an actor (i.e., a former angel) he is still able to perceive those angels who are approaching the human state.

The final "proof" that the actor is a fallen angel is the conversation between Damiel and Falk after Damiel has entered the human sphere. After telling his angel-companion Cassiel that he wants to enter the river, the flux of human passions and of history, Damiel wakes up on a deserted street with medieval clothing and armor lying beside him. The supernatural creature has made his entry into the world. He has a scar on his forehead, as if the clothing and armor, his "machina," fell down on him after his own fall. Damiel sells them in an antique shop and buys new clothes before trying to find the bunker where Peter Falk is shooting the film about the Second World War. When they finally meet, Falk is surprised — "Gee, I expected a much taller man, I don't know why . . ."³— clearly indicating that he actually knows to whom he is speaking. In order to help Damiel to get started, Falk wants to lend him a few dollars, but Damiel politely declines:

Damiel: I sold something.
Falk: The armor! Right? What did you get for it?
Damiel: Two hundred marks.
Falk: You got robbed, but that happens. Let me tell you
     something. I'm going back now thirty years! New York
     City . . . pawn shop, 23rd and Lexington: the guy gave me
     five hundred dollars.
Damiel: You were . . .
Falk: Yeah.
Damiel: You are . . . ? You, too?
Falk: Oh yeah! There's a lot of us.⁴

At this point it is clear that the angel Damiel has become a creature who enters the flow of history through his fall and who now, like Peter Falk, can also make a film about the historical past. What this narrative quite clearly suggests is that the actor is not only a fallen angel,⁵ but has become an actor who now has the suitable "knowledge" for performing history, just like Falk, who is shooting a movie about the Second World War.

It is also interesting to see what Wenders makes of the couple Damiel and Cassiel in his sequel film about them, *So Weit und so Nahe*, which is about the city of Berlin after the wall has been dismantled and the two Germanys have been unified. Damiel now has a daughter with Marion and is the owner of a restaurant ironically named "Pizza del'Angelo," while it is his wife who is connected to performing as a trapeze artist. Cassiel is involved in an intense struggle against the evil forces present in Berlin since the Second World War. As an angel Cassiel is able to identify those individuals, some of whom are willingly caught in the circles of evil, as present-day criminals, as well as those who more unwillingly continue to carry their fatal burdens of the past with shame. The troupe of trapeze artists to which Marion belongs becomes engaged in the struggle against these evil forces. In this film Wenders has changed some of the angelic conventions he created in *Der Himmel über Berlin*: in spite of being an angel, Cassiel can now intervene more actively in both the making and unraveling of the historical past. In the first film the angels were more or less forced, by their angelic existence, to serve as passive but introspectively suffering witnesses. Here they have become privileged witnesses who can intervene in the flow of history.

There is also another kind of "angel" in the two films, the two older veteran actors who have really experienced that past which in so many ways is present in the city of Berlin: Curt Bois and Heinz Rühmann, who have both died since the two films were made. Wenders cast them in roles as witnesses or representatives of the past. These specific roles can also be seen in relation to their respective careers, in particular during the Second World War. Curt Bois was a Jewish actor who fled to the United States during the Nazi period, where among other parts he played a minor role in *Casablanca*. In *Der Himmel über Berlin* he plays an epic storyteller called "Gedankenstimme Homer" (Homer's thinking voice) in the script. Looking like a homeless vagabond, he ends his melancholy recollections of the past with an invocation while stumbling on the stones in the empty (before the reunification of the city) field near the Berlin wall, which was once Potzdammer Platz, situated in the very center of Berlin. It was completely bombed out during the Second World War and is now being rebuilt.

The other actor, Heinz Rühmann, was quite prominent in Germany during the Nazi period and was a personal friend to some of its leaders. He also continued to be a popular actor after the war in spite of his "history." In *So Weit und so Nahe* he played the role of an old chauffeur who served the Nazis faithfully during the war and is now hiding in a ruin somewhere in Berlin together with his old car. He has survived with this mechanical memento and his memories, as a guardian and a historian of that past.

Bois and Rühmann do not only *play* characters who are survivors/ historians in the two respective films; like all actors, through their individual biographies as actors and human beings, they are also historians who represent certain aspects of the past. Their biographical and professional pasts have in a sense become inscribed in their bodies, as something which exists as an extension of their direct presence on the screen. Viewing them today, it is possible to perceive them as a complex and even enigmatic combination of actor, angel, witness, and historian.

"To write history means to quote history," Walter Benjamin supposedly wrote somewhere, although I have not been able to find the exact reference.[6] This is perhaps symptomatic for the notion of per forming history, which first quotes history, but then "forgets" the exact reference when the performance itself, the *here* and *now* of the theatre, fully absorbs the spectators.

In my epilogue I have intentionally brought this book to the place which most painfully, and powerfully, is the site for the history of the twentieth century, the city of Berlin. In this location the interactions between history and performance have been, and still are, more complex than in any other place I know. Perhaps another such highly charged location would be Jerusalem, the city where I have lived for the last thirty-five years. But in that city the burdens of history in combination with the ongoing political conflicts are still too complex to provide the freedom needed for performance.

Perhaps that is still the case for Berlin too, the city about which Walter Benjamin wrote in "A Berlin Chronicle" in the early 1930s. At that time Benjamin was already acutely aware of the haunting tensions between the daily life of this city and the presence of the ghosts of the dead:

> Reminiscences, even extensive ones, do not always amount to an autobiography. And these quite certainly do not, even for the Berlin years that I am exclusively concerned with here. For autobiography has to do with time, with sequence and what makes up the continuous flow of life. Here, I am talking of a space, of moments and discontinuities. For even if months and years appear here, it is in the form they have at the moment of recollection. This strange form — it may be called fleeting or eternal — is in neither case the stuff that life is made of. And this is shown not so much by the role my own life plays here, as by the people closest to me in Berlin — whoever and whenever they may have been. The atmosphere of the city that is here evoked allots them only a brief, shadowy existence. They steal along its walls like beggars, appear wraithlike at windows, to vanish again, sniff at thresholds like *genius loci*, and even if they fill whole quarters with their names, it is as a dead man fills his gravestone. Noisy, matter-of-fact Berlin, the city of work and the metropolis of business, nevertheless has more, rather than less, than some others, of those places and moments when it bears witness to the dead, shows itself full of dead; and the obscure awareness of these moments, these places, perhaps more than anything else, confers on childhood memories a quality that makes them at once

as evanescent and as alluringly tormenting as half-forgotten dreams.[7]

What makes the city of Berlin so powerful for Benjamin are "those places and moments when it *bears witness to the dead*" (my emphasis), a strategy through which the writing of his own life becomes a kind of performing history in the "theatre" of his own mind.

For Heiner Müller the "half-forgotten dreams" of Benjamin became a nightmare. Müller's writing as well as his theatrical practice bore witness to a constant, sometimes unresolved struggle to come to terms not only with his private memories, the story of his own family, his biography, but also with the collective identity of being German after the Second World War.[8] In the last section of the short speech Müller delivered in 1985, when receiving the Georg Büchner Prize of the German Academy for Language and Poetry, there are clear echoes of Walter Benjamin:

Woyzeck lives where the dog is buried, the dog's name: Woyzeck. We are all waiting for his resurrection with fear and/or hope that the dog will return as a wolf. The wolf will come from the South. When the sun is in its Zenith, he will be one with our shadow and in the hour of white heat History will begin. Not until History has happened will our shared destruction in the frost of entropy or, abridged by politics in the nuclear lighting be worthwhile: the destruction which will be the end of all utopias and the beginning of a reality beyond mankind.[9]

We have not reached that phase, however — the angel has not yet become a wolf. Today Müller, who took over the Berliner Ensemble at the end of his life, before that theatre closed, is buried in the same graveyard as Bertolt Brecht, its founder. And on Müller's grave, marked by a red block of granite, there are small pebbles, like those traditionally put on Jewish graves. The performances of history are indeed difficult to interpret.

I end as I began, by quoting from books in libraries. But while libraries are resources for our knowledge about the past, there are three libraries in Berlin from which it becomes more and more difficult to quote. The first are the library scenes in Wenders' *Himmel über Berlin*. All the angels gather in the Public Library in Berlin in order to "listen" to the readers' minds. This paradoxically shows that the angels are not reading the books themselves — they just overhear (eavesdrop on) the voices of the readers who are in the library.

The second library is the monumental statue by Anselm Kiefer in the Museum für Gegenwart-Berlin at the Hamburg Bahnhof. This

statue, and again I am quoting, "consists of two vast steel bookcases, thirteen feet high, standing end to end at a slight angle to one another, like pages of an open book. Each bookcase is filled with massive lead books, some of them empty, some containing images and substances which record the reality of our time."[10] It is monumental, as a repository containing references to the past like Paul Celan's famous poem "Der Tod ist ein Meister aus Deutschland" (Death Is a Master from Germany). The quotes from this monumental library will of necessity be unconventional.

The third library, from which it is impossible to quote anything but the void itself, is the "installation" by the Israeli artist Micha Ullman called *Library* (1995). This installation is situated *under* the square in central Berlin called Bebelsplatz opposite Humboldt University, just off the famous boulevard Unter den Linden. This is the place where the Nazis burned books on May 10, 1933. Walking on the completely empty square today, you cannot see the installation until you reach a place where there is a small window on the square instead of cobblestones. Beside the window there is a small plaque identifying this work itself, which also quotes Heinrich Heine's famous words that people who burn books will eventually burn people. Looking down through the small window, it is possible to see a subterranean room with white bookshelves, each containing approximately fifteen shelves. They are divided into smaller sections on each of the four walls. The perspective becomes distorted when looking down through the small window on the square; it takes a little while until you realize that the bookshelves are completely empty.[11]

NOTES

Preface

1. Barthes 1981, 65.
2. Levi 1989, 63–64.
3. Benjamin 1999, 463.
4. Rokem 1998b.

Introduction

1. I am using the now well-known Hebrew word "Shoah," destruction, instead of the more frequently used English word "Holocaust" here, because of the latter's ritual implications as a historical event.
2. There are numerous books on this subject. See, for example, Skloot 1988 and Schumacher 1998.
3. Shakespeare 1985, I, 1, 21.
4. Favorini 1994, 32.
5. Brecht 1978, 121.
6. Aristotle 1965, ch.9, 43.
7. Aristotle 1965, ch. 25, 65–66.
8. Aristotle 1965, ch. 25, 66.
9. Aristotle 1965, ch. 25, 66.
10. Vernant and Vidal Naquet 1990, 243.
11. Lindenberger 1975.
12. Certeau 1988, xxvii; emphasis in original.
13. See, for example, Carlson 1966.
14. Arasse 1989, 90.
15. This was the central topic of the conference published in Friedlander 1984.
16. Klossowski 1992, x.
17. Klossowski 1992, x–xi.
18. Airaksinen 1995, 13.
19. Airaksinen 1995, 14.
20. Scarry 1985.
21. Weiss 1966, 99.
22. Weiss 1966, 24; the stage instructions in this passage have been omitted; emphasis mine.
23. Sontag 1967, 165.

24. Weiss 1966, 4–5.

25. Telephone interview, March 6, 1999.

26. See, for example, Patraka 1996 and 1999 and Young 1993.

1. Refractions of the Shoah on Israeli Stages: Theatre and Survival

1. LaCapra 1998 has dealt with the general implications of this "working-through."

2. Zuckerman 1993.

3. Bernstein 1994, 47.

4. Felman and Laub 1992, 224; emphasis in original.

5. LaCapra 1997.

6. Kohansky 1981.

7. Feingold 1989, 116–118.

8. Todorov 1975, 25.

9. Todorov 1975, 25.

10. Todorov 1975, 31.

11. Todorov 1975, 33.

12. Diner 1992 has pointed out that there were no possibilities for the Jews in the ghettos in particular to develop any consistent strategies for survival.

13. In Harel 1987.

14. For a more detailed discussion of these plays and his *The Palestinian Woman*, as well as some of the major themes in his writing, see Rokem 1996c.

15. Sobol 1984, 14.

16. Sobol 1984, 8; Sobol 1992, 14.

17. Sobol 1984, 14; Sobol 1992, 14.

18. Sobol 1984, 14; Sobol 1992, 14.

19. Nora 1989.

20. Sobol 1984, 16.

21. Sobol 1998; my translation.

22. I have analyzed this ironic mode of the *deus ex machina* in Rokem 1995a.

23. See Yerushalmi 1997, who has examined *The Dybbuk* as a subtext (*langue*) for the Israeli theatre.

24. This performance has been analyzed by Hertzberg 1992; Rovit 1993; Urian 1993; and Rokem 1996a. Parts of this section have previously appeared in Hebrew: Rokem 1999.

25. Arte-ZSF (1993; 1 hour 29 minutes).

26. Set Productions (1994; 2 hours 30 minutes).

27. Young 1993, 237.

28. Roms 1996, 60.

29. Raz-Krakotzkin 1993–1994.

30. Chaudhuri 1995, 17.

31. Rokem 1987.

32. Levi 1989, 63–64.

33. This kind of performance situation of witnessing in *Arbeit macht frei vom Toitland Europa* can also be compared with two specific scenes examined in

the next chapter; in Peter Brook's production of *Marat/Sade*, where Corday, played by Glenda Jackson, whips de Sade with her hair; and in Ingmar Bergman's production of *Madame de Sade*, where the actress Agneta Ekmanner carries the stigmata on her palms and transforms herself into a witness of Christian suffering. Selma, lying outstretched on the descending table, also presents herself to us as a Jewish martyr-witness. This process of transformation into a "complete," but mute, witness to some extent also takes place in Sobol's *Ghetto*, where the ventriloquist Srulik loses his "voice," while the doll Lina is a mute witness who can only "speak" with the "voice" of Srulik. But here the metaphysical dimension has not been clearly worked out; it was not possible to integrate the Tora shrine fully in a performance situation, and the "muteness" is more technical than in *Arbeit macht frei vom Toitland Europa*.

34. A selection of ten of Levin's plays, in a translation by Barbara Harshav, will be published by Stanford University Press.
35. See Yaari 1996 for a general introduction to Levin's work.
36. Levin 1988, 117; my translation.
37. Levin n.d.a., 1. All quotations are from this English version.
38. Diner 1992.
39. Bernstein 1994.
40. Benjamin 1969, 257–258.
41. Benjamin 1969, 255.

2. Three European Productions about the French Revolution

1. Przybyszewska 1989.
2. Beauvoir 1990, 31.
3. Fischer-Lichte 1992.
4. Quoted in Williams 1988, 29.
5. Fischer-Lichte 1992, 182.
6. Quoted in Fischer-Lichte 1992, 183.
7. Williams 1988, 32.
8. Williams 1988, 33.
9. Brook 1982, 124–125.
10. Weiss 1966, 6; the stage directions have been omitted from this passage.
11. Jones 1986, 251.
12. Suvin 1988, 398–399. See also Koski 1993.
13. Palmstierna-Weiss 1995, 20–21; my translation from the Swedish; the last sentence is in English in the original.
14. Kiernander 1993, 71. See photos: http://members.tripod.com/~titoegurza/obras/1789.htm.
15. Miller 1977, 52.
16. Quoted in Kiernander 1993, 73; my emphasis.
17. *1789* 1972, 11.
18. There are several scenes at this point in the printed script which have not been included in the official video version of the production sold by the Théâtre du Soleil.

19. Kustow 1972, 6.
20. Kustow 1972, 5.
21. Klossowski 1992, 21.
22. The negative of the original photo has been reversed in order to enable this gesture of pointing at the actress in the program. This clearly shows the conscious intentions of the editors, who undoubtedly also consulted Bergman himself.
23. Program for *Markisinnan de Sade*, Kungliga Dramatiska Teatern 1989, 31; my translation.
24. Marker and Marker 1982, 25.
25. Marker and Marker 1982, 16
26. Marker and Marker 1982, 16.
27. Marker and Marker 1982, 24
28. Mishima 1990, 61; all translations from the Swedish text are my own. The reason for translating the Swedish translation into English in spite of the fact that an English translation already exists is that it is on a much higher stylistic level than the Swedish text.
29. Mishima 1990, 62.
30. Mishima 1990, 93–94.
31. Ekmanner 1998, 26; my translation.
32. Mishima 1990, 114.
33. Mishima 1990, 116–117.

3. Three American Productions of Danton's Death

1. Ginters 1996, 652. When this article was written there were almost 300 such productions, but since then that mark has been passed.
2. Reinhardt's first production was in 1916. Among the earlier productions of *Danton's Death* those by Leopold Jessner in different theatres in 1910, 1911, and 1913 are considered models for how the play has been produced. Even though the play itself was written in 1835, it has a much shorter production history, only in the twentieth century.
3. Drake 1938.
4. Davis 1998, 245–246; and McConachie 1998, 134.
5. This understanding of how European and American theatres have absorbed their basic ideological deep-structures is quite different from that charted by Joseph Roach in *Cities of the Dead*, which considers the relations between the cultures on both sides of the Atlantic. Roach's analysis focuses on much more popular performance traditions and cultural practices than the theatre productions dealt with here. Roach argues for a homogenic basis and perception of what he terms a "circum-Atlantic world (as opposed to a transatlantic one)" and insists "on the centrality of the diasporic and genocidal histories of Africa and the Americas, North and South, in the creation of the culture of modernity" (Roach 1996, 4). Each one of these distinct geographical areas has in a sense incorporated all the others by showing through its performance practices what it is not, and through substitutions and surrogates an "inter-

culture" has been created, which includes not only the colonies but the colonizing powers like England and France as well. This kind of intercultural practice Roach considers the key "to understand how circum-Atlantic societies, confronted with revolutionary circumstances for which few precedents existed, have invented themselves by performing their pasts in the presence of others" (Roach 1996, 5). This, however, seems to be something which the three American productions of *Danton's Death* were not able to achieve. Roach's dynamic genealogical model of cultural communication cannot, it seems, help us to understand why this play could not be transposed to an American context.

6. The anatomy of theatrical failure is much more complex for the theatre historian to analyze than different modes of success. Any explanation can give a partial answer, but it is impossible to know if it is sufficient.

7. It is worth noting the conclusion of Postlewait (1999), confronting the "seeming failure or evasion of American theatre" and the "apparent disjunction between stage and age" (113), that "[i]n the case of the Civil War, three generations of playwrights dramatized it, but they avoided not only the horror of battle (most difficult to put on stage) but also the major issues and problems over which the war was fought. The demands of putting history on stage are seldom met" (115).

8. For example, Reinelt 1995; Auslander 1992; Malkin 1999; and many others.

9. Blau 1982, xv.

10. Halperin-Royer 1998, 75.

11. Dycke 1927.

12. Unidentified review, New York Public Library, Theatre Collection, Lincoln Center.

13. Hammond 1927.

14. Brown 1938. See also Waldorf 1938, who reiterates the same view in a preview for the Welles production.

15. Watts 1938.

16. Pollock 1938.

17. Winchell 1938.

18. Benchley 1938.

19. Lockridge 1938.

20. Lockridge 1938.

21. Atkinson 1938a.

22. Atkinson 1938a.

23. Atkinson 1938b.

24. New York Public Library, Theatre Collection, Lincoln Center.

25. Blau 1982, 69–70.

26. Blau 1965.

27. In *Unmarked* (1993) and *Mourning Sex* (1997) Phelan not only has drawn on Blau's style of writing, but has also developed many of his ideas, in particular in her understanding of the notion of "disappearance." Blau is undoubtedly the *unacknowledged* source of inspiration in Phelan's books. Phelan's tactic is a form of "disappearance" in itself.

28. Ehrlich 1961, 68.

29. Blau 1982b, x.

30. Benjamin 1969, 258.

31. Benjamin 1969, 258.

32. Hobe 1965.

33. Oppenheimer 1965.

34. Chapin 1965.

35. Kerr 1965

36. Smith n.d.

37. Smith n.d.

38. Blau 1982b, 36

39. Blau 1982b, 40–41.

40. Blau 1982b, 45–46.

41. Blau 1982b, 48.

42. Blau 1982b, 56.

43. Houseman 1973, 62.

44. Houseman 1973, 63.

45. Houseman 1973, 63.

46. Boyd 1992, 1.

47. Boyd 1992, 1.

48. *Audience* (Alley Theatre newspaper), 1992, 10.

49. *Audience* 1992, 12.

50. *Audience* 1992, 1.

51. Kirkpatrick 1992.

52. Kirkpatrick 1992.

53. Rockwell 1992.

54. Littel 1929.

55. Houseman 1973, 59.

56. Max Grube, *The Story of Meininger*, quoted in Braun 1982, 16.

57. Houseman 1973, 61.

58. Houseman 1973, 61

59. Benchley 1938.

60. Atkinson 1938b.

61. Quoted in Callow 1996, 392.

62. Houseman 1973, 64.

63. Houseman 1973, 61.

64. Callow 1996, 409.

65. Blau 1982b, 44–45.

66. Taubman 1965.

67. Hobe 1965.

68. Thomson 1997, 108.

69. Bolton 1965.

70. Chapman 1965.

71. Chapin 1965.

72. Kerr 1965.

73. Taubman 1965.
74. Blau 1982b, 40.
75. Counsell 1996, 186.
76. Baker 1992b, 7.
77. Baker 1992b, 10.
78. Baker 1992b, 7.
79. Quoted in Baker 1992b, 10.
80. Counsell 1996 195.
81. Baker 1992b, 10.
82. Kirkpatrick 1992.
83. Büchner 1983, 23.
84. Przybyszewska 1989.
85. The screenplay for this film was created by Jean-Claude Carrière, one of Peter Brook's closest collaborators. Before doing this film, Wajda had directed Przybyszewska's play twice in Poland, first in 1975 at the Powszecny Teatr in Warsaw and in 1980. Reviewing the Warsaw production, one of the critics wrote that "Robespierre represents the attitude of a man of principle, which any time can turn into dangerous dogmatism, bringing self-destruction despite the chastity of his motives. Danton stands for revolutionary compromise which although much closer to the defective human nature, inevitably stains the moral purity of the idea . . . Robespierre will seal down the victory of the Revolution, which is going on amidst errors, ideological meandering and horrible mistakes, but implacably and inadvertently changing the face of the world" (Karpinsky 1975, 9, 13). In 1986 the Swedish director Suzanne Osten directed Przybyszewska's play at the Unga Klara theatre in Stockholm, where she is the artistic director. Osten sees her aesthetics as an alternative to that of Ingmar Bergman; it is therefore interesting that Bergman chose to direct a play about the French Revolution three years after Osten's monumental production. For more details on this production, see Rokem 1998b, 362–363; Osten 1986; and Osten and Zweigbergk 1990.
86. Baker 1992b, 11.
87. Baker 1992b, 7.
88. Rockwell 1992.
89. Kirkpatrick 1992; my emphasis.
90. Baker 1992b.
91. Thomas 1993, 27.
92. Halperin-Royer 1998.
93. Callow 1996, 409.
94. Nadel 1965.
95. Holmberg 1996, 167.
96. Wirth 1993, 60–61.
97. See also Fischer-Lichte 1995 for a formal semiotic analysis of this production.
98. Blau 1992, 158.

99. Blau 1992, 158.
100. Blau 1990, 353.
101. Blau 1982, 20.
102. Blau 1987, 169–170, emphasis in original.
103. Genet 1966, 75.
104. Genet 1966, 51.
105. Blau 1990, 280.
106. Blau 1990, 285.
107. The quote is from Blau 1990, 71; in Büchner 1983, 64, this line reads "Will the clock never rest?"
108. Büchner 1983, 7.
109. Büchner 1983, 118–119.
110. Blau 1990, 286.
111. Blau 1990, 286.
112. Blau 1990, 285.
113. Büchner 1983, 34.
114. Blau 1990, 285.
115. Büchner 1983, 35.
116. Büchner 1983, 36.
117. Büchner 1983, 72.
118. Büchner 1983, 72.
119. Büchner 1983, 73.

4. Theatrical Energies

1. There are numerous discussions on the notion of performance, a term which has been most prominent in American research. The article by Bert O. States (1996) sums up some of the major issues.
2. The ways in which actors and directors have used the notion of energy deserve a full-length study. My aim here is only to exemplify by citing directors who in different ways have influenced the contemporary theatre.
3. The historian Carlo Ginzburg (1992 and 1999) has examined the role of the witness in historical and legal discourses.
4. Plato 1937, 288–289.
5. Greenblatt 1988, 2.
6. Greenblatt 1988, 2.
7. Greenblatt 1988, 6; my emphasis.
8. Greenblatt 1988, 7.
9. Greenblatt 1988, 7.
10. Goldman 1975, 5.
11. Goldman 1975, 7.
12. Goldman 1975, 23–24.
13. Fischer-Lichte 1992, 182.
14. Fischer-Lichte 1992, 182.
15. Fischer-Lichte 1992, 189.

16. Fischer-Lichte 1992, 189.

17. Fischer-Lichte 1992, 189.

18. Certeau 1988, xxvii. See also my comments on these ideas in the introduction.

19. Certeau 1988, 9.

20. Schechner 1985, 124.

21. Schechner 1985, 119.

22. Schechner 1985, 124.

23. Schechner 1985, 118.

24. Barba and Savarese 1991, 54.

25. Barba and Savarese 1991, 54.

26. Barba and Savarese 1991, 55.

27. Barba and Savarese 1991, 55.

28. Barba and Savarese 1991, 55.

29. Barba and Savarese 1991, 57.

30. Brook 1982, 52.

31. Brook 1992, 107

32. Brook 1992, 108.

33. Aristotle's definition of *catharsis* in his *Poetics*, trying to cope with Plato's critique of the arts, has as a rule, but by no means always, been connected to the arousal of the contradictory emotions of pity and fear in the individual spectators. But Aristotle's definition of tragedy "as the imitation of an action that is serious, complete and possesses magnitude . . . accompanying through pity and fear the *catharsis* of such emotions [passions]" (Aristotle, *Poetics*, 6.1449b24–28, quoted from Ford 1995, 110) hardly provides us with any clear indication of how to describe or measure the success of a certain performance in this respect. The attempts by scholars to clarify Aristotle's terms have frequently been qualified by terms like "enigmatic," "puzzling," and riddlelike (Sparshot 1983).

34. All references to *Hamlet* are to Shakespeare 1985.

35. Freedman 1991, 9.

36. Rokem 1995a.

37. This portrait is a variation of the portrait of Hedda Gabler's father hanging on the wall of the back room in Ibsen's play. In Ibsen's play it is the "presence" of the father which brings Hedda to her suicide.

Epilogue

1. Wenders and Handke 1987, 122–123.

2. Wenders and Handke 1987, 123.

3. Wenders and Handke 1987, 137.

4. Wenders and Handke 1987, 138–139.

5. Rokem 1992.

6. When I first read this it was quoted by someone else. In the meantime Benjamin's *The Arcades Project* has appeared in an English translation, where this

quotation reads: "To write history thus means to *cite* history. It belongs to the concept of citation, however, that the historical object in each case is torn from its context" (Benjamin 1999, 476).

7. Benjamin 1979, 316.

8. Malkin 1999 has treated this aspect of his work.

9. Müller 1989, 106.

10. Anne Seymour, quoted in Lopez-Pedraza 1996, 73.

11. I want to thank Paul Mendes-Flohr for showing me this library the first time.

1789 — The French Revolution Year One. 1972. Texts collected and presented by
  Sophie Lemasson and Jean-Claude Penchenat; translated by Alexander
  Trocchi. *Gambit: International Theatre Review* 5, no. 20, 9–52.
Airaksinen, Timo. 1995. *The Philosophy of the Marquis de Sade.* New York and
  London: Routledge.
Arasse, Daniel. 1989. *The Guillotine and the Terror.* London: Penguin.
Aristotle. 1965. *On the Art of Poetry.* In *Classical Literary Criticism.*
  Harmondsworth: Penguin.
Artaud, Antonin. 1958. *The Theatre and Its Double.* Translated by M. C. Richards.
  New York: Grove Press.
Atkinson, Brooks. 1938a. "Mercury Theatre Reopens with Orson Welles'
  Production of 'Danton's Death.'" *New York Times,* November 5.
———. 1938b. "Orson Welles Frightening Little Playgoers in 'Danton's
  Death.'" *New York Times,* November 13.
Auslander, Philip. 1992. *Presence and Resistance: Postmodernism and Cultural
  Politics in Contemporary American Performance.* Ann Arbor: University of
  Michigan Press.
Baker, Christopher. 1992a. "An Interview with Richard Thomas." *Audience*
  (Fall) 3, 12–13.
———. 1992b. "Notes from the Dramaturg's Journal: *Danton's Death*
  in Rehearsal" (preceded by an anonymous introduction). *Audience*
  (Fall), 7, 10–11.
Barba, Eugenio, and Nicola Savarese. 1991. *The Secret Art of the Performer: A
  Dictionary of Theatre Anthropology.* London: Routledge.
Barthes, Roland. 1981. *Camera Lucida.* Translated by Richard Howard. New
  York: Hill and Wang.
———. *A Barthes Reader.* Ed. Susan Sontag. New York: Hill and Wang.
Beauvoir, Simone de. 1990. "Must We Burn de Sade?" Translated by Annette
  Michelson. In Marquis de Sade, *The One Hundred Twenty Days of Sodom,* 3–64.
  London: Arrow Books.
Beckett, Samuel. 1965. *Waiting for Godot.* London: Faber and Faber.
Benchley, Robert. 1938. "Great Caesar's Ghost." *New Yorker Magazine,*
  November 12.

Benjamin, Walter. 1969. *Illuminations*. Translated by Harry Zohn. New York: Schocken Books.

———. 1979. "A Berlin Chronicle." In *One-Way Street*, translated by Edmund Jephcott and Kingsley Shorter, 293–346. London: NLB Publishers.

———. 1991. "Über den Begriff der Geschichte." In *Gesammelte Schriften*, I, 2, 691–704. Frankfurt am Main: Suhrkamp Taschenbuch Verlag.

———. 1999. *The Arcades Project*. Translated by Howard Eiland and Kevin McLaughlin. Cambridge, Mass., and London: Belknap Press of Harvard University Press.

Bernstein, Michael Andre. 1994. *Foregone Conclusions: Against Apocalyptic History*. Berkeley: University of California Press.

Blau, Herbert. 1964. *The Impossible Theatre: A Manifesto*. New York: Collier Books.

———. 1965. Unpublished mimeographed program note for the production of *Danton's Death* at Repertory Theatre of Lincoln Center, New York Public Library for the Performing Arts, Lincoln Center, New York. 4 pp. (Parts of this program note have also been published in Blau 1982b, 70.)

———. 1982a. *Blooded Thought: Occasions of Theatre*. New York: Performing Arts Journal Publications.

———. 1982b. *Take Up the Bodies: Theater at the Vanishing Point*. Urbana: University of Illinois Press.

———. 1987. *The Eye of Prey: Subversions of the Postmodern*. Bloomington: Indiana University Press.

———. 1990. *The Audience*. Baltimore and London: Johns Hopkins University Press.

———. 1992. *To All Appearances: Ideology and Performance*. New York and London: Routledge.

Bolton, Whitney. 1965. "*Danton's Death* Magnificent Stage Spectacle." *Morning Telegraph*, October 23.

Boyd, Gregory. 1992. "The Alley Theatre Welcomes Robert Wilson." *Audience*. (Fall), 1.

Braun, Edward. 1982. *The Director and the Stage: From Naturalism to Grotowski*. London: Methuen.

Brecht, Bertolt. 1978. *Brecht on Brecht*. Edited and translated by John Willet. London: Methuen.

Brook, Peter. 1968. "Preface" to Jerzy Grotowski, *Towards a Poor Theatre*. New York: Simon and Schuster.

———. 1982. *The Empty Space*. New York: Atheneum.

———. 1992. "Any Event Stems from Combustion: Actors, Audiences and Theatrical Energy." Interview of Peter Brook by Jean Kalman. *New Theatre Quarterly* 8, no. 30 (May), 107–112.

Brown, Erella. 1989. *Allegory and Irony in the Satirical Work of Hanoch Levin*. Ann Arbor: UMI Research Press.

———. 1992. "Cruelty and Affirmation in the Postmodern Theatre: Antonin Artaud and Hanoch Levin." *Modern Drama* 35, 585–606.

———. 1996. "Politics of Desire: Brechtian 'Epic Theatre' in Hanoch Levin's

Postmodern Satire." In Linda Ben-Zvi, ed., *Theater in Israel*, 173–199. Ann Arbor: University of Michigan Press.

Brown, John Mason. 1938. "Danton's Death." *New York Post*, November 5.

Büchner, Georg. 1983. *Complete Plays, Lenz and Other Writings*. Translated by John Reddick. London: Penguin Books.

Callow, Simon. 1996. *Orson Welles: The Road to Xanadu*. London: Vintage.

Carlson, Marvin. 1966. *The Theatre of the French Revolution*. Ithaca, N.Y.: Cornell University Press.

———. 1993. "Body and Sign in *Marat/Sade*." Mimeographed paper presented at the symposium on Performance Analysis, Helsinki.

Certeau, Michel de. 1988. *The Writing of History*. New York: Columbia University Press.

Chapin, Louis. 1965. *Christian Science Monitor*, October 27.

Chapman, John. 1965. "*Danton's Death* a Spectacular Opener for Beaumont Theatre." *Daily News*, October 22.

Chaudhuri, Una. 1995. *Staging Place: The Geography of Modern Drama*. Ann Arbor: University of Michigan Press.

Counsell, Colin. 1996. *Signs of Performance: An Introduction to Twentieth-Century Theatre*. London and New York: Routledge.

Davis, Peter A. 1998. "Plays and Playwrights to 1800." In *The Cambridge History of American Theatre*, vol. 1, ed. Don B. Wilmet and Christopher Bigsby, 216–249. Cambridge: Cambridge University Press.

Diner, Dan. 1992. "Historical Understanding and Counterrationality: The *Judenrat* as Epistemological Vantage." In *Probing the Limits of Representation: Nazism and the "Final Solution,"* ed. Saul Friedlander, 128–142. Cambridge, Mass.: Harvard University Press.

Drake, Herbert. 1938. "The Playbill: Mercury Sets Schedule." *Herald Tribune*, August 7.

Driver, Tom F. 1967. *The Sense of History in Greek and Shakespearean Drama*. New York and London: Columbia University Press.

Dycke, Thomas van. 1927. "Danton's Death at the Century." *New York Telegraph*, December 21.

Ehrlich, J. W. 1961. *Howl of the Censor*. San Carlos, Calif.: Nourse Publishing Company.

Ekmanner, Agneta. 1998. "Förvandlas — om skådespeleri." In *Försök om Teater*, 7–36. Stockholm: Bonnier.

Favorini, Attilio. 1994. "Representation and Reality: The Case of Documentary Theatre." *Theatre Survey*, 35, no. 2, 31–43.

Feingold, Ben-Ami. 1989. *The Theme of the Holocaust in Hebrew Drama*. Tel Aviv: Hotzaat Ha-Kibbutz Ha-Meuchad (in Hebrew).

Feldman, Yael. 1987. "Deconstructing the Biblical Sources in Israeli Theater: *Yisurei Iyov* by Hanoch Levin." *AJS Review*, 12, no. 2, 251–277.

———. 1989. "'Identification-with-the-Aggressor' or the 'Victim Complex'? Holocaust and Ideology in Israeli Theater: *Ghetto* by Joshua Sobol." *Modern Judaism*, 9, no. 2, 165–178.

Felman, Shoshana, and Dory Laub. 1992. *Testimony: Crises of Witnessing in Literature, Psychoanalysis and History*. New York and London: Routledge.

Fischer-Lichte, Erika. 1992. *The Semiotics of Theater*. Translated from the German by Jeremy Gaines and Doris L. Jones. Bloomington: Indiana University Press.

———. 1995. "Passages to the Realm of Shadows: Robert Wilson's *King Lear* in Frankfurt." In *Understanding Theatre*, ed. Jacqueline Martin and Willmar Sauter, 191–211. Stockholm: Almqvist & Wiksell International.

Ford, Andrew. 1995. "Katharsis: The Ancient Problem." In *Performativity and Performance*, ed. Andrew Parker and Eve Kosefsky Sedgewick, 109–132. New York and London: Routledge.

Freedman, Barbara. 1991. *Staging the Gaze: Postmodernism, Psychoanalysis, and Shakespearean Comedy*. Ithaca and London: Cornell University Press.

Friedlander, Saul. 1984. *Reflections of Nazism: An Essay on Kitsch and Death*. New York: Harper & Row.

———, ed. 1992. *Probing the Limits of Representation*. Cambridge, Mass.: Harvard University Press.

Friedman, Regine-Mihal. 1991. "Violence du Sacrifice et Sacrifice de la Violence dans *Danton* de A. Wajda." *Athanor* 2, 126–136.

Genet, Jean. 1966. *The Balcony*. Translated by Bernard Frechtman. New York: Grove Press.

Ginsberg, Allen. 1956. *Howl and Other Poems*. San Francisco: City Lights.

Ginters, Laura. 1996. "Georg Buechner's *Dantons Tod*: History and Her Story on the Stage." *Modern Drama*, 39, no. 4, 652–667.

Ginzburg, Carlo. 1992. "Just One Witness." In *Probing the Limits of Representation: Nazism and the "Final Solution,"* ed. Saul Friedlander, 82–96. Cambridge, Mass.: Harvard University Press.

———. 1999. *The Judge and the Historian: Marginal Notes on a Late-Twentieth-Century Miscarriage of Justice*. Translated by Antony Shugaar. London and New York: Verso.

Goldman, Michael. 1975. *The Actor's Freedom: Toward a Theory of Drama*. New York: Viking Press.

Greenblatt, Stephen. 1988. *Shakespearean Negotiations: The Circulation of Social Energy in Renaissance England*. Berkeley: University of California Press.

Grimm, Reinhold. 1985. *Love, Lust and Rebellion: New Approaches to Georg Büchner*. Madison: University of Wisconsin Press.

Halperin-Royer, Ellen. 1998. "Robert Wilson and the Actor: Performing in *Danton's Death*." *Theatre Topics* 8, no. 1, 73–91.

Hammond, Percy. 1927. "The Theatres — 'Danton's [*sic*] Tod,' in Which Mr. Reinhardt Exercises His Great Gifts as a Picture-Maker." *New York Tribune*, December 12.

Harel, Vered. 1987. "An Interview with Yehoshua Sobol and Gedalia Besser — Directors at the Haifa Theatre." *Bamah* 103, 43–58 (in Hebrew).

Hertzberg, Judith. 1992. "Arbeit Macht Frei: Ein Theater — und mehr." *Theater Heute* 4, 4–7.

Hobe. 1965. "*Danton's Death*." *Variety*, October 27.

Holmberg, Arthur. 1996. *The Theatre of Robert Wilson*. Cambridge: Cambridge University Press.

Houseman, John. 1973. "Orson Welles and *Danton's Death*." *Yale Theater* 3, no. 3, 56–67.

Hunt, Albert, and Geoffrey Reeves. 1995. *Peter Brook*. Cambridge: Cambridge University Press.

Isser, Edward R. 1997. *Stages of Annihilation: Theatrical Representations of the Holocaust*. Cranbury, N.J.: Fairleigh Dickinson University Press.

Johnson, Walter. 1963. *Strindberg and the Historical Drama*. Seattle: University of Washington Press.

Jones, David Richard. 1986. *Great Directors at Work: Stanislavsky, Brecht, Kazan, Brook*. Berkeley: University of California Press.

Karpinsky, Maciej. 1975. "*Sprawa Dantona* at Teatr Powszechny. Directed by Andrzej Wajda." *Theatre en Pologne* 7, 9–13.

Kaynar, Gad. 1996. "'Get Out of the Picture, Kid in Cap': On the Interaction of the Israeli Drama and Reality Convention." *Theater in Israel*, ed. Linda Ben-Zvi, 285–301. Ann Arbor: University of Michigan Press.

Kerr, Walter. 1965. "Premiere at Beaumont." *New York Herald Tribune*, October 22.

Kiernander, Adrian. 1993. *Ariane Mnouchkine and the Théâtre du Soleil*. Cambridge: Cambridge University Press.

Kirkpatrick, Melanie. 1992. "Theater: Robert Wilson's *Danton's Death*." *Wall Street Journal*, November 5, A15.

Klossowski, Pierre. 1992. *Sade My Neighbour*. Translated by Alphonso Lingis. London: Quartet Books.

Kohansky, Mendel. 1981. "Perils of Realism." *Jerusalem Post*, May 22.

Koski, Pirkko. 1993. "Which Ghosts Are the Strongest? *Marat/Sade* in Finland." *Nordic Theatre Studies* 6, no. 3, 48–62.

Kruger, Loren. 1992. *The National Stage: Theatre and Cultural Legitimation in England France and America*. Chicago and London: University of Chicago Press.

Kustow, Michael. 1972. "Introduction to *1789*, the French Revolution, Year One." *Gambit: International Theatre Review* 5, no. 20, 5–8.

Lacan, Jacques. 1980. "The Mirror Stage as Formative of the Function of the I." In *Ecrits: A Selection*, translated from the French by Alan Sheridan, 1–7. London: Tavistock Publications.

LaCapra, Dominick. 1997. "Lanzmann's *Shoah*: 'Here There Is No Why.'" *Critical Inquiry* 23, 231–269.

———. 1998. *History and Memory after Auschwitz*. Ithaca and London: Cornell University Press.

Lerner, Motti. 1994. *The Kastner Trial*. N.p.: Or va-Tsel, n.d. (in Hebrew).

Levi, Primo. 1989. *The Drowned and the Saved*. London: Abacus.

Levin, Hanoch. 1988. *Plays I*. Tel Aviv: Ha-Kibbitz Ha-Meuchad (in Hebrew).

———. n.d.a. "The Boy Dreams." First draft-translation into English (no translator). Unpublished MS.

———. n.d.b. "The Sorrows of Job." Translated from Hebrew by Barbara Harshav. Unpublished MS.

Lindenberger, Herbert. 1975. *Historical Drama: The Relation of Literature and Reality.* Chicago and London: University of Chicago Press.

Littel, Robert. 1929. "'Danton's Tod.'" *New York Post*, December 12.

Lockridge, Richard. 1938. "The Stage in Review." *New York Sun*, November 5.

Lopez-Pedraza, Rafael. 1996. *Anselm Kiefer: The Psychology of "After the Catastrophe."* London: Thames and Hudson.

Lukacher, Ned. 1986. *Primal Scenes: Literature, Philosophy, Psychoanalysis.* Ithaca and London: Cornell University Press.

Malkin, Jeanette. 1999. *Memory-Theater and Postmodern Drama.* Ann Arbor: University of Michigan Press.

Marker, Lise-Lone, and Frederick J. Marker. 1982. *Ingmar Bergman: Four Decades in the Theater.* Cambridge: Cambridge University Press.

McConachie, Bruce. 1998. "American Theatre in Context, from the Beginnings to 1870." In *The Cambridge History of American Theatre*, vol. 1, ed. Don B. Wilmeth and Christopher Bigsby, 111–181. Cambridge: Cambridge University Press.

Miller, Judith Graves. 1977. *Theatre and Revolution in France since 1968.* Lexington, Ken.: French Forum.

Mishima, Yukio. 1967. *Madame de Sade.* Translated by Donald Keene. New York: Grove Press, Inc.

———. 1989. *Markisinnan de Sade.* Swedish translation by Gunilla Lindberg-Wada; adaptation for the stage Per Erik Wahlund. Stockholm: Schultz – Kungliga Dramatiska Teatern.

———. 1990. "Markisinnan de Sade." Mimeographed manuscript no. 32. Kungliga Dramatiska teaterns bibliotek; corrected and signed by Katarina Sjoberg, March 9. Play script of the Bergman production.

Müller, Heiner. 1980. *Der Auftrag*, Cotta's Hörbühne, SDT/BR/WDR. Radio-recording, 94 mins.

———. 1983. *Der Auftrag* (first published 1980). In *Herzstück*, 43–70. Nördlingen: Rotbuch Verlag.

———. 1984. *The Task.* In *Hamletmaschine and Other Texts for the Stage*, edited and translated by Carl Weber, 81–101. New York: Performing Arts Journal Publications.

———. 1989. "The Wound Woyzeck." In *The Battle*, 103–106. New York: Performing Arts Journal Publications.

———. 1995. *The Mission.* In *Theatremachine*, translated and edited by Marc von Henning, 59–84. London: Faber and Faber.

Nadel, Norman. 1965. *World Telegram & Sun*, October 22.

Nora, Pierre. 1989. "Between Memory and History: 'Les Lieux de Mémoire.'" Translated by Marc Roudebush. *Representations* 26, 7–24.

Oppenheimer, George. 1965. "*Danton's Death* Opens the Beaumont." *Newsday*, October 22.

Osten, Suzanne. 1986. "Why Are We Playing *The Danton Case*." Program for the Unga Klara Production, Stockholm, 4–7 (in Swedish).

Osten, Suzanne, and Helena von Zweigbergk. 1990. *Osten om Osten: Barndom, feminism och galenskap.* Stockholm: Alfabeta Bokförlag.

Outram, Dorinda. 1989. *The Body and the French Revolution: Sex, Class and Political Culture.* New Haven and London: Yale University Press.

Oz, Avraham. 1995. "Dried Dreams and Bloody Subjects: Body Politics in the Theatre of Hanoch Levin." *JTD: Haifa University Studies in Theatre and Drama* 1, 109–146.

Palmstierna-Weiss, Gunilla. 1995. *Scenografi.* Catalogue from exhibition in Stockholm. Stockholm: Waldemarsudde (in Swedish).

Parker, Noel. 1990. *Portrayals of Revolution: Images, Debates and Patterns of Thought on the French Revolution.* New York: Harvester Wheatsheaf.

Patraka, Vivian. 1996. "Spectacles of Suffering: Performing Presence, Absence, and Historical Memory at U.S. Holocaust Museums." In *Performance and Cultural Politics*, ed. Elin Diamond, 89–107. London and New York: Routledge.

———. 1999. *Spectacular Suffering: Theatre, Fascism, and the Holocaust.* Bloomington and Indianapolis: Indiana University Press.

Pavis, Patrice. 1995. "From Theatre to Film: Selecting a Methodology for Analysis. On *Marat/Sade* by P. Weiss and P. Brook." In *Understanding Theatre*, ed. Jacqueline Martin and Willmar Sauter, 212–230. Stockholm: Almqvist & Wiksell International.

Phelan, Peggy. 1993. *Unmarked: The Politics of Performance.* London and New York: Routledge.

———. 1997. *Mourning Sex: Performing Public Memories.* London and New York: Routledge.

Plato. 1937. "Ion." In *The Dialogues of Plato*, vol. 1, translated by B. Jowett, 285–297. New York: Random House.

Pollock, Arthur. 1938. "Orson Welles Does Buechner's 'Danton's Death' Over into a Little Thing of His Own, Enjoying Life as a Boy Prodigy." *Brooklyn Daily Eagle*, November 6.

Postlewait, Thomas. 1999. "The Hieroglyphic Stage: American Theatre and Society, Post–Civil War to 1945." In *The Cambridge History of American Theatre*, ed. Don Wilmeth and Christopher Bigsby, 107–195. Cambridge: Cambridge University Press.

Przybyszewska, Stanislawa. 1989. *The Danton Case and Thermidor.* Translated by Boleslaw Taborski; with an introduction by Daniel Gerould. Evanston, Ill.: Northwestern University Press.

Raz-Krakotzkin, Amnon. 1993–1994. "Exile within Sovereignity: Toward a Critique of the 'Negation of Exile' in Israeli Culture." *Theory and Criticism: An Israeli Forum* 4, 23–56; and 5, 113–132 (in Hebrew).

Reinelt, Janelle. 1995. "The Drama of Nation on Nations' Stages." Unpublished mimeographed ms.

Roach, Joseph. 1996. *Cities of the Dead: Circum-Atlantic Performance.* New York: Columbia University Press.

Rockwell, John. 1992. "Robert Wilson Tackles the French Revolution." *New York Times*, November 3, C 13.

Rokem, Freddie. 1987. "Acting and Psychoanalysis: Street Scenes, Private Scenes, and Transference." *Theatre Journal* 39, no. 2, 175–184.

———. 1990. "Jehoshua Sobol's Theatre of the Ghetto." In *Small Is Beautiful*, ed. Claude Schumacher and Derek Fogg, 140–146. Glasgow: Theatre Studies Publications.

———. 1992. "A Walking Angel: On the Performative Function of the Human Body." *Assaph: Studies in Theatre* 8, 113–126.

———. 1995a. "Der Deus ex Machina im Theater der historischen Avantgarde." In *Theater Avantgarde: Wahrnehmung — Körper — Sprache*, ed. Erika Fischer-Lichte, 324–368. Tübingen and Basel: Francke Verlag.

———. 1995b. "Sobol's Ghetto-Trilogy." *Machanaim* 9, 304–311 (in Hebrew).

———. 1996a. "Cultural Transformations of Evil and Pain: Some Recent Changes in the Israeli Perception of the Holocaust." In *German-Israeli Theatre Relations after the Second World War*, ed. Hans-Peter Bayerdörfer, 217–238. Tübingen: Niemeyer Verlag.

———. 1996b. "One Voice and Many Legs: Oedipus and the Riddle of the Sphinx." In *Untying the Knot: On Riddles and Other Enigmatic Modes*, ed. Galit Hasan Rokem and David Shulman, 255–270. New York and Oxford: Oxford University Press.

———. 1996c. "Yehoshua Sobol — Between History and the Arts: A Study of *Ghetto* and *Shooting Magda (The Palestinian Woman)*." In *Theater in Israel*, ed. Linda Ben-Zvi, 201–224. Ann Arbor: University of Michigan Press.

———. 1998a. "On the Fantastic in Holocaust Performances." In *Staging the Holocaust: The Shoah in Drama and Performance*, ed. Claude Schumacher, 40–52. Cambridge: Cambridge University Press.

———. 1998b. "'Performing History': Theater und Geschichte — Die Französische Revolution im Theater nach dem Zweiten Weltkrieg." In *Theater seit den 6oer Jahren*, ed. Erika Fischer Lichte, Friedemann Kreuder, and Isabel Pflug, 316–374. Tübingen and Basel: A. Francke Verlag.

———. 1999. "*Arbeit macht frei vom Toitland Europa* at the Akko Theatre Centre." *Theory and Criticism: An Israeli Art Forum*. 11, 389–399 (in Hebrew).

Roms, Heike. 1996. "'Arbeit Macht Frei vom Toitland Europa': Akko Theatre Centre." *Performance Research*, 1, no. 1, 59–62.

Rovit, Rebecca. 1993. "Emerging from the Ashes: The Akko Theatre Center Opens the Gates to Auschwitz." *Drama Review*, 37, no. 2, T138, 161–173.

Scarry, Elaine. 1985. *The Body in Pain: The Making and Unmaking of the World*. New York and Oxford: Oxford University Press.

Schechner, Richard. 1985. *Between Theatre and Anthropology*. Philadelphia: University of Pennsylvania Press.

Schumacher, Claude, ed. 1998. *Staging the Holocaust: The Shoah in Drama and Performance*. Cambridge: Cambridge University Press.

Shakespeare, William. 1985. *Hamlet, Prince of Denmark*. The New Cambridge Shakespeare, edited by Philip Edwards. Cambridge: Cambridge University Press.

———. 1997. *As You Like It*. The Norton Shakespeare. New York and London: W. W. Norton & Company.

Simon, Art. 1996. *Dangerous Knowledge: The JFK Assassination in Art and Film.*
Philadelphia: Temple University Press.

Skloot, Robert. 1988. *The Darkness We Carry.* Madison: University of Wisconsin
Press.

Smith, Michael. n.d. Theatre Review from the New York Public Library
Theatre Collection, Lincoln Center (no title, no indication of source).

Sobol, Yehoshua. 1984. *Ghetto.* Tel Aviv: Or Am (in Hebrew).

———. 1987. *Ghetto.* Translated and adapted by Jack Viertel. In *Plays of the
Holocaust*, ed. Elinor Fuchs, 153–230. New York: Theatre Communications
Group.

———. 1992. *Ghetto.* 2nd ed. Tel Aviv: Or Am (in Hebrew).

———. 1998. Program-note for *Ghetto*, Haifa Municipal Theatre (in
Hebrew).

Sontag, Susan. 1967. "Marat/Sade/Artaud." In *Against Interpretation and Other
Essays*, 163–174. New York: Farrar, Straus & Giroux.

———. 1978. *Illness as Metaphor.* New York: Vintage Books.

Sparshot, Francis. 1983. "The Riddle of Katharsis." In *Centre and Labyrinth:
Essays in Honour of Northrop Frye*, ed. Eleanor Cook et al., 14–37. Toronto,
Buffalo, and London: University of Toronto Press.

States, Bert O. 1996. "Performance as Metaphor." *Theatre Journal*, 48(1), 1–26.

Suvin, Darko. 1988. "Weiss's *Marat/Sade* and Its Three Main Performance
Versions." *Modern Drama* 31, 395–419.

Taubman, Howard. 1965. "*Danton's Death* at Beaumont." *New York Times*,
October 22.

Thomas, Richard. 1993. "Wilson, Danton and Me." *American Theater* (July–
August 1993), 24–28.

Thomson, Peter. 1997. *Brecht, Mother Courage and Her Children: Plays in Production.*
Cambridge: Cambridge University Press.

Todorov, Tzvetan. 1975. *The Fantastic: A Structural Approach to a Literary Genre.*
Ithaca, N.Y.: Cornell University Press.

Tornqvist, Egil. 1991. *Transposing Drama: Studies in Representation.* London:
Macmillan.

Urian, Dan. 1993. "The Holocaust and 'The Arab Question.'" *Assaph: Studies
in the Theatre* 9, 129–147.

Vernant, Jean-Pierre, and Pierre Vidal-Naquet. 1990. *Myth and Tragedy in Ancient
Greece.* Translated by Janet Lloyd. New York: Zone Books.

Waldorf, Wilella. 1938. "'Danton's Death' First Produced Here by Max
Reinhardt in 1927." *New York Post*, October 22.

Watts, Richard, Jr. 1938. "The Theatres." *New York Herald Tribune*, November 3.

Weiss, Peter. 1964. *Die Verfolgung und Ermordung Jean Paul Marats dargestellt durch
die Schauspielergruppe des Hospizes zu Charenton unter Anleitung der Herrn de Sade.*
Frankfurt am Main: Suhrkamp Verlag.

———. 1966. *The Persecution and Assassination of Jean-Paul Marat as Performed by
the Inmates of the Asylum of Charenton under the Direction of the Marquis de Sade.*
English version by Geoffrey Skelton; verse adaptation by Adrian Mitchell.
New York: Atheneum.

Wenders, Wim, and Peter Handke. 1987. *Der Himmel über Berlin: Ein Filmbuch*. Frankfurt am Main: Suhrkamp Verlag.

Williams, David, ed. 1988. *Peter Brook: A Theatrical Casebook*. London: Methuen.

Winchell, Walter. 1938. "'Danton's Death' Slow Drama of the French Revolution." *Daily Mirror*, November 3.

Wirth, Andrzej. 1993. "The Thrust Stage as Guillotine." *Performing Arts Journal* 43, no. 15, 1, 59–61.

Wolin, Richard. 1992. *The Terms of Cultural Criticism: The Frankfurt School, Existentialism, Poststructuralism*. New York: Columbia University Press.

Yaari, Nurit. 1996. "Life as a Lost Battle: The Theater of Hanoch Levin." In *Theater in Israel*, ed. Linda Ben-Zvi, 151–171. Ann Arbor: University of Michigan Press.

Yerushalmi, Dorit. 1997. "'I will not leave!': The Language of 'The Dybbuk' in the Plays of Aloni, Sobol and Levin." M.A. thesis, Tel Aviv University (in Hebrew).

Young, James E. 1993. *The Texture of Memory: Holocaust Memorials and Meaning*. New Haven and London: Yale University Press.

Zuckerman, Moshe. 1993. *The Holocaust in Israeli Press during the Gulf War*. Tel Aviv: Author's Press (in Hebrew).

INDEX